MW00413397

For the Sake of Zion

FOR THE SAKE OF ZION

Reform Zionism
A Personal Mission

Richard G. Hirsch

URJ Press, New York
World Union for Progressive Judaism, Jerusalem

All rights reserved.

No part of this book may be reproduced, stored in a retrieval system, or transmitted without express written permission from the author. This excludes brief quotations used only for the purpose of review.

For permission to reprint, please contact:

URJ Press
633 Third Avenue
New York, NY 10017-6778

(212)650-4124
press@urj.org

All quotes from the Torah come from *The Torah: A Modern Commentary*, edited by W. Gunther Plaut © 2005. All quotes from Prophets and Writings come from *The Tanakh: A New Translation of The Holy Scriptures* © 1985 by The Jewish Publication Society. Used with permission.

Unless otherwise noted, all translations from Hebrew are the author's.

Library of Congress Cataloging-in-Publication Data

Hirsch, Richard G.
    For the sake of Zion : Reform Zionism : a personal mission / Richard G. Hirsch.
        p. cm.
    Includes index.
    ISBN 978-0-8074-1188-9
    1. Reform Judaism.   2. Zionism and Judaism.   3. Reform Zionism.
4. Reform Judaism—Israel.   5. Israel and the diaspora.   6. World Union for Progressive Judaism.   7. Hirsch, Richard G.   I. Title.
    BM197.H57 2010
    296.8'341--dc22

                                                                    2010045234

This book is printed on acid-free paper.
Copyright © 2011 by Richard G. Hirsch
Manufactured in the United States
1 2 3 4 5 6 7 8 9 10

To Our Grandchildren

Your old men shall dream dreams,
Your young men shall see visions.

(Joel 3:1)

For the sake of Zion I will not be silent,
For the sake of Jerusalem I will not be still,
Till her victory emerge resplendent
And her triumph like a flaming torch.

(Isaiah 62:1)

Contents

Preface

The world Jewish condition is undergoing continuous transformation mainly because of developments in the State of Israel. Whereas the Jewish population in Palestine at the end of the 19th century (when Theodor Herzl founded the World Zionist Organization) was approximately 78,000 people, and still only 640,000 on the eve of the establishment of the state in 1948, by the second decade of the twenty first century the Jewish population of Israel already comprises the largest Jewish community in the world (5,700,000 people). Demographers project that within another generation or two, the majority of world Jewry will live in Israel.

The intention of this book is to demonstrate how this revolutionary change in demography and in Jewish status has already affected worldwide Reform/Progressive Judaism. The ultimate purpose is to issue a clarion call to the leadership of the liberal Jewish movements to recognize and exploit the potential opportunities for a more intensive participation in the Zionist cause. If we indeed wish to serve as true partners, then this obligates us to assume full responsibility, as well as to seek equal rights. The ongoing struggle for complete recognition enhances the democratic spirit in the Jewish state. The creative institutions and programs we have established enrich the spiritual, educational, and cultural character of Israeli society.

Without the presence of the dynamic liberal religious movements active in the Diaspora, Israeli society will not be fully representative of *K'lal Yisrael* (the worldwide community of Jews). Conversely, our liberal religious movements abroad will become less relevant in the ongoing venture to perpetuate the Jewish people and its heritage.

For these reasons, I have constantly stressed that the transfer of the international headquarters of the World Union for Progressive Judaism to Jerusalem in 1973 and the commitment to build a robust, effective Progressive religious movement in Israel comprise the most significant developments in the Reform Movement since its establishment in the United States in the nineteenth century.

I consider it a privilege to have been given responsibility for helping to shape and direct the ongoing relationships of Reform/Progressive Judaism both to the Jewish state and the Zionist movement. This book records some of my institutional decisions and actions and describes my ideological convictions from the perspective of a personal mission. I named this mission "Reform Zionism" to send a clear signal that Reform Judaism should search for a new enhanced Zionist emphasis.

In this book I do not attempt to present an objective or complete account either ideologically or chronologically. I assume that in the course of time some scholar will assess the developments from an impartial historical perspective.

Many people have assisted in the publication of this book and I acknowledge with gratitude their contributions:

To Asher Weill, my editor. Grounded in a broad secular culture, he is a knowledgeable, devoted, critical Zionist. He has been a tough taskmaster, posing sharp questions and demanding cogent answers. During our many hours of discussions, we have established an enduring friendship, rooted in a shared vision for our movement and the Jewish state.

To Michael H. Goldberg, editor in chief of URJ Books and Music, for his gracious cooperation in seeking the highest standards of publication.

To Debra Hirsch Corman for her painstaking copyediting.

To my devoted secretary, Yvonne Marcus, for typing endless versions of the manuscript.

To colleagues and good friends who contributed to a publication fund: Austin and Nani Beutel, Leslie and Dee Bergman, Gerard and Ruth (*z"l*) Daniel, Dr. Arthur and Betty Roswell.

To colleagues who read the manuscript and made invaluable comments: Austin Beutel, Bobby Brown, Gerard Daniel, Paula Edelstein, Rabbi Stuart Geller, Mike Grabiner, Terry Hendin, Rabbi Naama Kelman, Rabbi Rich Kirschen, Rabbi John Levi, Paul Liptz, Professor Michael A. Meyer, Rabbi Joel Oseran, Shai Pinto, Rabbi John Rosove, Al Vorspan, Rabbi Yoshi Zweiback.

To my life partner, Bella, who has been my most perspicacious and constructive critic during almost six decades of our married life.

To our children—Dr. Ora Hirsch Pescovitz, Dr. Raphael Hirsch, Rabbi Ammiel Hirsch, and Dr. Emmet Hirsch— who bless us with their love and enrich our lives by giving us *nachas* (joy of fulfillment) in their professional careers and in rearing our grandchildren to perpetuate our Jewish values.

To the lay and professional leaders of our Movement who are dedicated to the cause of creating an exemplary Jewish people in Israel and throughout the world.

May we all fulfill the dictates of the Ethics of Fathers (*Pirkei Avot* 2:2): "Let all who work with the community work with them for the sake of Heaven, for then the merit of their fathers sustains them and their righteousness endures forever."

R.G.H.
Jerusalem, November 2010

Introduction

In the Ethics of the Fathers, we are taught that when a person reaches the age of eighty, he is capable of "special strengths" (*Pirkei Avot* 5:24). Now that I have entered the ninth decade of my life, I feel it is time to put into perspective the special strengths I have acquired in three separable but interrelated areas of activity.

From 1962 to 1973, I was the founding director of the Religious Action Center of Reform Judaism in Washington, D.C. From 1973 to 1999 I served as the professional head of the World Union for Progressive Judaism (WUPJ), the international movement of Reform Judaism whose headquarters moved to Jerusalem when I accepted the appointment (upon retirement, I was named honorary life president of the WUPJ), and I have held and still hold many positions in the World Zionist Organization and Jewish Agency for Israel. In all these areas I was privileged to be offered rare opportunities for leadership and service to the Jewish people.

Over the years, colleagues who have worked with me have learned that my favorite phrase in defining leadership responsibility is, "It is not the position that accords honor to the person but the person who accords honor to the position" (Babylonian Talmud, *Taanit* 21b). It is my conviction that no matter what job description is given to a person, he or she shapes the position anew. In effect every person defines a job by what they do with it. Whenever I engaged a new person for a position I said, "We are giving you a *n'kudah*, a point of departure. You can stand on the point without expanding or changing it. However, if you are creative, innovative, and conscientious, you can expand the *n'kudah* beyond all expectations. The *n'kudah* is like a pebble. If you throw a pebble into a pond it can sink without trace, or it can create a ripple effect that will broaden your horizons and the perceptions and aspirations of all those with whom you work. It is entirely up to you." I have always tried to practice what I preach.

In this book I have decided to concentrate on those aspects of my career that relate to Zionism, Israel, and the Jewish people. Elsewhere, especially in my previous book, *From the Hill to the Mount: A Reform Zionist Quest* (Jerusalem: Gefen Publishers, 2000), I have written about social action concerns and issues of conscience in the United States. From my perspective, the activities in which I was engaged in America before immigrating to Israel are inextricably related to my activities in Israel.

Zionism and Israel have been a constant factor in my life. As a child growing up in Cleveland, Ohio, I was fascinated by the drama of a revivified Jewish people aspiring to re-create a homeland of their own in the Land of Israel. Because my wife's mother and siblings and their families lived in Israel, we maintained an intimate family relationship with the country. We visited Israel whenever possible and welcomed family members on visits to our home in America. With no sense of pride but with great satisfaction, I recount these facts in order to reaffirm our family's affinity for Israel and my own personal convictions. I stress the word "personal" because these relationships reflected the private values of our family and were not directly related to any movement responsibilities.

My interests began to assume institutional proportions with the outbreak of the Six-Day War in 1967. For me personally, and I believe for the Jewish people as a whole, that cataclysmic event became a transformational milestone. In some ways the Six-Day War had greater impact than even the establishment of the State of Israel itself nearly twenty years earlier. From 1948 when the state was established (the partition plan was actually adopted by the United Nations on November 29, 1947) until May 1967, Israel had become a symbol of hope for the renewal of the Jewish people. Following the destruction of European Jewry in the Holocaust, Israel had integrated hundreds of thousands of new immigrants and enabled them to begin reconstructing meaningful lives. The Jewish population of the new state had grown from 640,000 to over 2.5 million, and it had begun to develop a strong socioeconomic infrastructure. The blockade of the Straits of Tiran at the entrance to the Gulf of Aqaba in 1967 by President Gamal Abdel Nasser of Egypt threatened to destroy the state and stifle the Jewish population. Was it conceivable, only one generation after the horrors of the Holocaust, that the world would acquiesce in the destruction of the Jewish state?

Leaders of the American Jewish organizations frantically began to engage in lobbying efforts with the American administration and members of Congress to buttress support for breaking the blockade and eliminating the threat to Israel's southern approaches.

In my capacity as director of the Religious Action Center, I had established a close working relationship with many of the key leaders of the Catholic Church and the major Protestant denominations. We had worked in collaboration on important issues of civil rights, anti-poverty legislation, and other social concerns. We had testified jointly before the Senate and Congress. In the course of our work together we had developed firm personal relationships. Indeed, I often found myself spending more time with my Christian friends than with my Jewish colleagues.

Despite the clear commitment of the Christian organizations to take a strong stand on the crucial moral issues confronting American society, when it came to the potential destruction of the State of Israel, the major Protestant and Catholic establishments were either silent or issued pallid statements of neutrality (see chapter 7).

The month of May 1967 leading up to June 5 was the most difficult period in my life. I was angry, frustrated, anxious, bewildered, and dismayed. The gamut of emotions prevented me from sleeping or eating. In fact, toward the end of the month, I discovered that I had lost fifteen pounds.

In the event, the Six-Day War was a miraculous victory. It signified that the Jewish people had learned the lesson of history. No longer would Jews be led like sheep to the concentration camps and crematoria. Henceforth, Jewish destiny would be determined by the Jewish people itself.

During the summer of that year, after the Six-Day War was over, I began to ponder on the ramifications of the war. My criticism of Christian colleagues inevitably led me to criticism of our own Reform movement. Where did Reform Judaism stand in relationship to Israel?

Through my work in developing the Religious Action Center, my basic premises had been validated. Before the establishment of the Commission on Social Action of Reform Judaism and the Religious Action Center, individual Reform Jews had been among the most ardent proponents of issues of social justice. However, the synagogue as an institution was quiescent and for the most part irrelevant in shaping the moral values of American society. Through the involvement of synagogues in social concerns and the stands taken by the Religious Action Center, we had developed policies of collective action. Reform Judaism as a movement activated synagogues and their members to understand that Judaism obligated concern for and action toward the aim of *tikkun olam*, "improving the world."

Having learned the lesson of collective action with regard to social issues, I aspired to apply the lesson to Israel and Zionism. Where did Reform Judaism stand in relation to these vital issues? To be sure, long before the establishment of the state, individual American Reform rabbis and lay leaders had been active Zionists. Indeed, the most prominent American Zionist leaders, Abba Hillel Silver and Stephen S. Wise, were both Reform rabbis. However, during the heyday of their leadership, the movement as a whole had been non-Zionist.

As I saw it, Reform Judaism as a movement had failed in its relationship to Zionism. The Union of American Hebrew Congregations (UAHC) and the Central Conference of American Rabbis (CCAR) had established special commissions for Jewish education, for youth, for study, for worship, for synagogue administration, and for other areas of responsibility. So why was there no commission on Israel? The World Union for Progressive Judaism, which had assumed responsibility for encouraging the development of Reform Judaism around the world, had earmarked less than $10,000 in its annual budget for Israel. It had engaged two rabbis to develop congregations in Israel, both of whom had indicated after the Six-Day War that they were considering leaving the country because of lack of support. In the summer of 1967, I decided to take action. I wrote a number of articles directed to the leadership of the Reform movement, some edited excerpts of which follow:

> The war of 1967 has dramatically demonstrated that Israel in reality has become more than Israel in anticipation. The living experience has altered, and even improved on the theory. For twenty years, Israel has been an inspiring light, and our vision has become readjusted. The threat to extinguish the light made the remembrance of darkness more vivid. Israel has come to assume a significance far beyond an "insurance

policy" role against anti-Semitism. The possibility that the
Arabs could carry out their threat to destroy Israel meant that
something beyond the lives of fellow Jews was at stake. The
life of the Jewish people as an entity was being threatened.
The destiny of the Jewish people was inseparable from the
destiny of the State of Israel. The inexpressibly profound
reaction of American Jews was in response not only to the
danger confronting Jews, but to the danger confronting all
that for which Jews stand. In June 1967, it became clear that
the destiny of the People of Israel was inseparable from the
destiny of the State of Israel.

What the State of Israel is to American Jews and what it
will yet become is difficult to define. Israel is the product
of many sources of inspiration and tragedy, having different
meaning for different people. Since the nineteenth-century
rebirth of Zionism, its supporters have been embroiled in
controversy concerning the character, purpose, direction,
and meaning of a Jewish state. Let the debates continue. The
process of defining and redefining our essence and existence
is integral to the character of the Jewish people. It is not necessary to resolve all the ideological questions to know that,
however defined, what happens in the Land of Israel has a
capacity to stir Jews as no other phenomenon or institution
can.

The majority of young Jewish intellectuals on college campuses who, in the past, moved into the civil rights movement
and later into the peace movement with a passion bordering
on religious fervor, were either indifferent to or repelled
by Jewish institutional life and the synagogue. To be sure,
not all our young people were moved by the events of June
1967. But the vast majority of our youth identified as Jews as
never before. Let us recognize frankly that for many young
Jews, what neither the synagogue, the Hillel Foundation, nor
the Jewish community centers could do, Israel was able to

do. Let us recognize that for many Jews, the State of Israel, seven thousand miles away, offers a more tangible expression of Jewishness than the synagogue on the next block.

The foregoing is not intended as a criticism of American Jewish institutional life. Rather it is intended to motivate us to accept the new role that Israel has come to play in our lives and its potential for enriching American Jewish life. It is no diminution of the synagogue to say that the Jewish soul also expresses itself poignantly through what happens to the State of Israel. Rather than fight it, let us try to understand, accept, and exploit it.

The driver who narrowly avoids an accident on the highway will hopefully drive more carefully afterwards. But after the sharp image of possible death fades, there is a tendency to return to normal driving habits. In the same way, there is a similar danger that American Jewry, now stirred by the miraculous deliverance of the State of Israel, will return to its previous routine. The task of American Jewish leadership should be to assess the recent events and to channel the passions aroused into constructive programs of enduring significance.

Let us begin with Reform Judaism. Both Reform Judaism and political Zionism trace their origins to neo-messianism, but the moods were diametrically opposite. The former was grounded in hope for Jews in a gentile world, while the latter was mired in hopelessness for Jewish survival in the gentile world. Reform Judaism evolved in an atmosphere of optimism. The nineteenth-century spirit of liberalism, progress and enlightenment, and the emancipation of the Jews called for a radical new approach to Jewish theology. Whereas Orthodox Judaism maintained that the Jews were living in exile as punishment for their sins, Reform Judaism in essence declared that if we choose to integrate into an enlightened world and be considered as citizens of the countries in which we live, we cannot wait with our baggage packed for a Messiah who will redeem us from exile and take us back to the Land of Israel. Let us find a solution to the problems of mankind and we will find a solution to the problems of the Jews.

The noted Pittsburgh Platform of 1885 summarized the thinking of classical Reform Jews by stating, "We no longer consider ourselves a nation, but a religious community, and, therefore, expect neither a return to Palestine nor sacrificial worship under the sons of Aaron nor a restoration of any of the laws concerning a Jewish state." Anti-nationalism thus became a basic plank in Reform Judaism. Every effort was made to eliminate from the liturgy references to the return to Zion.

Conversely, political Zionism evolved in an atmosphere of pessimism for the future of European Jewry, born out of despair; a recognition that complete emancipation and equality for the Jews could not be realized. Anti-Semitism on the one hand and assimilation on the other would lead to the ultimate dissolution of the Jewish people. In the eyes of the Zionists, the only hope for survival lay in the reestablishment of a Jewish homeland in the Land of Israel.

Reform Judaism and political Zionism were therefore inevitably destined to clash. In retrospect, the clash was greatly responsible for the limited appeal that Reform Judaism held for Jews of Eastern European origin in America. They had fled from Europe to escape persecution, which they had suffered because they had been seen as members of an alien nation. In America, Reform Judaism in effect told them they were not a nation but only a member of a religion; that the Land of Israel, for which they prayed daily, should be of no special concern to them. Small wonder then, that the Eastern European Jews accused the classical Reformers of perverting the basic character of Judaism.

Had Reform Judaism remained committed to the platform
inaugurated at Pittsburgh, the movement would inevitably
have degenerated into a splinter sect similar to that represented by the anti-Zionist ideology of the American Council
for Judaism. Fortunately, Reform Judaism did not retain its
anti-Zionist stance. The Columbus Platform of 1937 officially recognized the transition. The Central Conference of
American Rabbis declared, "In the rehabilitation of Palestine, the land hallowed by memories and hopes, we behold
the promise of renewed life for many of our brethren. We
affirm the obligation of all Jewry to aid in its upbuilding as a
Jewish homeland, by endeavoring to make it not only a haven
of refuge for the oppressed, but also the center of Jewish
culture and spiritual life."

But although the Reform rabbis changed their stance
in 1937 and the Union of American Hebrew Congregations adopted a pro-Zionist position, even in the 1960s, the
Reform movement has yet to embrace the full consequences
resulting from the establishment of the State of Israel. It has
still not fully appreciated that the contemporary "new look"
of Reform Judaism was in great measure derived from the
inspirational impact of Israel. The development of a Jewish
homeland has been the single most important factor. Israel
has restored balance and perspective to Reform Judaism,
necessitating the strengthening of our ties with the Jewish people. Israel has enriched the consciousness of Jewish
peoplehood and, in so doing, has revitalized Jewish history
and culture.

American Jewish culture needs the stimulus that comes
from Israel, just as Israel needs the stimulus that comes from
the Diaspora. The revival of Hebrew as a spoken tongue has
given new meaning to Hebrew as a holy tongue. The Jewish Festivals, all of which are associated with the Land of
Israel, have assumed a new significance. In sum, the reality

of a Jewish state has infused new life into Reform Judaism
and implanted new idealism, purpose, and hope in American
Jewry.

Reform Judaism as a movement and Reform Jews as individuals both draw sustenance from and give nourishment to
Israel. But the relationship of Reform Judaism to Israel has
yet to be developed to its full potential. Israel is a living laboratory of the Jewish soul. Until now the Reform movement
has entered the laboratory hesitantly, gingerly, making small
experiments here and there. The Six-Day War proved the
value of the laboratory. Israel, the people, the land, and the
state are all essential to the continued creativity and development of Reform Judaism. Let us now enter the laboratory in
earnest, knowing that our experiments have borne fruit and
thus justify the expenditure of major resources and energy.

During the summer of 1967 I drew up a plan of action and
proposed the establishment of a UAHC-CCAR Commission
on Israel and the adoption of a detailed platform recommend-
ing educational programs in North America on all levels:
religious schools, youth, college, and adult. The recommendations included the establishment of camps, seminars, study
tours, and language immersion classes in Israel for laypeople,
rabbis, and Jewish educators.

I also proposed that a full-time director of the Israel Commission be appointed to implement the programs recommended. My plan was the main subject for discussion at the
fall staff meeting of the UAHC. At the time, the key phrase in
Washington political circles was "the reallocation of national
resources." I recommended that we reallocate our Reform
Jewish national resources, namely that we take a major slice
for Israel out of our existing budget. Although the content
of all my proposals was received positively, the leadership
balked at the budgetary implications. The UAHC was already

facing a budget deficit, and no head of a department would agree that his budget be cut in order to accommodate the new Israel program. I was confronted with a serious dilemma. I realized that in these circumstances, my grand vision would not get off the ground. So in desperation I agreed that temporarily, in addition to serving as director of the Religious Action Center, I would also serve as director of the Israel Commission. Since I believed that the Israel program represented the thrust of the future, I volunteered to raise funds outside the regular operating budget of the Union. In the fall of 1967, I embarked on a mission to Israel. On my return a resolution was formulated for the November 1967 Biennial Convention of the UAHC, which reads as follows:

> We authorize the Board of Trustees of the UAHC to create a National Committee on Israel, among whose purposes shall be: to advance, in cooperation with the World Union for Progressive Judaism, the cause of Progressive Judaism in Israel, to support existing congregations and to create new congregations; to initiate a camp program in Israel to encourage the development of adult programs, including, if feasible, settlements under the auspices of Progressive Judaism; to conduct various campaigns to strengthen our relations with the people of Israel and to educate our members and the community at large on issues involving Israel; and to encourage the formation of corresponding committees in every region and congregation. In order to finance this work, the Committee is hereby authorized to solicit from the entire constituency of American Reform Judaism, as a voluntary offering, one dollar per year per person—man, woman, and child.

The resolution, including the levy of one dollar per person, was accepted with enthusiasm. However, the campaign raised only one-tenth of its potential. It was then that I recognized that in order to raise a substantial amount of money, it was essential to solicit foundations and private donors for specific projects.

At the same time, I urged the WUPJ to adopt a serious program of helping to develop the fledgling liberal movement in Israel. My advocacy led to my being appointed chairman of the WUPJ's Commission on Israel, as well as director of the URJ's Israel Commission.

In that capacity I proposed that we invest a major effort in expanding the Israel Movement for Progressive Judaism. Since Reform Judaism had accepted by now that Israel was central to Jewish destiny, it was essential for us to develop a strong, dynamic movement in the country. The basic premise of American Jewry at the time was that there were two equal foci of Jewish life, American Jewry and Israeli Jewry, parallel to the two ancient centers of Babylon and Jerusalem. I contended that the Six-Day War had demonstrated that this premise was no longer valid. Now Israel had become the center stage for the enactment of the Jewish drama. If we as a movement remained in the audience, applauding or criticizing the actors from our comfortable seats, we were defaulting on our responsibilities as Jews. We were also, by our own negligence, in danger of relegating the Reform movement to a tangential, marginal, and irrelevant status within world Jewry. Our task as I saw it was to transform our role from spectator to actor. We could not be content with minor roles. We had to become major players on the Jewish stage. We were fully aware of the discrimination we would confront in Israel, but this could not serve as a pretext for noninvolvement.

In the years that followed, I began to advocate the thesis that in order to become major players on this Jewish stage, we had to join the World Zionist Organization and the Jewish Agency for Israel, the leading international organizations of world Jewry based in Israel. Again, we were fully aware of the allegations of politicization and ineffectiveness directed

against these institutions, but we could not allow these to ab-
solve us from sharing responsibility as partners in the vital
tasks undertaken by world Jewry: the struggle to rescue Soviet Jewry and the Jews of Ethiopia and other endangered
communities; the efforts to absorb immigration; settling the
land; influencing Jewish education; and enhancing the qual-
ity of life in Israel. To move our international headquarters
to Jerusalem and yet not to join the national institutions of
Jewish life would be tantamount to ushering the bride to the
wedding canopy, but refraining from placing the ring on her
finger.

Our challenge as a movement was to become a full partner
in the exhilarating drama of *binyan haaretz*—the upbuilding
of Zion. Were we aware of the shortcomings and disabilities
in Israeli society? Indeed we were. Were we cognizant that
often the reality of Israel seems far distant from the dream?
To be sure. But would Reform Judaism have been better off
if we only lived with the dream? Is it not a blessing to be able
to wrestle with the reality? As a movement we had to commit
ourselves to fulfilling the spirit epitomized by the prophet Jeremiah: "There is hope in your future, says the Lord, because
your children shall return to their land" (Jeremiah 31:17). In
the final analysis, without the reality of Israel, we would not
have been able to sustain the dream.

On a Personal Note

This book does not purport to be an autobiography, and some of the account in this chapter is expanded upon in my previous book, *From the Hill to the Mount: A Reform Zionist Quest*. Nevertheless, I feel that some background is necessary for the reader of this book to understand to what extent my formative years had an impact on the future direction my life was to take.

I was born in Cleveland, Ohio, in 1926. Our home was a typical American Jewish home of that time. Our family was active in the local Conservative synagogue and in other Jewish organizations. My father had become a lawyer, but because he was unable to make a living during the Depression, he acquired an interest in a small business. My mother administered the office in our home. Unfortunately, at the age of only forty-three my father became seriously ill and was confined to a wheelchair with paralysis. He was unable to talk, but he retained his intellectual acuity and his pleasant disposition, until he passed away twenty years later.

My best friend was my brother Jay, four years younger than was I. Because I was in school in Cincinnati, Jay decided to enter university and medical school at the University of Cincinnati. For many years as a student doctor he lived in the Hebrew Union College (HUC) dormitory and administered the small infirmary there. We organized a student basketball team to play in the Jewish Community Center league. Jay was the star of the team and in later years would often joke to his many rabbinical friends that he was the only person in history to ever receive a basketball scholarship at HUC! Although I was not as good as my brother, I was also a fairly good athlete and played on the first team. Those were the days when you did not have to be seven feet tall to play basketball. Jay was the recipient of many scholastic awards and became a professor of psychiatry at the University of Illinois College of Medicine. Tragically, he developed a brain tumor and passed away in 1997.

As a child and later as a teenager, I was unusual in only one respect. Unlike my contemporaries, I actually enjoyed Hebrew school and relished studying the Hebrew language. I fell in love with the Zionist idea and became active in the Young Judea youth movement. I discovered that I enjoyed public speaking, and so at the age of thirteen, I entered the Young Judea national oratorical contest. Unexpectedly, I won the national prize. A number of articles about me appeared in the press, and I became somewhat of a hero in our local community. Rabbi Abba Hillel Silver, the doyen of American Reform rabbis and a prominent leader in the national Jewish community, asked me to deliver a talk at the opening meeting of the Cleveland Zionist Federation in the fall of 1940. Because of the looming crisis in Germany, many hundreds of people were in attendance. My participation added to my notoriety, and I became known as a youth leader and a public speaker.

Even though before that time I had never really thought about what occupation I would enter, other people began to say, "Dick wants to be a rabbi." Some of my closest friends expressed the thought jokingly, because I was a rambunctious boy and hardly fitted the image of a rabbi. I was encouraged by my parents, and since I had finished high school at sixteen, I went for my freshman year to Western Reserve University in Cleveland and, in the fall of 1944, entered a combined program as a sophomore at the University of Cincinnati and as a freshman in the rabbinical school of HUC.

In those days, the student body was very small. In my freshman class there were eight students and there were only forty-two students in the entire school. Some of the students in the senior class had been sent to take over pulpits of ordained rabbis who had gone into the chaplaincy during World War II. A high percent of my fellow students came from Orthodox backgrounds and had studied in a yeshivah. I was shocked to discover that it was those students with yeshivah backgrounds who tended to distance themselves from tradition. Some of them even became fervent defenders of the classical German Reform tradition. Conversely, students like myself who had entered HUC with no traditional experience and no background in Talmudic studies tended to seek more tradition. Today, of course, most of the students entering HUC come from Reform backgrounds.

I enjoyed my studies at HUC as well as my extracurricular activities in the community. However, I was always critical of the lack of an intensive Jewish environment. The religious services at the College chapel on Shabbat were conducted in the classic Reform mode, and the students did not even don *kippot* or prayer shawls. The food in the dining room was not kosher. Instead of the College serving as a paradigm for a new, more traditionally oriented Reform Judaism, it was a bastion for the reinforcement of classical Reform Judaism.

My main disappointment related to the burning issue of Zionism. World Jewry had suffered the trauma of the Holocaust. The British were turning the survivors of the concentration camps away from the Land of Israel. The Jewish community in Palestine was engaged in an epic struggle to create a state. But from my perspective, most of the faculty and the student body were insufficiently involved. In 1947 an emissary from Palestine came to recruit students to fight for the Haganah (later to become the Israel Defense Forces). I was the only one to sign up. When I informed my parents, my mother became distraught. The situation with my father was desperate, and my mother and brother begged me not to leave at that time. My mother did, however, agree that I could go as soon as the War of Independence was over.

In 1948 I went to Professor Nelson Glueck, who had become president of the Hebrew Union College in 1947, and asked him to permit me to take a year's leave of absence to study at the Hebrew University of Jerusalem. Dr. Glueck made every effort to dissuade me. He urged me to wait until my ordination in 1951. A number of other rabbis had gone to study after ordination, and Glueck himself had received a doctorate in Germany following his ordination. He told me that because I was a good student, I would be considered as a faculty member. I told Dr. Glueck that I had no interest in being an academician. Besides, I said, I felt a compulsion to go now. He warned me that the faculty would give no guarantee that I would get credit for the year of study and that I would be expected to pass stringent tests on my return. I accepted his warnings. Reluctantly, he authorized my leave of absence. I was the first undergraduate student to study in Israel and was very pleased that in subsequent years many other students followed suit, although HUC still refused to grant them automatic credits. How gratifying it was when in 1970 the College decided to make the first year of study in Jerusalem compulsory.

So I spent the academic year of 1949–50 in the newly established State of Israel. To this day I look upon that year as the most formative in my life. During the summer I worked on Kibbutz Hazorea and Kibbutz Ginegar, performing a variety of tasks in the fields and in the kitchen. Although my friends assured me that I had picked up the Hebrew language quickly, I discovered to my dismay that I could not fully comprehend plays in Hebrew at the theater or follow intellectual discussions on the radio. I panicked. How was I going to understand the lectures at the Hebrew University? This was before the intensive Hebrew-language *ulpan* system that was later developed. So I moved to Jerusalem. Fortunately, I developed a friendship with a teacher with whom I met daily to practice my Hebrew, and I worked on the language day and night. Since it was the first semester after the war, the university did not commence until December. Fortunately, I made great progress and was able to participate in the classes alongside the regular students. I had the privilege of hearing lectures from some of the great teachers at the university in those days: Martin Buber, Gershom Scholem, Ernst Simon, Hugo Bergman, Benjamin Maisler (later Mazar), Yehezkiel Kaufman, Yosef Klausner, and others. In the recess between Purim and Passover, I worked on archeological excavations at Khirbet Kerach (Beit Yerach) in the Jordan Valley.

At the time approximately fifty students from overseas were attending the university, many of them on scholarships from the American GI Bill of Rights. The university had made no provision for special programs for foreign students, so we organized a foreign student association and I was elected chairman. We made many suggestions to the university administration, most of which were adopted when it developed programs for overseas students.

On my return to Cincinnati, I passed the oral and written tests and was given full credit for the year. I was even asked to teach the Hebrew course for the incoming first-year students. However, the return to life at HUC proved traumatic. I had been so conditioned to the vitality of Israeli life, the crises, the mass absorption of immigrants, the shortage of food, water, and basic supplies, and the numerous other challenges of living in the incipient state that it was difficult to get adjusted to the leisurely pace of the College. I met with the leadership of the Cincinnati Jewish Federation and helped to organize a special division, in order to encourage young adults to participate in the local community and to raise funds for Israel and overseas Jewish needs. No HUC student had ever before been active in the Federation. I recommended that we initiate a fund-raising campaign among the HUC faculty and student body so that they should experience the gratification of giving of their own resources. Since I had made the recommendation, I was asked to serve as chairman. I experienced numerous difficult moments when I discovered that some faculty and students, even those whose origins were in Europe and had lost relatives in the Holocaust, were unwilling to give according to their capacity or, indeed, at all.

My greatest disappointment came as a result of my senior sermon. Every senior was obliged to deliver a sermon in the College chapel at the Shabbat morning services attended by the faculty and the student body. I decided to preach on my experiences in Israel and to develop the ideology that I had formulated about the inextricable relationship between Reform Judaism and Zionism. I criticized the Reform movement for not coming to terms with the revolution that had occurred with the establishment of the Jewish state. The following is an excerpt from my sermon (November 18, 1950):

> Reform Judaism has displayed neither the foresight nor
> the courage to concede that there is no longer a dichotomy
> between Zionism and Judaism. It has been unwilling to grant
> that almost everything included under the generic term

"Zionism" is by very definition an integral part of Judaism, inextricably associated with our concept of the peoplehood of Israel. . . . If Reform Judaism wants to influence Israel, and we have every privilege and duty to do so . . . then let us enter actively into the work of revitalizing the Jewish state. Let us include as an integral part of our general Jewish education program what today is known as Zionist education. Let us inspire our members with the need for American aliyah and the pioneering spirit. Once Reform Judaism articulates in deeds the close relationship between Israel and American Jewry, it will find that what was originally intended as a service to Israel has, in turn, increased the strength and significance of Reform Judaism in America. The difficult burdens of family responsibility will bring the rich blessings of family love.

In retrospect the message I preached at HUC at the age of twenty-four was a harbinger of what I have been advocating ever since. However, I was totally unprepared for the furor that ensued. The majority of the faculty and the students reacted negatively. How could I advocate *aliyah* for American Jewry? How could I in effect say that without Zionism, there is no Reform Judaism?

To this day, colleagues who were fellow students remember how even the revered Leo Baeck, who was teaching at HUC, met with me in the chapel after services and in his own gentle manner tried to explain to me the errors in my views. It was difficult for me to comprehend how this saintly man, after so many years in Theresienstadt, whom I respected so much for his character, learning, and personal courage, did not consider himself a Zionist. Even after Israel had come into being, people like Baeck, Nelson Glueck, Ernst Simon, Judah Magnes, Hugo Bergman, and many others were still advocating a binational state.

For weeks after delivering the sermon I engaged in continuing debate with my friends at HUC. It made me realize how far I was from the mainstream of our movement and how far we still had to go in order to bring Reform Judaism closer to Zionism.

After ordination, I served for two years at Chicago's Temple Emanuel as assistant to Rabbi Felix Levy. I respected Rabbi Levy for his keen intellect and integrity and was pleased that he and his wife considered me a member of their family. Rabbi Levy was an ardent Zionist and had been president of the CCAR when the Columbus Platform, adopted in 1937, revised the anti-Zionist stance of the Pittsburgh Platform of 1885. Rabbi Levy told me that the now famous Columbus Platform was not considered a major issue at the time. Many of the members were not even on the floor during the vote. Early in the proceedings the delegates were presented with a proposal not to adopt any platform at all. The vote, by a show of hands, resulted in an 81–81 tie. Rabbi Levy cast the deciding vote to keep the platform on the agenda. In his book *Turning Point: Zionism and Reform Judaism*, Harold R. Greenstein states, "The number of men present when the final vote was taken on the Zionist plank represented but a fraction of the total conference membership."* So even the much-heralded Columbus Platform reflected a minority position within the Reform movement.

From 1953 to 1956, I served as co-rabbi at Temple Emanuel in Denver, Colorado. The most important event that happened there was that I met my life partner, Bella. My congregation held a summer camp high up in the Rocky Mountains. In the summer of 1954 we were ready to open

---

*See Michael A. Meyer, *Response to Modernity* (New York: Oxford University Press, 1988), pp. 318–20. For a full account of this event, see Howard R. Greenstein, *Turning Point: Zionism and Reform Judaism* (Chico, CA: Scholars Press, 1981), pp. 28–30.

the camp but desperately needed a nurse. Several days before the camp opened I received a call from a pediatrician who knew how anxious we were. He said that one of his patients had brought her sick child to his clinic and was accompanied by a cousin who was a nurse visiting from Israel. He suggested I contact her. She came for an interview and after considerable persuasion agreed to accept the position of camp nurse. Camp closed at the end of the summer on a Sunday. The following Tuesday we flew to my parents' home in Miami, and on September 5, 1954, Bella and I got married. Bella, who had been reared in the Soviet Union in a town on the border of Siberia, had left Russia in 1946, lived in various displaced persons' camps, the last being Bergen-Belsen, signed up with the Haganah, left on an illegal ship from Marseilles, and landed in Israel on May 14, 1948, the day the state was declared, on the first ship to enter the new Jewish state. When we returned from our honeymoon just before Rosh HaShanah, Bella entered a synagogue for the first time in her life.

In April 1956 I accepted a call to become regional director of the Chicago Federation and the Great Lakes Council of the Union of American Hebrew Congregations. It was a prestigious position, particularly for a rabbi who was only twenty-nine years old.

I initiated many new projects. I was selected as the representative of the Chicago rabbinate to serve on a prime-time religious television program. This enabled me to become a well-known figure in the Chicago community.

A major area of concern was interreligious social action. Chicago was a city with complex interracial demographic problems. Many areas were threatened by transmigration of racial groups. One such area was the district surrounding the University of Chicago. In order to preserve the integrity of the university and to preclude it being overwhelmed by slums, a revolutionary plan called the Hyde Park–Kenwood urban renewal program was developed. The plan was to be brought before the city council for discussion. The Catholic archdiocese and the Protestant Council of Churches had engaged experts on their behalf to develop their respective positions on the complex and intricate issues involved in the plan.

The day before the church experts were to present their views on the proposed plan to the city council, I received a call from the head of the Chicago Council of Churches, who said that they thought it was important for a Jew to testify and asked if I would agree to do so. I willingly agreed. I prepared two pages of biblical and Rabbinic quotes on the Jewish stance toward social justice, the elimination of poverty, and equality for all men. The church experts presented detailed opinions based on months of preparation. I presented a few generalized quotes drawn from Jewish sources. After I finished my remarks, members of the city council remonstrated with me sharply. "Rabbi, have you even read the plans?" to which I had to respond in the negative. "Rabbi, do you not think it is presumptuous of you to come before this body and preach pious platitudes to us? We would be pleased to hear from you when and if you know what you are talking about."

Unfortunately, to my chagrin the entire incident reached the Chicago press. An emergency meeting of the UAHC Chicago Federation was convened, and I was severely criticized for behaving irresponsibly. I had embarrassed the entire Jewish community. Why had I not consulted anyone? Why had I not tried to find out if the Jewish community even wanted to take a policy stand? Why did I speak without knowing what I was talking about?

The entire incident was traumatic, but it taught me an important lesson. A responsible leader must be well prepared. A responsible leader must consult with those he represents and win their approval for his position. I was determined to make amends. I spent the next few months studying the subject in depth and meeting with nationally recognized experts. In due course I became knowledgeable on urban renewal and related subjects. I even wrote a book, *Judaism and Cities in Crisis*, on the topic of urban problems and their impact on Jewish concerns.

The knowledge I had acquired enabled me to be the key Jewish organizer in a conference on religion and race that was organized by the Catholic, Protestant, and Jewish communities of Chicago. It also helped to prepare me for my next position in Washington.

We spent five years in Chicago. It was there that Bella gave birth to our four children, in three and a half years. We had agreed that we would raise our children with Hebrew as their mother tongue, with no thought at that time of immigrating to Israel. We made every effort to visit the country as much as possible to visit Bella's family and to inculcate a love of Israel in our children. In 1958, I helped to organize and lead the first National Federation of Temple Youth (NFTY) mission to Israel. The first Reform synagogue in Israel, Har-El in Jerusalem, had been established earlier in the year, and I was asked to bring them their first *sefer Torah*. That was my first contact with the nascent movement of Progressive Judaism.

In 1959, at the UAHC Biennial the leadership recommended establishing a center for social action in Washington. A prominent liberal lay leader named Kivie Kaplan was prepared to purchase a building in Washington to house the center. The proposal provoked heated controversy, especially among the larger congregations in the UAHC. The debate was so intense that it was decided to postpone the decision until the next Biennial in 1961 and in the interim to consider the issue in depth within the movement. In 1961 the establishment of a center was endorsed. I have told the story in my book *From the Hill to the Mount: A Reform Zionist Quest,* and there is no need to repeat it here.

I was asked to serve as the founding director of the new Religious Action Center. I considered the appointment to be a once-in-a-lifetime opportunity to found a new institution representing Reform Judaism in Washington on the critical issues confronting American society. I served as its director from 1962 until 1973. The Religious Action Center housed the Leadership Conference on Civil Rights. It was in our center that the civil rights legislation of the 1960s was drafted. I offered Martin Luther King Jr. the use of our offices whenever he visited Washington. My years in Washington enabled me to be in the forefront of the civil rights revolution that was in the process of reshaping American society. The Washington years were turbulent, exciting, and rewarding, because as a social activist I was in the pulsating heart of events that were changing the world.

Then came the Six-Day War and its aftermath. And my life and that of my family once again took a radical new turn.

PART ONE

Ideological Underpinnings

Chapter One

Why Reform Zionism Is Different

In 1967, still under the shock of the traumatic experiences of the Six-Day War, I spent many hours pondering the relationship of Reform Judaism to Israel. I had grown up in Cleveland, Ohio. Our family was affiliated with The Temple, commonly called Silver's Temple, in acknowledgment of the exceptional role played by its distinguished spiritual leader, Rabbi Abba Hillel Silver. Rabbi Silver was not just an acknowledged leader in the Jewish community; he was probably the best-known and most respected citizen in Cleveland. He was internationally renowned as an author, a scholar, and an orator. His major claim to fame was his activity as a Zionist and his advocacy of a Jewish state. Indeed, it was he who had appeared before the United Nations in 1947 representing the Jewish Agency for Israel to state the case for the recognition of the Jewish state.

I held Rabbi Silver in high esteem. He was a person of intellectual integrity who was never afraid to espouse unpopular causes and to take a minority position on controversial issues. The most conspicuous manifestation of his independence was his continuing criticism of President Franklin D. Roosevelt

---

An earlier version of this chapter was published in the *CCAR Journal: A Reform Jewish Quarterly,* Fall 2008.

and the policies of his administration with regard to European Jewry. The vast majority of American Jews idolized and idealized Roosevelt. Not Abba Hillel Silver. He found ample opportunity to criticize Roosevelt unsparingly for minimizing Hitler's threat to decimate European Jewry and for failing to take any meaningful action to rescue the Jews. Silver engaged in bitter disputes with Rabbi Stephen S. Wise and other Jewish leaders over the Roosevelt administration's policies toward the Nazi persecution of the Jews. In retrospect, Silver's criticism of Roosevelt was validated by historical research carried out following the Second World War. However, precisely because of my esteem for Silver's forthright leadership and my respect for his historic Zionist role, I raised two fundamental questions. The first question was why he had not made a major effort to instill Zionism in his own congregation. Silver was forthright in affirming his Zionist views in lectures to the community at large. However, he made no effort to change the classical Reform character of his congregation. The main synagogue service was held on Sunday morning rather than on Saturday, in keeping with the pattern of classical Reform. To be sure, a Shabbat morning service was also held, but it was sparsely attended. The siddur was an abbreviated set of prayers in leaflet form, and the service lasted no more than fifteen minutes. This prayer meeting was considered a purely warm-up introduction for the main event, a lecture delivered by the rabbi before a packed congregation. Rabbi Silver was adamant in refusing to countenance bar and bat mitzvah ceremonies. He contended that to permit such celebrations was to encourage pupils to forsake Jewish studies after the bar mitzvah was over and done with. My brother, four years younger than I, was forced to have his bar mitzvah in a small Orthodox synagogue whose rabbi was a close friend of our family.

In contrast, the Zionist-inclined rabbis of my generation assumed that those rabbis who ardently espoused peoplehood as the essence of Jewish identity were the very same rabbis who had wanted to introduce their congregations to a more intense level of observance. At the time, I considered Rabbi Silver's persistent affirmation of classical Reform to be fundamentally incongruous. It was only much later when I had delved more deeply into his writings that I understood that he was able to delineate intellectually between classical Reform Judaism and Zionism and saw no contradiction in being a fervent advocate of both. I began to comprehend that in his mind there was no inconsistency. He was deeply committed to classical Reform Judaism and believed that its message truly projected the future for American Jews. At the same time he painstakingly strived to persuade the Reform movement to accept the Jewish state as an existential and political necessity for the perpetuation of Jewish peoplehood.

For me it was fascinating to see how the non-Zionist congregation tolerated and even took pride in their rabbi's activities on behalf of Zionism. They welcomed the huge attendance at the Sunday morning service and lecture, in which many members of the larger Jewish community, including Orthodox Jews, participated. They appreciated that Rabbi Silver's prestige and visibility elevated the status of the congregation in the eyes of both the Jewish and the general community.

When the American Council for Judaism was established by anti-Zionist Reform rabbis in 1943, its ideological stance depended on defining Jewish identity as a faith. Its adherents' rejection of Zionism was a rejection of the concept of Jewish peoplehood. The council was committed to reinforcing the ideology and observance patterns of the nineteenth-century classical Jewish Reformers. For them, opposition to Zionism was not only political, but essentially theological in nature. The Jews, they maintained, were not a people but a community defined by faith. Therefore, it was seen as essential to eliminate all vestiges of peoplehood from the liturgy and ritual.

When the classical Reformers eliminated the *kippah*, the tallit, the observance of kashrut, and other traditional rituals, they did so ostensibly for ideological reasons. However, their major motivation was to expunge those observances that could be seen as symbols of Jewish peoplehood.

As I began to develop my own concept of what the character of the Progressive movement in Israel should be, I posited that at the very least we should restore those elements that the classical Reformers had rejected. If the *kippah*, tallit, and kashrut were symbols of Jewish peoplehood, then these and other manifestations of peoplehood should be preserved. The liturgy had to restore the references to Zion. From the moment our spiritual leaders in Israel created our own prayer books, the siddurim and High Holy Day *machzorim* were exclusively in Hebrew.

For me a key test of Jewish peoplehood was the obligation that all food served in our institutions would be kosher. When we built Beit Shmuel, our cultural center and youth hostel in Jerusalem, I instructed the architect to design a *n'tilat yadayim* (ceremonial basin for the washing of the hands) with the relevant prayer inscribed in the marble in Hebrew. As it happened, we had to wage an extended battle with the Orthodox authorities in order to secure the right to engage a *mashgiach* (kashrut supervisor). We finally prevailed and received a license of kashrut despite initial attempts to reject the application.

Some Reform Jews from abroad who visit our Progressive movement synagogues in Israel still question the traditional character of our services. Where is Reform Judaism? they ask. It is necessary to explain to them that Israel is the one place in the world where Jews live in the totality of Jewish peoplehood. It is natural for any Israeli to accept that when a male Jew prays he should cover his head and that in public institutions the food served should be kosher and therefore acceptable for Jews of all persuasions.

The forms of Jewish observance are shaped by the historic experiences of Jewish peoplehood. The return to the Land of Israel was not merely a physical move to an ancient land, but reflected a spiritual, cultural, and intellectual return to Jewish peoplehood. The restoration of Hebrew as the spoken tongue was in itself a manifestation of the Jewish experience as rooted in the Bible.

When we decided that the name of the Israel movement would be "Progressive Judaism" (*Yahadut Mitkademet*), we indicated that we expected to develop a movement that would be progressive and pluralistic in character, but fundamentally different from traditional European or American Reform Judaism. We expected to draw knowledge and inspiration from classical Reform Judaism, but we were committed to developing a movement that would be indigenous to Israel. We anticipated that we would be influenced by the Reform movements overseas, but we also aspired to make our own mark on these movements. We were committed to becoming fully integrated in Israeli society. We hoped to convince Israeli society to understand that without an alternative liberal and progressive Judaism, Israel would be incomplete, and our movement would be unfulfilled unless it would be rooted in Israel.

Another question I posed was why Rabbi Abba Hillel Silver and Rabbi Stephen S. Wise did not attempt to organize a Zionist movement within Reform Judaism. After all, these two rabbis were the most notable and respected Zionist leaders in the American Jewish community. However, both in their own view and in the perspective of their supporters, their Reform Jewish identity was incidental to the leadership roles they played in American Jewry as a whole. They had neither the time nor the inclination to organize one segment of the American Jewish community into a Reform Zionist movement, particularly since the majority of the members in those days were either non-Zionist or anti-Zionist. In truth, it probably never entered their minds, even after a group of Reform rabbis organized the American Council for Judaism as the anti-Zionist voice of American Jews in 1943.

Nevertheless, in 1967 I could not help but conjecture what would have transpired had they done so. The Orthodox Mizrachi Zionist movement was a small minority when they became a political movement. They were active as a separate force within the Zionist organization from its inception. They encouraged *aliyah*. They established numerous educational and welfare programs, as well as synagogues in Israel. As a consequence, they were deeply active in the pre-state era and were a major force when the state was declared. They established a political party, the National Religious Party, which became prominent in the Knesset and the government. They were recipients of significant government support for their institutions and programs, mostly as a consequence of exercising their political power in coalition negotiations.

I never advocated that we should establish a political party. However, had activists within the Reform and Conservative movements organized a liberal Zionist movement before the establishment of the state, our status within the Zionist movement and subsequently in Israel would have been radically different. We would not be constantly facing powerful opposition from the Orthodox political parties and indifference from secular Israelis.

Following the Six-Day War, I posed key questions to myself and other leaders of our movement. Was it too late to make a major effort to build an Israeli movement of liberal Judaism? Was it too late to identify as a movement within the Zionist movement as a whole? To those who had doubts,

I asked, What was the alternative? Not to take action? I was fond of quoting the Roman senator Cato: "Never is one so active as when one does nothing." If we failed to rectify the defaults of our past, we would eventually become even more marginalized.

Abba Hillel Silver's best-known scholarly work is *Where Judaism Differs: An Inquiry into the Distinctiveness of Judaism*, in which he brings his vast knowledge of both classical and Jewish sources to illuminate the distinctive character and values of Jewish civilization in comparison with other religions and cultures. I began to conjecture that what was necessary for the post-1967 generation was to introduce a new ideological perspective to be called Reform Zionism. The task confronting the Reform movement was, to paraphrase Silver, to make it clear where Reform Zionism differs. This ideology would develop two new approaches: to Zionize Reform and to reform Zionism. This task required a complete rethinking of our Reform ideology.

I reviewed the history of Zionist ideology through resolutions of the Central Conference of American Rabbis. The Columbus Platform, adopted in 1937, was in effect a negation of the anti-Zionist planks in the Pittsburgh Platform of 1885 and was seen as a major turning point in the development of Reform Judaism. Indeed, *Turning Point* is the title of a book written by Howard R. Greenstein on the Columbus Platform. Yet, as Greenstein himself has pointed out, "The majority of the CCAR was still in the non-Zionist camp. The number of men present when the final vote was taken on the Zionist plank resolution represented but a fraction of the total conference membership."*

---

*See Michael A. Meyer, *Response to Modernity* (New York: Oxford University Press, 1988), pp. 318–20. For a full account of this event, see Howard R. Greenstein, *Turning Point: Zionism and Reform Judaism* (Chico, CA: Scholars Press, 1981), pp. 28–30.

Furthermore, the Columbus Platform itself did not reflect a clear-cut Zionist position. The authors encouraged the return of the Jewish people to Zion, but in their view the return was unrelated to the "messianic goal" of "universal brotherhood, justice, truth, and peace on earth." They perpetuated the classical Reform view that particularism and universalism were two separable, unintegrated components of Reform Jewish theology.

Subsequently, even in 1976, the Centenary Perspective adopted by the CCAR did not tie the "messianic hope that humanity will be redeemed" to the traditional messianic hope, the precondition of which is that the Jewish people will be redeemed.

Without underestimating or deprecating the value of platforms and resolutions, I was aware of their limited efficaciousness. In my career, I had written many resolutions on a host of issues. However, I was also aware that all too often groups adopting resolutions were under the illusion that words were a substitute for action. Furthermore, my experience had led me to believe that resolutions disseminated to and by the public media had limited influence. I contended that the resolution process impacted more on the individuals and groups adopting the resolutions than on the groups to whom the resolutions were addressed. In the final analysis, the resolution process educates the formulators of the resolution more than the addressees.

In retrospect, if Reform Zionism had been limited to resolutions and proclamations of the various Reform bodies, by now Reform Judaism would have become totally marginalized within Jewish life. We would have become spectators in the Coliseum rather than gladiators in the arena. We would be sitting in the bleachers of the Diaspora watching the Jews in Israel wrestle with their problems.

Therefore, I believed, resolute action should take precedence over resolutions. What gave meaning, purpose, and incentive to our Reform Zionist ideology was the application of the dictum from Ethics of the Fathers, *Lo hamidrash hu ha-ikar elah hamaaseh*, "It is not the idea that is essential, but the deed [in Zion]" (*Pirkei Avot* 1:17). Indeed, it has been the deed that has inspired the idea, not the other way around. It is no coincidence that the first Association of Reform Zionists of America (ARZA) think tank was held in 1992, a full twenty-five years after we had begun to take decisive action to build the movement in Israel and fifteen years after we had moved the World Union for Progressive Judaism to Jerusalem and joined the World Zionist Organization and the Jewish Agency for Israel. Most movements, as well as individuals, tend to preach what they practice, rather than practice what they preach.

I was convinced that we had to apply the lessons learned from our experiences in social action. Before we had organized the Commission on Social Action of Reform Judaism and the Religious Action Center in Washington, many rabbis and lay leaders had been active in progressive causes as individuals. However, the synagogue as an institution was uninvolved and therefore inconsequential. The establishment of the commission and the center mobilized the movement for collective action. That process stimulated social action by the synagogue as an institution and has activated congregational programs. Even more significant, individual members who had until then not considered social issues to be of particular Jewish concern came to see social action as an inherent mandate of Judaism.

Similarly, I was convinced that it was insufficient to assume that Zionist activities of individual rabbis and lay leaders would activate the Reform movement. To "Zionize" the movement as a whole required collective action. We had to learn from our Orthodox colleagues and to adopt their methods. So what if our movement did not have rights in Israel? We had learned from the civil rights struggle in the United States that a movement that does not fight for its rights will never win them.

Also, we had learned that if a movement does not exercise those rights it has, no matter how limited they may be, it loses them. Therefore, instead of complaining from abroad about discrimination against liberal Jews in Israel, it was incumbent upon us to act, to create facts on the ground. Thus we endeavored to build synagogues and institutions and to develop educational, cultural, and social action programs to serve Israeli society in general.

The establishment of a vibrant, dynamic movement of Progressive Judaism in Israel was the key objective. The development of such a movement is not philanthropy, but affects Progressive Judaism in the Diaspora directly. A universal religion is not bound by geography. If Reform Judaism appeals only to American Jews and not to Israelis, then serious doubt would be cast on the authenticity of Progressive Judaism in the Diaspora.

For those who knew the Israeli milieu, it was predictable that the development of a liberal religious movement would be considered a foreign transplant by much of the general Israeli public. The first liberal rabbis in Israel would have to be American- or European-trained, and therefore the nature of worship might be considered strange and even "non-Jewish." Reform Judaism projected the image of an assimilatory movement, perhaps of value to help American Jews retain their Jewish identity, but incapable of serving the spiritual needs of Israelis.

Professor Nelson Glueck had erected the Hebrew Union College–Jewish Institute of Religion (HUC-JIR) building in Jerusalem that was dedicated in 1963. He had courageously insisted on constructing a small synagogue in the building and had prevailed after an extended political and legal struggle. However, HUC-JIR was primarily a school for archeology to replace the American School of Oriental Research, with which Glueck had been associated in East Jerusalem and which, after the War of Independence and the subsequent division of the city, was inaccessible. Even though there were Shabbat morning services at HUC-JIR, the focus of the institution was to pursue archeological research. Glueck did not envisage the establishment of a major liberal movement. In fact, because of ongoing differences with Rabbi Maurice N. Eisendrath, president of the Union of American Hebrew Congregations and an active leader in the World Union for Progressive Judaism, and because of institutional rivalries between HUC-JIR and the UAHC, Glueck refused to be involved with the establishment of a Progressive movement in Israel.

The fledgling movement was at pains to stress the difference between American Reform and the Israeli movement. The use of the term "Progressive Judaism" rather than "Reform Judaism" was intended to project an image of a more traditional movement, rooted more intensively in the Israeli environment. However, over the years, the effort to draw a clear distinction between the Israeli movement and the American movement has not succeeded. The Israeli public at large still sees the Israeli movement as a transplant of the American movement.

I must admit that I anticipated that by now, nearly four decades after we moved the international headquarters to Jerusalem, we would have made greater progress. I had hoped and expected that we would have more congregations, more educational institutions, more professional and lay leadership, and more participants in our multifaceted spiritual, cultural, and educational programs. Nevertheless, we have made great strides. Israelis of all ethnic origins are identifying with our congregations, establishing new congregations, sending their children to our kindergartens and schools, participating in our study groups, inviting our rabbis to officiate at weddings and other life-cycle events, bringing their children as bar and bat mitzvah to our synagogues, and, of special significance, entering HUC-JIR to study for the rabbinate.

However, our true achievement is not in numbers, but in our very presence in Israel. I contend that the most significant decision made by Reform Judaism in the twentieth century was to move the international headquarters of Progressive Judaism to Israel and to develop the institutions and programs of Progressive Judaism in the country. The Union of American Hebrew Congregations moved its headquarters from Cincinnati to New York in order to be in the center of Jewish action in America. The World Union for Progressive Judaism moved its headquarters from New York to Jerusalem in order to be at the pulsating heart of Jewish destiny.

We are here and we are insiders, not outsiders. We need Israel and Israel needs us. Our presence strengthens Israel and it strengthens the Reform movement in the Diaspora. The very presence of the movement in Israel shows the world that Israel is a pluralistic state (even if not as much as we would like). If we were not here, the controversy over the relationship between religion and state would be less intense. Our membership in the World Zionist Organization and the Jewish Agency demonstrates that the Jewish people is a democratic people. Paradoxically, it is the very opposition of the Orthodox to our legitimacy that actually gives us legitimacy, as well as enhanced visibility. Perhaps not every secular Jew has recognized our presence, but the Chief Rabbinate and Orthodox Jewry know very well that we are here. Judgments rendered by Israel's High Court of Justice reaffirm our rights as an authentic Israeli movement. In so doing, they also reinforce the legitimacy of the Reform movement abroad. Just as the State of Israel has become a source of pride for Diaspora Jewry, so the movement in Israel has enhanced the Jewish identity of Diaspora Reform Judaism.

Chapter Two

Liberal Judaism in Israel

The American liberal Jewish religious movements are a success story. They include in their membership the vast majority of American Jews affiliated with synagogues and a significant number of unaffiliated Jews who identify as Conservative, Reform, or Reconstructionist. These movements have established major academies of learning, national synagogue and rabbinical organizations, and a network of congregations sustaining Jewish education, innovative worship experiences, Jewish cultural creativity, social action, and advocacy. The synagogue as an institution has become the symbol of Jewish identity and the place to develop a Jewish way of life. The liberal rabbi has become a respected leadership figure and the bearer of Jewish knowledge and values. In sum, the liberal movements have become the primary foundation for the perpetuation of Jewish life in America.

But like generals who plan for the next war using the strategies of the previous one, the leaders of the two major movements in America are not adequately defining the strategic goals for Jewish survival, nor are they developing the arsenal to wage the battles of the future.

An earlier version of this chapter appeared in *CCAR Journal: A Reform Jewish Quarterly*, Spring 2007.

The major fault of the leadership of the Reform and Conservative movements is the failure to project the probable
demographic conditions and character of Jewish life in the
twenty-first century.

Professor Sergio DellaPergola, the preeminent Jewish
demographer, has provided a projection of the world Jewish population in 2050. Given a median fertility rate, Israel
will have a Jewish population of 8,230,000, whereas the total
Diaspora population will be 6,251,000, of whom 5,036,000
will be in the United States and Canada. Approximately 55
percent of world Jewry will live in Israel, and less than 35
percent will live in North America. The remaining 8 percent
will live in other countries of the Diaspora.

In the Diaspora, the Jewish fertility rate is lower and the
death rate higher than in the general population. The low
fertility rate, aging of the population, assimilation, and increasing intermarriage and non-marriage combine to make a
negative demographic trend. Because of its high fertility and
low mortality rate, Israel is the only place in the world that
will experience a natural increase in its Jewish population.
Already, one-half of all Jewish children under fifteen years
of age live in Israel, as do more than two-thirds of children
receiving Jewish education of any kind.

This projection of Jewish demography should lead the
American liberal movements to two clear-cut conclusions:
the State of Israel needs liberal Judaism, and liberal Judaism
needs the State of Israel.

The rapid growth of the *haredi* (ultra-Orthodox) population in Israel should be of increasing concern. It is estimated
that today 550,000 or 11 percent of Israeli Jews are *haredi*.
By the year 2020 it is projected that the *haredim* will reach
one million or 17 percent of the Israeli Jewish population.
The ultra-Orthodox have an average 6.5 children per family, whereas the average in the secular Jewish family is 2.6

children. In Jerusalem, where a majority of the city council is ultra-Orthodox, 65 percent of the children are in *haredi* schools. It is projected that the imbalance in the capital will be even greater in the future, because the out-migration of secular Jews from Jerusalem is increasing rapidly.

Statistics indicate that a very high percentage of immigrants from Western countries are Orthodox, whereas the majority of those who leave Israel for other lands are secular, many of them highly educated. In contrast, a high percentage of the *haredi* population is among the poorest elements of society and in socioeconomic terms is expanding the underclass economic component of Israeli society. Overwhelmingly, they do not serve in the army. They tend to be underskilled, underemployed, and underproductive. They are not integrated into society at large and are often not involved in the social issues confronting Israel. Moreover, for the most part, they do not accept the Zionist ideology that represents the underlying premise of the Jewish state.

This demographic pattern is of great consequence. Most significant is the negative image of Judaism that is projected. For many secular Israelis, the *haredi* way of life represents the real, authentic Judaism. Other expressions of Judaism, whether Conservative or Reform or even modern Orthodox, appear less legitimate in the eyes of the average secular Israeli Jew. In effect, the secular Israeli is saying, "The *haredi* way might be the true Judaism, but it is not for me. I reject it."

Many years ago, when we first began to formulate the objectives for Progressive Judaism in Israel, I projected that eventually we would probably constitute only one of many possible options of religious Jewish expression in the country. At the time, I had high hopes for the role of modern Orthodoxy. There were many enlightened voices within the Mizrachi movement who had traditionally aligned themselves with liberal political elements. Ever since the establishment of the state, the National Religious Party had maintained what was termed "the historic covenant" with the Labor Party.

In those days, I conjectured that the enlightened Orthodox forces would eventually rebel from within against the stringent, anachronistic interpretation of halachah (Jewish law) by the Orthodox establishment. As an example, I would cite the development of Protestantism. Martin Luther, originally a Catholic priest, started his historic revolution from within the church and initiated Protestantism as a revolt against the excesses and corruption of what he saw as the closed autocratic Catholic hierarchy. In a similar way, the Chasidic movement evolved from within Rabbinic Judaism as a rebellion against its rigid authoritarianism. Similarly, I assumed that ultimately a modern Orthodox liberal movement would develop from within fundamentalist Orthodoxy.

In regard to our own Progressive movement, I was convinced that in the milieu of Israel, where Judaism as a faith was a manifestation of Jewish peoplehood, Progressive Judaism would become more traditional than in the United States and would be more likely to view halachah as a guide rather than as an immutable set of rules. I believed that eventually a liberalized Orthodoxy and a more traditional liberal Judaism would find much in common and would be able to reconcile some of the major differences without losing their independent identities.

However, in the light of recent developments, my early conjectures have not been validated. Within the Israeli political system, the forces of modern liberal Orthodoxy have become less relevant and less visible. In a recent election, the National Religious Party entered into an alignment with the National Union, a right-wing political movement. The move was made necessary, they claimed, because otherwise the NRP leadership feared they would not have sufficient votes to gain representation in the Knesset.

The struggle over the Jewish character of Israel is an ever-present factor in the country. Theodor Herzl's *Der Juden-staat*—literally "The Jews' State"—could be translated either as "The Jewish State" or "The State of the Jews." The accepted Hebrew translation calls it *M'dinat HaY'hudim*, "The State of the Jews." I personally prefer the translation "The Jewish State," meaning a state that is Jewish in character as well as in name.

However, in effect, the Orthodox establishment views the state as *M'dinat HaYahadut*, meaning "The State of Judaism." They would prefer that the state be governed by halachah, which in their worldview takes precedence over the democratic and civil character of Knesset legislation. Indeed, the Orthodox establishment has yet to recognize the significant distinction between the Diaspora conditions, where Jews live as a minority in a non-Jewish environment, often without civil rights, and the conditions in the modern state where Jews are the majority. In effect, whereas the Orthodox establishment left the *galut* (exile) behind them, they brought the Judaism of the *galut* to Israel.

The clash between the two worldviews of *M'dinat HaY'hudim* and *M'dinat HaYahadut* is inevitable and irreconcilable. As long as there are religious political parties, the proponents of the *M'dinat HaY'hudim* position will need to be eternally vigilant to prevent further incursions into affairs of state by the proponents of the *M'dinat HaYahadut*. In order for a nation to guarantee freedom of religion, it must first guarantee freedom from religion. Because the State of Israel has been unable to guarantee the latter, it has been unable to guarantee the former.

The only solution appears to be some form of separation of religion and state. Since halachah, as interpreted by the Orthodox Rabbinate, cannot meet the special needs of all citizens in a complex democratic society, it cannot have exclusive control over issues such as marriage, divorce, abortion, conversion, burial, and medical ethics. Until the state can meet all needs by setting up alternative civil frameworks, the religion-state issues will continue to fester as an open wound. In this ongoing fight, there are no permanent winners—only permanent losers.

Through the courts, Reform Jews have been the prime opponent of religious coercion. We should not diminish efforts to pursue our rights through the judicial and legislative frameworks. However, let there be no illusion. Religious belief, knowledge, commitment, and observance cannot be legislated or adjudicated. Even if we should eventually achieve some form of separation, even if we should win rights through the courts and the Knesset, this would not lead to a greater degree of observance of Jewish tradition among secular Israelis.

The Jewish state needs a synthesis of Zionism and Judaism. It is possible to reinterpret halachah in consonance with the needs of a modern Jewish society and in a way that will be conducive to a more hospitable environment for all religious streams. This was the view of Rabbi Eliezer Berkowitz, an eminent Orthodox scholar. Writing at the time of the "Who is a Jew?" crisis in the 1980s, he said, "Within halachah there are possibilities for an approach between the various ideological groupings of the Jewish people. The responsibility of striving for unity in the spirit of *Ahavat Israel* [Love of Israel] is equally binding on all of us. Halachah has to be stretched to its limits in order to further Jewish unity and mutual understanding."*

At the present time, Israeli society is still concerned primarily with the urgent task of resolving the Israeli-Palestinian conflict and secondarily with socioeconomic issues and the

---

*Eliezer Berkowitz, *Not in Heaven: The Nature and Function of Halakha* (Ktav Publishing House, 1983), 106–112.

well-being of its citizens. Some issues of religion and state have been relegated to a back burner. However, these issues will eventually come to the fore again in full-blown controversy, especially if and when the foreign policy and defense issues near resolution.

Since, as we have pointed out, it is unlikely that the middle ground will come from within Orthodoxy, a significant option can and should come from liberal Judaism. The liberal approach to Judaism, as reflected in the two main movements, Masorti (Conservative) and Progressive Judaism (Reform), has the obligation to play a major role.

In the American environment, Jewish identity has been contracted. Whereas previous generations of American Jews were identified as being a nationality, in the contemporary context Jews tend to be defined as a religious community. Jewish participation in the four faith frameworks (Catholic, Protestant, Muslim, Jewish) elevated the role of the synagogue to the counterpart of the church and mosque, and the rabbi as the counterpart of the minister, the imam, and the priest. Vestiges of cultural ethnicity, such as Jewish food, music, and art still exist, but as dimensions of Jewish peoplehood are being deemphasized, the Jewish ethnic identity is being transformed.

The contraction of Jewishness to religion distances American Jews from Israeli Jews, where they comprise a nationality. The divergent definitions between "religionized" American Jewry and "nationalized" Israeli Jewry potentially widen the misunderstanding between Israel and the Diaspora and detract from their sense of common destiny. There are also differences between Israel and the Diaspora in terms of socioeconomic conditions, the character of society and government, psychological experiences, and geopolitical developments. All these can lead to conflicting views on major issues.

The most effective counterbalance to a diminished American Jewish ethnicity is closer affinity with Israel, the essence of Jewish peoplehood. For liberal American Jews, the closer the relationship to liberal Judaism in Israel, the greater the sense of identification. The more traditional nature of liberal Judaism in Israel is itself a manifestation of living in a nation characterized by Jewish peoplehood.

The success or failure of liberal Judaism in Israel is the ultimate test for liberal Judaism in America. The degree of success of American liberal Judaism needs to be evaluated from the perspective of the ultimate goal—preservation of the Jewish people and its heritage. We believe that knowledge of Judaism, commitment to worship, observance of tradition, and application of Jewish ethics will enhance the lives of individual Jews and the Jewish people as a whole. Yet, the reality is that only a small percentage of those affiliated with American Reform, Conservative, and Reconstructionist congregations fulfill the prerequisite criteria of practicing liberal Judaism.

This phenomenon has led some critics to define the liberal movements as "sociological" rather than "theological" in character. By "sociological," they mean that they have succeeded because they represent an easier, more aesthetic, more palatable way for members to have exposure to Jewishness. However, in general, most of our members do not practice what we preach. Therefore, contend our critics, liberal Judaism is a Diaspora phenomenon—not only incapable of having serious impact on the daily lives of its adherents, but incapable of rooting itself in the predominantly Jewish environment of Israel.

A realistic analysis of Israeli society suggests that neither the opposition of the Orthodox nor the lack of rights for liberal Judaism fully explains the inability to develop a more significant non-Orthodox Judaism in Israel. Many non-Orthodox and secular Israelis are in search of more meaning and purpose in life. If those seekers and searchers discover that liberal Judaism can meet their spiritual, educational, and cultural needs, then the movement will flourish as an indigenous, legitimate expression of Judaism.

Therefore, the true test of whether liberal Judaism is a universal religious movement is the extent to which it can have an impact on Jews in Israel. Israel is the testing ground for the determination of Jewish authenticity. If liberal Judaism can flourish only in a non-Jewish environment and not in a Jewish environment, then we will be like fish that can live out of water—and a fish that lives out of water is not a fish.

Liberal Judaism in America can never achieve a proper relationship with Israel until there is a strong liberal movement within Israel itself. Until then, not only will the average Israeli consider us outsiders, but we shall also consider ourselves outsiders—a Diaspora creation flourishing in gentile soil, but foreign to that of the Land of Israel.

Liberal Judaism projects a viable option of a Judaism that is relevant, egalitarian, aesthetic, and moral. We proclaim that in Judaism laws and ritual observance are inseparable from the ethical code. The very word *halachah* derives from the Hebrew root "to walk, to go forward, to progress." In its very essence halachah should be progressive.

To retain the spirit of Judaism, halachah should not send forth a cloud of darkness, obfuscating the path through life, but it should ignite a pillar of enlightenment to illuminate life's goals. To keep the Sabbath holy, it should not degenerate into a day of stone throwing, burning garbage, and demonstrating, but should allow Jews of all shades of observance to capture a glimpse of peaceful harmony in the world, the community, and the home. In relating to social and economic issues, such as poverty and unemployment, rabbinical leaders would do well to heed the dictum of the Kotzker Rabbi: "Rather than taking care of your body and another man's soul, take care of his body and your own soul." To claim that our biblical forefathers were cartographers divinely appointed to set Israel's geographical boundaries for all time is not to preserve, but to pervert Judaism. To categorize Israeli political leaders who "seek peace and pursue it" as enemies of the people—and in the name of God, no less—is to desecrate God's name. To declare that it is a religious duty to oppose negotiations with adversaries is to violate the spirit of the Rabbinic dictum "Who is a hero among heroes? He who converts an enemy into a friend" (*Avot D'Rabbi Natan* 23). As Jews, we should aspire not to a Pax Romana, a peace imposed by military might from on high, but to a *sh'lom emet*, a peace of truth among equals.

To support liberal Judaism in Israel is not philanthropy, such as is support for universities, hospitals, yeshivot, and a host of other worthy causes. To support liberal Judaism in Israel is inseparable from investing in liberal Judaism in the Diaspora. In developing the Israeli movement, we affirm the viability of liberal Judaism throughout the world.

Do all liberal Jews abroad understand that through the movement in Israel their own Jewish identity is being tested? Unfortunately, some do not. Nevertheless, even if we have not persuaded all our own members to recognize our efforts, even if we have not convinced all secular Israelis to recognize us, at least we should be grateful that the Orthodox establishment has unanimously, albeit unwittingly, extended recognition to us. Just see how they advance our cause and publicize our efforts. Initially, the "Who is a Jew?" controversy erupted over the issue of recognition of conversions performed by non-Orthodox rabbis living abroad. The controversy raging since 1997 is over conversions performed in Israel for Israeli citizens by our rabbis living in Israel (see chapter 8). The controversy is also over participation of the Reform and Conservative representatives in local religious councils. In the 1970s not every Israeli was aware of the presence of the developing liberal movement in Israel. Today, again thanks to our Orthodox colleagues' vociferous objections, every Israeli knows that liberal Judaism is here, and growing in numbers and influence.

The more the Orthodox attempt to impose religious coercion in Israel, the stronger liberal Judaism becomes, and the more they fear us—and for good reason. If a liberal alternative to Orthodoxy gains a stronger foothold in Israel, the Orthodox political monopoly will be undermined.

In order to retain their own legitimacy, the Orthodox feel the need to delegitimize the non-Orthodox movements. However, both history and the Torah have sealed their fate and ours. Freedom both for and from religion is destined to prevail.

Given the above considerations, the liberal movements in Judaism must reevaluate their relationship to Israel and especially to their own movements in Israel. The World Zionist Organization program of 1968 espoused as the first aim of Zionism "the unity of the Jewish people and the centrality of the State of Israel." The word "centrality" was a cause for continued ideological controversy, particularly when the North American Jewish population was twice the size of that of Israel. However, in light of the subsequent demographic changes and political developments, it should now be clear that Israel is central, not only ideologically but also demographically. The American liberal movements need a radical new approach. No geographical borders can separate Jewish minds, hearts, and destiny. The Eastern Seaboard of the United States cannot serve as the boundary for institutional responsibility or for financial obligations and commitments.

In this regard, the leaders of the Jewish Federation system in North America have led the way. From their inception, they understood that in order to foster the concept of a global Jewish people, it is essential to inculcate in local leadership a sense of global responsibility. They have highlighted overseas needs—Israel, Soviet Jewry, Ethiopian Jewry—as the prime objectives

of their fund-raising efforts. Although in recent years the allocations to overseas needs have been diminished in relation to
domestic allocations, nevertheless the Federations would never
contemplate the elimination of overseas needs altogether. They
recognize that assuming global responsibility enhances a more
intensive Jewish identity in local communities.

Would that our American liberal movements adopt the
same global perspective! In effect, the American movements
remain "America Firsters." The American liberal movements
have never considered their international counterparts to be
a primary obligation. The American institutions have developed effective fund-raising mechanisms for sustaining and
expanding their local programs, but they have not included
the Israeli and international counterparts as integral components of their campaigns. Therefore, the international and Israeli movements have had to fend for themselves. Since the
primary sources of funding are in North America, the world
movements have, in effect, been forced to compete with
the American movements for funding—with generally inef-
fectual results. Until the American movements incorporate
global needs into their regular funding goals, their leadership
will be defaulting on their responsibility. Raising funds is not
only necessary to sustain and expand the Israeli movements,
but the very process of fund-raising serves an educational
purpose. One of the things that sets apart American Jewry
from other religious and ethnic groups is the assumption of
responsibility for world Jewry.

The leadership of the Federations comes from within the
Conservative and Reform movements. How is it possible that
when it comes to our liberal movements in Israel, that same
leadership has not extended the scope of its responsibility to
include Israel? By contrast, Orthodox Jewry has met its own
challenge of responsibility. True, their contributions to the
Federations have been limited because they focus on direct

contributions to build and expand the network of Orthodox educational and welfare institutions in Israel. More than this—they have exploited the political clout of the religious parties in Israel to mobilize Israeli government funding.

We in the liberal movements have demonstrated our capacity to broaden the scope of Judaism to incorporate a liberal Jewish approach to education. Witness the growing network of Tali ("Augmented Jewish Studies") schools, our innovative kindergartens, early childhood training centers, and the youth movements. We have fostered new kinds of creative Jewish cultural expression (the programs of Beit Shmuel–Mercaz Shimshon, Beit Daniel, the Leo Baeck Education Center, and similar activities—see chapter 17), and we have created a program of social action and advocacy, centered in the Israel Religious Action Center and advocated in our congregations.

In order to exploit our potential for greater impact in Israel, we need a massive influx of material and human resources. Since we cannot expect significant Israeli government funding, we must rely on the American movements to recognize and assume their global responsibilities.

In Proverbs 29:18 we are taught, "Where there is no vision, a people deteriorates." If American liberal movements fail to be captivated by the vision of future opportunities and obligations in Israel, those failures will deleteriously impact on their capacity to thrive and progress in America. Advancing the Israeli and international movements is no less a vested interest of American Reform Judaism than is the concern for the American movements.

Now is the time to reaffirm our confidence in the future of the Jewish people, the Jewish state, and liberal Judaism in Israel. This confidence is epitomized by the prophet Jeremiah: "I am mindful of the plans I have made for you, declares the Lord, plans for your well-being, not for evil, to give you a future and a hope" (Jeremiah 29:11).

Chapter Three

Israel-Diaspora Relations

Not long ago I was riding in a taxi to Kennedy International Airport. The driver's name was Motke Goldstein. Speaking with a heavy Yiddish accent, he informed me that he was a Holocaust survivor. When he discovered I was on my way home to Israel, he waxed enthusiastic. "Most of my family is there. Israel is all I think about. I live and breathe Israel. Israel is my whole life." "If that's the way you feel," I probed, "why don't you join us and come there to live?" "What, me live in Israel?" he declared. "Never! There's too much corruption and hypocrisy, and just look how people have lost their idealism." "But are there not similar shortcomings here in New York?" "Sure," he responded, "but here it doesn't bother me. If I lived in the Jewish state, I couldn't stand it."

In his own way, Motke the driver demonstrated a profound insight into Israel-Diaspora relations. Many Jews in the Diaspora, even those who are not able to articulate an ideology in intellectual terms, understand that Israel is the paramount setting for the fulfillment of Jewish aspirations. Such a Jew as Motke, whose entire life centers around Israel, expects Israeli society to reflect the highest standards, while the failure to attain those standards can often serve as a rationale for distancing oneself from the country.

Not only Jews like Motke are disillusioned by the growing gap between Jewish expectations and Israeli reality. All recent polls reflect an increasing distance between American and Israeli Jews, particularly among the younger generation. They point to many factors, among them indifference: large segments in both populations are simply disinterested in what happens to their fellow Jews over the ocean. Others allude to conflicting positions on issues of foreign policy: many American Jews disagree with policies adopted by the Israeli government, even as many Israelis do not understand the lack of support among American Jews for Israel's policies. Still others blame the crises in the global economy and the subsequent reduction in American Jewish funding of Israeli causes and institutions.

I contend that the real explanations are much more complex. They presage radical changes that are likely to revolutionize the character of Israel-Diaspora relations. It is incumbent on Jewish leadership in both Israel and America to study and analyze the ever-changing conditions of Jewish life, to reject anachronistic ideologies and the outmoded institutional frameworks of the previous century, and to establish new organizational structures and innovative programs in order to respond to the needs for creative Jewish survival in the twenty-first century.

A number of factors play a part in the current changing relationship.

Comprehending the Historical Background: Emancipation and the Origins of Israel-Diaspora Relations

The contemporary differences between Jewish identity in the Diaspora and in Israel are a consequence of the impact of the Emancipation in Europe at the end of the eighteenth century. It is essential to study the dilemma then confronting

Jews as individuals and European Jewry as collective communities: How can Jews fully participate in the prevailing non-Jewish democratic society as individuals and at the same time retain their collective Jewish identity? How can Jews be both a part of the social order and yet stand apart from it? The question was first posed not by Jews, but by the intellectual and political leaders of the French Enlightenment. How could they proclaim "Liberty, Equality, Fraternity" for all human beings and yet exclude the Jews? How could they with integrity proclaim the Declaration of the Rights of Man and not grant equal rights of citizenship to the Jews in their midst? They wrestled with the dilemma for years until they resolved the issue by conferring equal rights on Jews who affirmed their loyalty to France and demonstrated the capacity to acculturate within the indigenous French milieu. In 1806, Napoleon convened an Assembly of Jewish Notables, most of whom were Orthodox, and posed a series of questions to determine whether the Jews were capable of being loyal French citizens. The questions were posed in order to elicit a response to the fundamental issue of Jewish identity. Are the Jews to be regarded as a "nation," a "separate people," or members of a "church"—that is, a people distinguished from other citizens only by their religious beliefs? Confronted by the choice of enfranchisement as adherents of the Jewish faith or exclusion from citizenship as members of a "separate people," the participants in the Assembly of Jewish Notables agreed to minimize the nationalist and ethnocultural dimensions of Jewishness. They agreed to pave the path to integration with the bricks of conscious deculturation. They formally responded to the issue that had been framed in the French Constitutional Assembly of 1789 by Count Clermont Tonnerre, who was an ardent advocate of equality for Jews. He had declared, "To Jews as a nation—nothing; to the Jews as individuals—everything."

As a consequence of the acculturation process, many Jews went far beyond what was expected of them. In France they even founded exclusive Jewish societies for those who did not want to associate with other Jews. Many of them converted to Christianity, especially the more integrated and established among them. The son of the French chief rabbi, Emanuel Deutz, converted to Christianity, and his son-in-law, who had begun his studies for the rabbinate, became a Catholic priest.

What transpired in France characterized the process of Emancipation everywhere. Despite all the efforts to redefine Jewish identity so as to conform to the challenges of integration, pernicious manifestations of anti-Semitism still continued to erupt. It was, after all, in France, after a century of Jewish efforts to acculturate to the French milieu, that the most infamous wave of anti-Semitism erupted. The trial accusing Captain Alfred Dreyfus, a distinguished Jewish officer in the French army, of treason demonstrated that the virus of anti-Semitism was as virulent as ever.

Partially in response to the Dreyfus trial and partially in response to other anti-Semitic manifestations, Theodor Herzl formulated his proposals in his treatise *The Jewish State* and established the foundations for political Zionism. His fundamental hypothesis was that Emancipation had failed. The twin dangers of anti-Semitism and assimilation continued to threaten the existence of the Jewish people. It was clear to Herzl that no matter how hard Jews tried to redefine their identity as a religious community and thereby to conform to the demands of equal citizenship, the non-Jewish world continued to define the Jews as an outcast people. Long after Herzl's death, Hitler demonstrated the validity of Herzl's hypothesis. German fascism did not care what Jews believed. Conversion to Christianity offered no protection. The Nuremberg Laws decreed that Jewishness was determined by birth.

If one of a person's grandparents was Jewish, that was enough to send the person to a concentration camp.

So, posited Herzl, if the world still defines Jews as a people, then let us indeed reconstitute ourselves as such. Let us return to the biblical land of our origin, to the Land of Israel, and there regain our identity as a people and in so doing renew our Jewish cultural heritage.

It is important to acknowledge the inherent contradiction. For the majority of world Jewry the Emancipation initiated a positive revolution, opening wide the gates of opportunity for Jews as individuals and for Jewish communities as a collective. Little wonder that when Herzl proposed his vision for a Jewish state, the vast majority of emancipated Jews were opposed, and that Herzl's major support came from the Jews of Russia and Eastern Europe, who had never tasted the fruits of Emancipation.

It is my contention that the dilemma first posed by the Emancipation has never been resolved. The fundamental differences between Diaspora Jewry and Israeli Jewry are grounded in divergent reactions to the Emancipation. The Zionist movement was founded by people who maintained that the process of Emancipation was a failure that threatened the very existence of the Jewish people. Conversely, the Jewish communities in the Western democracies are testimony to the success of Emancipation. The democratic process has enabled Jews to rise to the heights of success in all economic, political, academic, and cultural arenas of the Diaspora, especially in American society. Jews are prominent in every field of American endeavor,* far beyond their proportion in the population of the United States. The collective American

---

*According to all demographic projections, by the middle of the twenty-first century, only 8 percent of world Jewry will be living outside Israel and North America. Therefore, I stress American Jewry.

Jewish community has a multitude of successful institutions perpetuating Jewish continuity, including synagogues, universities, colleges, day schools, Federations, community centers, museums, camps, and a host of other institutions. Yet despite all this fruitful creativity in American Jewish life, intermarriage, assimilation, and anti-Semitism persist as ongoing threats to Jewish survival.

I would pose this question to American Jews. What if we were to resurrect Napoleon and ask him to frame similar questions that would determine the character of Jewish identity and the place of Jews in American society today? I believe that the vast majority of American Jews would choose the responses of early nineteenth-century French Jewry rather than the late nineteenth-century response of Herzl and the Zionist movement.

The generations of American Jews born after the Holocaust live in a society that prides itself on guaranteeing the rights of the individual. Indeed, the fundamental principle of Western democracy is to grant equal rights and civil liberties to every person, irrespective of gender, national origin, race, or creed. Each person is to be judged on the basis of individual merit. Society is expected to be oblivious to a person's ethnic or religious identity. This fundamental premise found expression when John F. Kennedy became the first Catholic president and when Barack Obama was elected as the first African American president. The secular nonsectarian character of American democracy has enabled Jews to progress in every sphere. That is why American Jewish communal institutions devote enormous efforts to defend the principle of separation of church and state.

Modern Zionism accepted the fundamental democratic principle of judging each person on the basis of individual merit. However, in contrast to America, Zionism proclaimed as its major objective the guarantee that the Jews *as a people* should have equal rights among the family of nations. It is this hypothesis that many American Jews and non-Jews alike find difficult to comprehend. For many, the definition of Jews is as a religious community parallel to that of Protestants, Catholics, or Muslims. In their view, the premise that Jews are a people contradicts the fundamental principles that have enabled Jews to succeed in American society. Moreover, the term "peoplehood" cannot be found in any English dictionary. In fact, it is a concept used only by Jews. It was first coined by Mordecai M. Kaplan to express the commitment of Jews to *K'lal Yisrael*, the totality of the Jewish people, and the concept that every Jew is responsible for every other and for the entire Jewish people. The term "peoplehood" implies recognition that Jews share common values, norms, culture, history, and a common destiny.

The Jewish state was created not as an end in and of itself, but as a means to preserve the Jewish people. In fact, Zionism has restored the Jews as a people. Those who reject the concept of Jewish peoplehood have difficulty in relating to the Jewish state, even as many Zionists have difficulty in relating to Jews who do not perceive Jews to be a people.

Living as a Jew: Divergent Relationships to Society in the Diaspora and in Israel

In the Diaspora Jewish life is *voluntary*. The degree of a person's identity as a Jew is a question of freedom of choice. Jewishness is experienced in the home, the synagogue, the Jewish community and its institutions. Jewishness is experienced through observance of the Sabbath and Festivals and in life-cycle events such as birth, marriage, and death. The phrase "Jew-by-choice" has been used to describe non-Jews who convert to Judaism, but in effect, every Jew born into the

Jewish people becomes a "Jew-by-choice." Every person can make a personal decision regarding the extent of his or her identity as a Jew. Even when Jews take group action through Jewish organizations such as advocating stands on civil rights or social justice issues, the action is legitimated by an accepted democratic process that encourages individuals to band together in order to exert influence on public policy. But the organizations take action on a limited number of specific issues of Jewish concern. Jews as a group are not responsible for the character of the American society as a whole.

In Israel, in contrast, Jewish life is in effect mandatory. Every Jewish citizen (except for those ultra-Orthodox or religious women who are exempt from military service) is obligated to serve in the Israeli army. Every person is obligated to pay taxes to the Jewish state. The official language is Hebrew (along with Arabic); public holidays are the traditional Jewish Festivals and those that have been added as a consequence of historical experience. It is impossible to distinguish between the private and public sectors, between universal and particular concerns, between humanness and Jewishness. All issues are both universal and particular. All issues are denominated as Jewish both by those who live in the state and those who live outside it. Take the issue of poverty and the growing gap between the rich and the poor in Israeli society. This is legitimately characterized as a failure of a Jewish society to fulfill its mandate of biblical values. Not only the secular state but its Jewish component is held accountable.

Because Israel was established as a Jewish state it is ipso facto the testing ground for applying traditional Jewish ethical standards. In effect, the State of Israel is a framework for judging how Jews who live in a sovereign Jewish state should create a just society. How do Jews use political power? How do they relate to the minority groups in their midst, particularly those who are not only disadvantaged but also challenge

the ideological foundations of the Jewish state? How should a
Jewish society deal with Jewish triumphalism, with prejudice
against non-Jews, and with instances of flagrant violation of
civil liberties and freedom of conscience? How do Jews relate to others when they are the victors and not the victims,
or when they are seen as the oppressors rather than the oppressed? The guiding principle of American society is to judge
Jews as individuals. In the Jewish state, the guiding principle
is that Jews should be judged as a people.

Conflicting Jewish Identities

A phenomenon of Jewish life in America has been the contraction of Jewish identity. At the turn of the twentieth century, when large masses of Jews entered the United States,
they identified themselves and were identified by others as
an ethnic group, similar to other immigrant groups, such as
the Irish, Germans, Greeks, and Italians. Today in America,
Jews are more identified as a religious community, on a par
with Catholics, Protestants, and Muslims. In many instances,
it amounts to "religionization" without "religiosity," individuals who declare themselves to be Jews but do not necessarily
practice Judaism. Some of these Jews can be termed "ali-
mony" Jews. They are willing to pay for support of Judaism
but prefer not to live with it.

In other instances, there is a search for spirituality. This
search often leads to New Age religious expression and an
emphasis on personal faith. In itself the search for spiritual
experiences is salutary, but all too often it is accompanied
by a rejection of Jewish peoplehood and by distancing from
the State of Israel. Rather than being perceived as a reinvigoration, it becomes a replacement for Jewish identity. This
trend threatens to reintroduce the reformist ideology of the

nineteenth century, but to clothe it in twenty-first-century garb. If the emphasis on individuality is not refracted through the prism of Jewish peoplehood and a sense of the collective Jewish experience, Jewish identity will be weakened and Judaism as a faith will be diminished.

Conversely, in Israel, Jewish identity is in danger of being "nationalized." Among secular Israelis, there is an innate desire for what is perceived to be normalization. This can lead to a form of Jewish assimilation. Assimilation leads to what has been defined as post-Zionism. Post-Zionists advocate that Israel should take its place as a "normal" state and aspire to become an integral part of the region. Ties to world Jewry and to the Jewish heritage are weakened as a result.

The trend toward nationalization of Jewish identity is evident not only among secular Israelis, but among the Zionist Orthodox. Their opposition to disengagement from Gaza and West Bank settlements reflects a merger of interests between Orthodox religious Zionist movements and right-wing political forces. In some instances, the negative reaction among Orthodox youth to disengagement has led to a weakening of bonds to Israel as a Zionist state. A major effort should be made to reconcile the differences and to prevent religious Zionists from succumbing to the tendency of separating loyalty to Judaism from loyalty to the state. No action of the government can serve as a pretext for juxtaposing faith and citizenship. Love of Judaism and allegiance to Zionism are inextricable.

Discarding Anachronistic Ideology

Every successful revolutionary movement must change its ideological perceptions in light of changing circumstances. Only a revolutionary movement that fails to achieve its objectives will retain its principles intact. A movement that is dynamic and progressive has to strive for relevance. To be relevant is to adapt basic principles to changing conditions. Therefore, the fundamental premises of Zionism, some of which were controversial in their original formulation, should undergo a constant process of reevaluation. In some instances, even though the terminology may remain the same, the connotation changes in response to developing circumstances.

To illustrate this, let us consider a Zionist ideological issue that generated controversy in the past, but that in the light of current developments appears to have lost relevance. This is what I refer to as the Babylon-Jerusalem two-foci hypothesis. This theory once reflected the view of the majority of American Jewry. The Jerusalem Program adopted at the 1968 World Zionist Congress proved highly controversial. It stated as the first aim of the Zionist movement, "The unity of the Jewish People and the centrality of Israel in Jewish life." At the time, the idea of "centrality" was unacceptable to many Diaspora Jews, including Zionists. Instead, American Jews adopted the two-foci hypothesis. Its proponents pointed to ancient Babylon, where a major center of Jewish life had evolved, and they projected American Jewry as a latter-day Babylon. At times Babylon outnumbered the Jewish community in Palestine and exceeded it in cultural creativity. Furthermore, the Babylonian community provided material resources to sustain the struggling Jewish community in Palestine.

No wonder that American Jewish leaders compared their community to ancient Babylon. Was not the American Jewish community the main political and financial supporter of Israel? Did not the American Jewish population far outnumber the Israeli Jewish population? By what right did Zionists proclaim that Israel is the center? In 1969 I wrote an article in the *Jerusalem Post* in which I stated that after the Six-Day War it should have become obvious that "Israel is Broadway

and America is Off Broadway." The article was severely criticized by many American Jewish leaders.

But by now the Jewish population of Israel is already larger
than the Jewish population of the United States, and demographers project that by the middle of the twenty-first century
the majority of world Jewry will live in Israel. I do not think
that my "Broadway–Off Broadway" metaphor would generate
such controversy today. It is widely recognized that Israel is
now the center stage for the enactment of the Jewish drama
and that Jewish destiny will be determined in great measure
by historic developments occurring to and affecting Israel.

Furthermore, the use of the word "centrality" has lost any
connotation of superiority. To say that New York is the center
of American Jewish activity is merely a statement of fact. To
acknowledge that the major Jewish organizations have their
headquarters in New York does not deprecate in any way the
Jewish communities of Chicago, Miami, Philadelphia, or Los
Angeles.

On the other hand, the present Jewish condition has contributed to a dilution of classic Zionist ideology. Take for example, the hypothesis of *sh'lilat hagalut*, the negation of the
Diaspora. Classical Zionists including Herzl believed that in
the long run, the Diaspora Jewish communities would not survive. Once the Jewish state was established, those who wanted
to remain Jews would move to the Land of Israel. Those who
remained behind would eventually assimilate. Philosophers
like Jacob Klatzkin went so far as to state that the Diaspora is
"nothing more than a life of futile struggle and pointless suf-
fering, of ambiguity, confusion and eternal impotence. It is
not worth keeping alive."

The argument for the negation of the Diaspora is no longer tenable. It failed to take into consideration many factors,
foremost among them the impact of Israel on the condition of
Diaspora Jewry. The very existence of the state and its struggle

to establish itself instilled inspiration, hope, and confidence into Diaspora Jewish life. The *sh'lilat hagalut* hypothesis has in effect been turned on its head. It is universally recognized that it is not feasible for all of world Jewry to live in the Jewish state. In countries of distress, the Jewish population has decreased. At present the largest realistic pool of potential immigrants remains the former Soviet Union. However, in the long term, the largest potential pool of immigrants is to be found among Jewish populations in the affluent countries. The Zionist movement should intensify its advocacy of *aliyah* from those areas. However, no responsible Jew would want Jews who choose not to immigrate to disappear. If over the last sixty years Diaspora Jewry considered its prime task to be the strengthening of the Jewish state, over the next sixty years it is the state that must strengthen the Diaspora.

World Jewry has come to recognize that the destiny of Israel and that of world Jewry are interdependent. What makes world Jewry distinctive is its identification with Israel. What makes Israel a special state is its interdependence with world Jewry.

The Religion and State Dilemma

I have dealt at length elsewhere in this book on the issues of religion and state. However, it is essential to repeat that for Diaspora and especially American Jews, this issue is a primary cause of disagreement with Israel. The principle of separation of church and state as enshrined in the American Constitution guarantees equal rights for all faiths. All of them have equal status and freedom of opportunity. As we have seen, in Israel the Orthodox Rabbinate has full authority over issues of personal status, which includes birth, marriage, conversion, divorce, and burial. The powers of the Chief Rabbinate, the

local rabbinical courts, and religious councils enable Orthodoxy to control personal status issues through a monopolistic
and stringent interpretation of halachah, without reference to
the needs of individuals living in a modern society. The imposition of Jewish law rather than that of civil law as in most
modern democracies often creates unjust conditions for individuals who have no recourse to the civil court system.

Furthermore, the inextricable relationship between the religious authorities and religious political parties enables the
forces of a narrow interpretation of Judaism to wield political
influence far beyond their electoral strength. The existence of
separate, independent religious educational systems height-
ens the divisiveness within Israel society. The curricula of
the ultra-Orthodox school systems concentrate on the study
of Talmudic and Rabbinic sources, depriving their pupils of
a core education in mathematics, the sciences, English, and
other subjects so essential to a modern society. The ultra-Orthodox education system creates an underclass of unemploy-
able or underemployed persons, thus consigning them to a
lower socioeconomic class within society at large.

Approximately 50 percent of American Jews do not associate themselves with any synagogue movement, 6 to 10 percent
are Orthodox, and the remainder are Reform or Conservative. With rare exceptions, the leaders of the Federations, the
communal agencies, and other major Jewish institutions are
drawn from the Conservative and Reform movements. They
will not forever tolerate a condition whereby those who represent their views of a liberal Judaism do not have equal status in Israel.

Therefore, the issue of religion and state is not a narrow,
isolated, tangential issue, which is how many Israelis perceive
it. It actually lies at the heart of the entire Jewish enterprise.
Unless religion-state issues are confronted head-on, Israel
will cease to be the state of the entire Jewish people. There is

a danger that many Jews in the Diaspora will cease to identify with the State of Israel, just as Israeli Jews are in danger of ceasing to identify with the Diaspora. As I have emphasized before, if all Jews do not feel at home in Israel, Israel will not be home for all Jews.

Demographic Patterns in the United States

All demographic projections indicate that the American Jewish population is declining. According to the latest National Jewish Population Survey of 2001, Jews were estimated to number 5.2 million persons, as compared to 5.5 million in the previous survey. In general, Jews dwell in the major metropolitan urban areas, which tend to have the lowest birth rate. Jews are high on the list of those who choose not to marry or who marry late in life or intermarry. In a recent census, 2,345,000 Americans reported that although they had Jewish grandparents, they no longer consider themselves Jewish.

The rate of intermarriage was estimated to be 47 percent. More and more Jews contend that it is prejudicial or racist to oppose intermarriage. Whereas in the past, as many as 25 percent of non-Jews who intermarried converted to Judaism, today the number of converts to Judaism who are intermarried has decreased to approximately 5 percent. The children of converts to Judaism have a much higher rate of intermarriage than do children both of whose parents are Jewish.

In the past the American Jewish population grew through immigration from Europe, the Soviet Union, and Israel, but the economic crisis that began in 2008, with the accompanying wave of unemployment, seems to have lessened the attractiveness of immigration to America. The declining American Jewish population has had an impact on Jewish participation in American politics. In the 1940s Jews numbered 3.7 percent of the American population. At the beginning of the twenty-first century, given the increase of the general American population, Jews now account for only 1.8 percent. This decline is likely to lead to a reduced influence on issues of special Jewish concern.

All these factors will inevitably lead to potential conflicts between Jews in Israel and the Diaspora. In addition to those listed above, other more contemporary issues complicate Israel-Diaspora relations even further:

1. *American Jewry is becoming more knowledgeable and sophisticated.* Modern technology provides instant information about all developments worldwide. In the age of the Internet and the computer anyone can acquire information on Israel at the same time as Israeli citizens. I recall an incident during the Intifada when a friend called from America to inform us that CNN had just announced that a suicide bomber had blown up a bus in our neighborhood, even before it was announced in the Israeli news media. The image projected exposes the blemishes as well as the virtues, the corruption as well as the heroism, the internecine divisiveness as well as the remarkable bonding in times of crisis.

2. *American Jewry as a whole can no longer be relied on to give unequivocal support to Israel's political actions.* In the past, whenever Israel's existence was threatened, such as in 1948, 1967, and 1973, American Jewry rallied overwhelmingly in support. But when Israel's very existence is not considered to be at stake, the support of American Jewry becomes more tenuous. Furthermore, American Jews are influenced by American politics. During the presidency of George W. Bush, the administration was considered to be solidly behind Israel's foreign policy. However, when the foreign policy of President Barack Obama was defined as

more "evenhanded," Jewish critics of Israel became more outspoken. Studies, such as those by Steven Cohen and Ari Kelman, conclude that members of the younger generation of American Jews are distancing themselves from Israel. They record that "feelings of attachment may well be changing, as warmth gives way to indifference, and indifference may well give way to downright alienation." Almost 50 percent of American Jews under thirty-five years old indicated that destruction of the State of Israel would not be seen by them to be a personal tragedy.*

3. *The passing of the Holocaust generation.* Some sixty-five years have elapsed since the world learned of the Holocaust and since the War of Independence created the Jewish state. During that time, the tragedy and the struggle for survival often involved American Jews' own relatives. But for the younger generation the trials and tribulations of the past have been relegated to history. Moreover, the historic events that motivated Diaspora Jewry to mobilize mass political support and emergency funding for rescuing endangered Jews in North Africa, Arab lands, the Soviet Union, and Ethiopia no longer exist. No such stirring causes are likely to arise in the future.

4. *The Arab-Israel issue.* The passage of time has not necessarily been favorable to Israel. The more time elapses, the more the world forgets the original cause for the conflict. It was the Arabs who rejected the 1947 Partition Plan, the original two-state solution, and who have waged continued warfare against the Jewish state. At the same time, the disabilities, the misery, and the frustrations of the Arab population in Gaza and the occupied territories in the West Bank have become more visible. The overt imbalances in

---

*Steven M. Cohen and Ari Y. Kelman, "Beyond Distancing: Young Adult American Jews and their Alienation from Israel," Andrea and Charles Bronfman Philanthropies, 2007.

the United Nations have made it impossible for Israel to be judged equitably and UN forums have been exploited to disseminate prejudice against Israel and to condone manifestations of anti-Semitism. American Jews have inevitably been influenced by the constant bombardment of anti-Israel and anti-Semitic propaganda emanating from the UN and some of the media.

5. *The impact of the economic crisis.* The drastic recession of 2008–9 (and the Madoff affair) is likely to produce fundamental and permanent changes in the financial situations of organized Jewish communities. Almost every Jewish institution has been forced to cut budgets, staff, and programs. In some instances it is anticipated that communal organizations and even some synagogues will either disappear or need to merge with other institutions in order to stay alive. Some have indicated that in any case these changes should have been initiated for the sake of efficiency and good governance. The shortage of funds expedited the opportunity and gave incentive for change.

As for the local Jewish Federations, they have been experiencing a decreasing donor base for many years. It is to be anticipated that policies will be adopted to contribute proportionately more funding for local causes than for Israel and overseas needs. If there needs to be a choice between nurturing Israeli institutions or domestic Jewish causes, more emphasis will be given to local needs.

Another factor has been that Israel appears to have weathered the economic crisis better than America and most other countries. There is a belief that by now Israel has matured economically and is capable of taking care of itself with less support from Diaspora Jewry.

So what is the future of Israel-Diaspora relations? It is unlikely that Israel-Diaspora relations will ever return to those we experienced in past. Institutions such as the Jewish Agency for Israel, the World Zionist Organization, the American Jewish Joint Distribution Committee, the World Jewish Congress, the Jewish National Fund, and Keren Hayesod are dependent on advancing Jewish causes and interests through a collaborative partnership between Israel and the Diaspora. In the light of current conditions they are not likely to survive in their present form in the long run. For years I have advocated that some of these organizations should merge or at least drastically reorganize in order to meet the changing needs and character of twenty-first-century Jewish life and the interrelationship between Israel and the Diaspora.

The raising of material resources is not only essential to maintain Jewish educational, religious, and communal programming, but funding of institutions demonstrates a commitment to the preservation of Jewish values. In a world where both Israel and the Diaspora are committed to Jewish survival, it is essential that joint sponsorship and equitable sharing of financial resources be encouraged.

The reorganization of Jewish institutional life cries out for the development of new leadership in both the Diaspora and Israel. This leadership must be dedicated to a worldview of Jewish peoplehood. From the American perspective, without the closest affinity and ties to Israel, American Jewry will become just another faith community. Millions of Diaspora Jews will continue to assimilate and intermarry and potentially disappear.

From the Israeli perspective, without the closest affinity and ties to Diaspora Jewry, Israel will become a state like all other states. In terms of Jewish identity, Orthodox Jewry will become a nationalistic right-wing, autocratic minority. Secular Israeli Jews will have little contact with Jewish tradition or with fellow Jews abroad.

In his address to the First World Zionist Congress in Basel in 1897, Theodor Herzl declared, "Zionism is a return to the Jewish fold even before it becomes a return to the Jewish land." That was the original objective of Zionism—to preserve the Jewish people and to secure its future. That remains the premise and the purpose of responsible Jewish leadership dedicated to a partnership of interdependence between Israel and the Diaspora.

Chapter Four

The Diaspora's Right to Dissent

During times of extreme crisis in Israel, Jews the world over tend to adopt a united front. When the State of Israel is threatened with extreme danger—as in 1948 with the War of Independence and its aftermath, in 1967 preceding the Six-Day War, or in 1973 with the Yom Kippur War—the Holocaust-induced psyche tends to be reactivated and to become a passionate, compelling force for Jewish unity. However, when the survival of Israel is not at stake, the Jewish propensity for contentiousness comes to the fore. Such was the case in the events surrounding the Sinai Campaign of 1956. The military initiatives taken in coordination by Israel, Great Britain, and France were condemned by the United States and other countries. Many Jews openly disagreed with Israel's policies at the time, and Jewish communities were unable to function as a united body.

One of the distinguishing characteristics of Western democracy is the existence of controversy over issues of public policy. Many years ago an article in *Look* magazine declared that "Jews are like everyone else, only more so." To elaborate on that thought, one could safely state that Israel is like the other Western democracies, only more so. The peculiarities of the Israeli electoral system tend to induce political instability and continual crises in foreign and domestic policies.

During my days in Washington I came to understand and to appreciate the American political process. The two-party system concentrates the debate over controversial issues. Divergent positions on major issues are reconciled not only in discussions between the political parties, but in debates within each party. In contrast, in Israel the debates over major controversial issues are exacerbated by the existence of multiple parties. The vested interests of each party tend to take precedence over the objective of reconciling legitimate differences for the welfare of society as a whole. In Israel, politics are far more intense and public issues are debated at a level many decibels higher than in America.

The inability to forge an enduring peace with the Palestinians generates continuing dissension on foreign policy, as well as on domestic issues. Divergent approaches to geographical borders, the West Bank settlements, Gaza, Islamic fanaticism, the threat of a nuclear-armed Iran, the status of minorities, and the religion-state controversies all complicate the Israeli political process.

Diaspora Jews who are well-informed on political developments in Israel, and especially those who are committed Zionists among them, are knowledgeable about the controversies and do not hesitate to express their views. Beginning with the first Lebanon War in 1982, the justification for which was not overwhelmingly endorsed, criticism of Israel's policies among Diaspora Jewry has become more frequent and outspoken. Various public opinion polls indicate that support of Israel among Diaspora Jews is weakening steadily.

Disaffection, especially among the younger generation of Diaspora Jews, is predicated not only on disagreement with specific aspects of Israeli politics but increasingly on the lack of committed affinity with the very existence of a Jewish state. Some Diaspora Jews have even become involved in movements seeking to divest support of commercial and academic enterprises in Israel and efforts to delegitimize the state.

I have often been asked to respond to fundamental questions: Do Diaspora Jews have the right to take positions on Israeli policy issues? To what extent is it responsible for Diaspora leaders to take public stands that are contrary to the official policy of the Israeli government? Do American Jews, whose children do not serve in the Israeli army, have a right to comment on war and peace issues? If American Jewish leaders have the right to dissent from Israeli policy, how and where should they express themselves?

In January 1988 in response to these issues, I sent the following letter to Reform and other Jewish leaders as my recommended guidelines to responsible American Jewish leadership, which, I contend, is as valid today as it was then:

Dear Friends in the Diaspora,

You have a vital stake in the policies adopted by the Israeli government. What happens in Israel and to Israel reflects on the values of Judaism and the ethical standards of all Jews. The mutual obligations inherent in the dictum "Every Jew is responsible for every other Jew" do not stop at geographical borders. No one has the right to demand that you share with Israel the fruit of your hands without at the same time being willing to receive the fruits of your heart and mind. How paradoxical that some of the very Israelis who proclaim for themselves the right to define "Who is a Jew?" in the Diaspora would deny Diaspora Jewry the right to help define "What is a Jewish state?" Shall Diaspora Jewry address all the foreign nations of the world on general issues of conscience and not address the state that bears our name on Jewish issues of conscience?

So the issue before us is not whether you have the right to
speak out. Of course you have the right, yea, even the obligation. The issue is how do you speak, what are your actions,
what is your motivation, and what are the consequences?
And here I would respectfully submit that careful attention
should be paid to the political setting in which Diaspora
Jewry finds itself.

Permit me to use as an example the tragedy that occurred
in 1982 in the Palestinian refugee camps of Sabra and Sha-
tilla in Lebanon. Then representatives of the State of Israel
engaged in or condoned acts that violated Jewish ethical
standards. By chance I was not in Israel at the time. Had
I been in the country, I would have added my name to the
lists of those who placed advertisements in the Israeli press
and would have attended the rally of four hundred thousand
Israelis who gathered in protest in front of Tel Aviv city hall.
However, had I been in the United States, I would not have
added my name to the advertisements that appeared in the
American press, nor would I have participated in the public
demonstration against Prime Minister Begin at the meetings
of the Council of Jewish Federations in Los Angeles. I would
have found other ways to express my moral indignation.

Why the difference in the course of action I would have
selected? I am the same person in both places. I hold the
same views whether in Israel or the United States. However,
the context is different. The *context* should be a factor in
determining the *content* of the action. An appropriate message in one setting may not necessarily be the appropriate
message in another setting. In the Diaspora, Jews need to
be sensitive to the public media's penchant for sensational-
ism. Diaspora Jewry should insist on the need for a balanced
presentation of the facts by the press and public officials.
There are a host of alternative ways to express concern
and criticism. At times, private communications and quiet

diplomacy are as effective as public statements. At times, visits with Israeli ambassadors and representatives are called for. The sending of delegations or the organizing of fact-finding missions may be even more dramatic than public statements. And of course, there are times when a widely disseminated public statement is the best way to manifest Jewish responsibility.

How does a Diaspora individual or organization determine what is the proper course of action? There are no hard and fast rules. Each situation is different, even as each person is different. Everyone must take action in accord with his or her own personal convictions. It is to be assumed that the definition of what is responsible Jewish action will depend on individual predilections and varying circumstances.

In a sense, it is easier to be a Jew in Israel than in the Diaspora. Here in Israel our reaction to events can be direct, simple, immediate. Our target audience is the Israeli government and the Israeli population. The options for you as Diaspora Jews are more complex. You have to be aware that your public actions impact primarily on your own government and only secondarily on the Israeli government. You have to pose more sophisticated questions. What are the consequences of your actions on the formulation of American foreign policy and the shaping of American public opinion? In sum, responsible action for Diaspora Jews requires you to balance Jewish conscience with Jewish consciousness.

When it comes to an issue such as proposed amendments to the Law of Return that would invalidate conversions performed by non-Orthodox rabbis abroad, the right of Diaspora Jews to oppose the legislation should be unquestioned. They have every justification to question the right of the Knesset, a civic body in which sit a majority of secular Jews, to pass judgment on religious acts performed by Jews abroad.

But, it is widely believed by Israelis, that when it comes to foreign policy or issues affecting Judea and Samaria, these are internal matters on which Jews abroad, whose sons and daughters do not serve in the Israel Defense Forces, have no right to pass judgment. And in the Diaspora heated debates have arisen over the right to dissent on such issues. The real issue, however, is not the right of dissent, but responsible participation in the political process, and this participation is dependent on the circumstances.

The Jew in the Diaspora not only has to judge what is right, but has to exercise right judgment. If he is circumspect, it is not because an Israeli has told him what to do, but because he imposes on himself a sense of responsibility and discipline. He has to be more concerned about the public consequences of expressing the truth as he sees it than does the Jew who lives in the Jewish state. The question "Is it good or bad for the Jews?" is rarely raised in Israel but is a legitimate one in the Diaspora.

This is not in any way to be construed as limiting the freedom of expression of Diaspora Jewry. Quite the contrary, the bonds binding Jewish communities to Israel and to each other are inextricable. Neither oceans nor boundaries nor citizenship can negate the interdependence of Jewish destiny. It is inevitable that the character and policies of Israeli society affect Diaspora Jewry, just as the conduct of Diaspora Jewry impacts Israeli Jewry. That is the price and the privilege of Israel-Diaspora interdependence.

Chapter Five

The Settler Movement: A Reform Zionist Critique

The most vexing problems confronting the Israeli-Palestinian conflict involve issues relating to the status of East Jerusalem and the Israeli settlements in the West Bank of the Jordan River. After the War of Independence in 1948, Jordan claimed jurisdiction over East Jerusalem and the West Bank. However, with the exception of the United Kingdom, the international community did not recognize Jordan's annexation as legitimate. In 1988, Jordan ceded its claim to the West Bank to the Palestine Liberation Organization as the sole representative of the Palestinian people.

Preceding the outbreak of the Six-Day War in 1967, the Israeli government pleaded with King Hussein of Jordan not to become involved in hostilities should they break out. Nevertheless, on May 30, 1967, the Jordanian government signed a mutual defense treaty with Egypt that obligated it to initiate military action against Israel should war break out.

Initially, Israel had no plans to capture territory controlled by Jordan. Only after the war had commenced did Israel decide to attempt to capture East Jerusalem, especially the Old City with its Jewish Quarter and the Western Wall. Moshe Dayan, the minister of defense, then ordered the Israeli army to halt its advance. However, when Israeli intelligence reported that King Hussein had ordered his troops to with-draw eastward across the Jordan, the decision was made to capture the entire West Bank, for strategic and defensive purposes.

This brief recounting of the historical facts is cited to dem-onstrate that the initial Israeli policy was not in any way expan-sionist. It was only after that war that the full consequences of the inadequacy of Israel's borders became a major issue for discussion.

In November 1967, the United Nations Security Council unanimously adopted Resolution 242. This called for "with-drawal of Israeli armed forces from territories occupied in the recent conflict" and for respect for the rights of every state in the area to live in peace within secure and recognized boundaries. It was only later that dissent arose over the in-terpretation of the text of the resolution. The Arab nations and their allies claimed that the true meaning of the resolu-tion was withdrawal from *all* the occupied territories, whereas the United States claimed that the absence of the word "all" clearly suggested that there should be adjustments to the frontiers. Political leaders such as David Ben-Gurion and Levi Eshkol were prepared to return the entire West Bank to Arab sovereignty. However, at a conference in Khartoum, in September, 1967, the Arab League declared "the three nos" of continued belligerency: "no peace with Israel; no recogni-tion of Israel; no negotiations with Israel."

The failure to initiate any discussion between the State of Israel and the Palestinians and Arab states regarding the sta-tus of the West Bank has led to a vacuum. Each of the parties has formulated its own policies. Israel argues that the east-ern border was never defined and that according to the 1994 agreement with Jordan, and the Oslo accords with the PLO of 1993, the final status of the West Bank will be determined only when a permanent agreement is reached between Israel and the Palestinians. On the other hand, Palestinians contend that the presence of Israeli settlers, as well as military forces, is a violation of the Palestinian right to statehood and sovereignty.

Within the Israeli public there are many divergent views. On the one hand are those who would withdraw from most or even all of the West Bank for the goal of establishing a separate Palestinian state that would coexist in peace with Israel. On the other extreme are those who would annex the entire West Bank and promote transfer of the Arab population or some form of individual citizenship with Jordan.

The failure to arrive at a resolution leads to a continuing exacerbation of the problem. The Jewish population of the West Bank has grown at a steady pace. In 2010 it was estimated that over 350,000 Israeli settlers lived in the West Bank and that over 200,000 Jews lived in those parts of East Jerusalem that were annexed by Israel. The Arab population was estimated to be 2,400,000, including Jerusalem. The Arab population is growing at a faster rate than the Jewish population because of its higher birth rate.

On the assumption that a peace agreement will eventually be formulated, it is assumed that large Jewish settlement blocs such as the towns of Ariel, Maaleh Adumim, Givat Ze'ev, and Beitar Ilit, together with some settlements of major strategic importance, will remain within the borders of Israel. This would be facilitated through land exchanges with the Palestinian state. The bulk of the territories in the West Bank would thus become the geographical base of the new Palestinian state. Should this happen, it will require a significant withdrawal of many settlements in the West Bank, and tens of thousands of people.

Various polls over several years have indicated that in exchange for a true peace, the majority of Israelis, perhaps even a majority of settlers, would support withdrawal from most of the territories. Nevertheless, a decision to withdraw would precipitate extreme and possibly violent opposition from well-organized militant and radical elements among the Jewish West Bank population. These elements are overwhelmingly Orthodox. They and their rabbinical leaders claim that their stance is grounded in fundamental principles of halachah and Jewish tradition. Among them are many who are prone to violence and who in the past have engaged in incitement or attacks against Arabs.

At issue is a debate between two diametrically opposed schools of Zionism. The school represented by the settlement movement believes in *Eretz Yisrael Hashleimah,* "the total Land of Israel," having the Jordan River as its eastern border. For them, control over the God-given territory as related in the Bible is weightier than all other considerations. The second school acknowledges the historical right to the Land of Israel but believes that pragmatic considerations such as the prevailing demographic composition of the population and the democratic character of the Jewish state take precedence over retention of all the territories now in Israeli control.

Do Diaspora Jews have a right to participate in this debate? Does Reform Jewry as a worldwide religious movement have a right to take sides in this conflict? I submit that Diaspora Jews have not only a right, but an obligation, both as individuals and as a movement. If they have the right to speak out on internal policies affecting the fate of Jews in Argentina or in the former Soviet Union, do they not have the right to speak on issues affecting the Jews in the Jewish state?

To be sure, there are political ramifications to taking a stand, but above and beyond the political aspects, over which there may be legitimate differences, there is a profound religious issue, to which we must respond. We have before us two conflicting concepts of holiness. There are some religious Jews who, professing love of the Holy Land and obedience to God, fan the flames of religious fanaticism, violate the civil liberties of minority groups, advocate rule by force, and prevent the evolution of conditions leading toward peaceful compromise. In my eyes, their version of Judaism is a perversion. Their love is blind, their messianic beliefs false, and their zealotry dangerous. Their deeds defame the holy faith, desecrate the Holy One, and defile the Holy Land.

As religious Jews, we declare that the concept of *Am Ha-Kodesh*, "Holy People," takes precedence over *Eretz Ha-Kodesh*, the "Holy Land." We should repudiate those forces that, by silence or inaction, condone religious and political intolerance, verbal and physical acts of violence, and anti-gentile as well as anti-Jewish acts of racism. The alliance between political radicalism and religious extremism is unholy and un-Jewish. Unless these threatening trends are reversed, the Diaspora will be alienated, the democratic fabric of Israeli society will be rent asunder, and the Zionist vision of national and spiritual renewal will be dissipated.

My position on the issue of the West Bank settlements is fundamentally political. If Israel does not relinquish the bulk of the West Bank (as it did the Gaza Strip) in favor of a Palestinian state, it will be forced to incorporate millions of Arabs into Israeli society. Unless the majority of its citizens are Jewish, the Jewish character of the Jewish state will be undermined and could eventually disappear. Moreover, if the Arabs are not given full rights as citizens, then Israel will not be a democracy. A society in which a significant percentage of the population sees itself as second-class citizens cannot remain democratic, nor will it remain peaceful.

There is only one conclusion. If Israel is to remain both Jewish and democratic, the West Bank and Gaza cannot be incorporated into Israel. So much for the political aspect. However, the rationale of the settler movement is not only politically

based. It is no coincidence that the overwhelming majority of
the settlers are Orthodox. They are heavily influenced by their
rabbis, who proclaim to follow the dictates of biblical tradition.
Therefore, the positions of the settler movement need to be
refuted from a religious as well as from a political perspective.
It is in this context that I present my views.

The claim that the settlers are applying halachah is subter-
fuge. In reality they exploit halachah in order to achieve their
political objectives. They abuse rather than use tradition and
in so doing distort the spirit and letter of Judaism.

The contention of the religiously motivated settlers is that
the Jewish people were given the Land of Israel by God as part
of an eternal covenant with Abraham and his seed (Genesis
12:1ff.). The Bible is replete with God's commitments. The
reestablishment of Jewish sovereignty over the Land of Israel
is termed in the Aramaic *athalta d'geula*, "The beginning of
the [time of] redemption." To quote the spiritual mentor of
the movement, Rabbi Zvi Yehuda Kook (son of the revered
Chief Rabbi of the Holy Land, Avraham Isaac Kook), "This
land is ours in its entirety, including all its borders and parts,
which the Creator of the universe bequeathed to our forefathers Abraham, Isaac, and Jacob. We are all commanded to
conquer it and settle it. Therefore, there is no permission or
right or license for any of us, or for our government, to dissect
parts of these, our lands and to transfer them to a foreign entity, God forbid. For 'the entire territory will be (within) your
border . . .' (Deuteronomy 11:24)."* They base their position
on an interpretation by Nachmanides of Maimonides that the
commandment of *yishuv haaretz*, "settling the land," is one
of the 613 precepts of Judaism: "We have been commanded
to inherit the land and not to leave it in the hands of others

---

*Rabbi Zvi Yehudah Hacohen Kook, *Lin'tivot Yisrael Volume III, Second Edi-
tion* (Amutat Hoshen Lev, 5757), 313.

among the nations or to leave it desolate, for we have been commanded to conquer it and to settle it." Another Rabbinic statement declares, "Fulfillment of the command to inhabit the land is equivalent to fulfilling all the other commands" (*Sifrei D'varim, R'eih* 12:29).

The basic contention of the settlement movement is that the Land of Israel is holy and that its very holiness determines the boundaries of the state. Therefore nothing can stand in its way, not the Arabs, not the nations of the world, and certainly not the Israeli government. It is every Jew's obligation to fight until all the Land of Israel is in the control of the Jewish people and free from the rule of others.

These religious convictions motivate the actions of the radical elements among the settlers. They oppose negotiations that might lead to withdrawal in whole or in part. They are likely to be oblivious or insensitive to the human rights of the Arab inhabitants. They have consistently violated decisions of the government and the Israel Defense Forces, prevailing by their persistence over a succession of Israeli governments that have not been strong enough to enforce their own policies. Certain members of the Knesset and even cabinet members have given both tacit and overt approval by demonstrating alongside them. Ministers of the government charged with implementation of settlement policy have more often than not given in to the demands of the settlers. Some liberal modern Orthodox rabbis, however, have declared that the halachic interpretations of the settler rabbis are contrary to the authentic spirit of halachah. Here are three such contentions:

1. The settlers quote from Deuteronomy 7:1: "When the Eternal your God brings you to the land that you are about to enter and possess, and [God] dislodges many nations before you—the Hittites, Girgashites, Amorites, Canaanites, Perizzites, Hivites, and Jebusites, seven

nations much larger than you . . ." However, all the rabbinic commentators are in agreement: the Arabs of today are not the descendants of the inhabitants of Canaan in biblical times. Therefore, what applied to those nations who have disappeared is of no relevance. Judaism recognizes the legitimacy of Christianity and Islam. The Arabs of Palestine are considered to be the sons of Noah, who have lived side by side with Jews and to whom Jews sold land during the Sabbatical year.

2. The commandment to conquer the land was a one-time command and is no longer valid. According to halachah, the command could be activated again only as a renewal of prophecy. However, prophecy ceased approximately twenty-five hundred years ago and is not in the Diaspora likely to be renewed. Moreover, there were periods in Jewish history when those who resorted to armed force were opposed by the recognized rabbinic leadership. During the final days of the Second Temple, those who took up arms were castigated, whereas Rabbi Yochanan ben Zakkai, who compromised with the Roman authorities, was praised as the hero who had preserved the Jewish heritage.

3. *Pikuach nefesh*, the "saving of life," is a fundamental Jewish precept for the sake of which any commandment except three—idolatry, adultery, and murder—can be broken. Even Rabbi Ovadiah Yosef, the preeminent sage of the Shas political movement, quotes the dominant insight of Jewish tradition "And you shall keep My statutes and My commandments, so that you shall *live* by them" (Leviticus 18:5). The Rabbinic Sages added, "That they should live by them and not that they should die by them." It follows, therefore, that for the sake of preserving life, the State of Israel is obliged to seek compromise.

No secular, democratic society of today can be governed by halachic interpretations. Biblical and Rabbinic promises of previous millennia cannot be invoked as the basis for drawing borders in the twenty-first century. Neither Abraham nor Joshua nor Maimonides was a cartographer engaged for eternity by the Jewish people. No biblical or medieval text can justify the shedding of blood to keep intact the post-Six-Day War borders of 1967. No Judaic tradition can condone, let alone sanction, the declaration that it is a religious duty to oppose negotiations with enemies. To use religion as the pretext for disregarding the rights of others is to distort Judaism. To make a battleground out of the Temple Mount or the Tombs of the Patriarchs is to demean Judaism. To violate the decisions of the government and its law enforcement officials is to undermine both the democratic process and Jewish morality.

In establishing the State of Israel we affirmed the legitimacy of nationalism for ourselves. We cannot fail to affirm it for the Palestinians. In order to respect the rights of the Palestinians to integrity and security, we are obligated to seek territorial and political compromise.

We Jews are not like the Greeks or the Romans. The Greeks evolved a code of justice within each city-state and between them, but there was no commitment to establish justice between the Greeks and the conquered peoples surrounding them. The Pax Romana, the peace that prevailed in the Roman Empire for 350 years, imposed Roman sovereignty and civilization over conquered peoples. But both the Greek and Roman concepts of government were based on the maintenance of military control over others.

We Jews believe not in Pax, literally the absence of a state of war, but in *shalom*—wholeness, integrity, well-being. *Shalom*, from the word *shaleim* (complete), is a product of righteousness between nations. That is our objective, our challenge, our vision. In the words of Isaiah, "For the work of righteousness shall be peace, and the effect of righteousness, calm and confidence forever" (Isaiah 32:17).

The more intense our relationship to Israel, the more acute appear the moral dilemmas confronting Progressive Judaism, and the more essential it is to confront them. Our movement, with its emphasis on social justice, has been infused with the Zionist vision of integrating the renewal of the Jewish people in a Jewish society grounded in social and economic justice. However, our participation in Israeli society has made us aware of several deficiencies in the public and personal standards of morality.

Are we the Chosen People? Is Israel the Promised Land? Is this the Jewish state for which our forefathers prayed for three millennia? How can we reconcile the dream with the reality? How do we ensure that the restoration of sovereign power deals with the acceptable use and the unacceptable abuse of that power? In sum, how do we till the soil of our Zionist dream without sullying our souls in the Zionist reality?

There are no easy answers to these and other profound dilemmas. Within our movement were rabbinic leaders who opposed transfer of the WUPJ international headquarters to Jerusalem and affiliation with the World Zionist Organization. They were concerned that too close an identification with Zionist institutions would compromise Progressive Judaism's pristine commitment to ethical universalism.

They do not understand that here in Israel, Jewish values are tested neither in theory nor in the abstract. Here, there is no artificial dichotomy between the political-historical-particularist dimension and the religious-spiritual-universalist dimension. Here, Jewishness and humanness, particularism and universalism, body and soul are inseparable. That is the source of our anguish and our rapture, our frustration and our exhilaration. That is the essence of Zionism.

One of the root meanings of the Hebrew word *am* (people) is "family." *Am Yisrael* (the People of Israel) is one large, close-knit family. Within the confines of the family, shared experiences and crises bind us together. Our obligations to members of the family dictate special relationships. We laugh and we cry with each other. We express our innermost anxieties and our uppermost aspirations. Within the family we let our hair down and we talk our hearts out.

Let it be so in this moment of history when our values as a people are being severely tested. Since the establishment of the state, we have attained new levels of achievement and inspiration. We have been honest with each other even as we have tried to be true to Jewish values. Let us continue to keep our ears and minds open to each other and to the higher call of Israel's destiny. The words of the prophet Malachi should serve as the guideline for the Israel-Diaspora discourse: "Then those who revere the Lord spoke one to the other and the Lord heard and paid heed" (Malachi 3:16).

Chapter Six

Yitzhak Rabin:
Friendship and Tragedy

Bella and I had become friendly with Yitzhak Rabin and his wife, Leah, when he was appointed Israel's ambassador to the United States following the Six-Day War. We were privileged to spend the first Shabbat with them after their arrival in Washington. They came to our home every Sukkot to eat in our sukkah, and we had many opportunities to be together at diplomatic policy discussions and on social occasions.

I grew to admire Rabin for his integrity, his diplomatic skills, his keen analytical powers and his persistent search for peace. I was impressed with the position he adopted that as an independent state, Israel did not have to rely on prominent American Jews to act as go-betweens with the American government. Israel had to learn to stand on its own, in recognition that there might be occasions when Israeli policy positions would differ from policies advocated by American Jewish groups.

Being a close friend, I was aware of his shortcomings. He had a temper of no mean proportions. After he had become prime minister, he appeared on Israeli television in a pre–Rosh HaShanah interview in September 1974. At the time of the interview, heated coalition negotiations were under way for a new government. The National Religious Party demanded as its price for entering into the government that the Law of Return be amended to preclude recognition of conversions performed by non-Orthodox rabbis in the Diaspora. A fake advertisement had been placed in the Israeli press by an organization called "Movement for Unity of the Nation." The advertisement featured a notice in the *New York Times* reporting that a Reform rabbi had officiated at a marriage ceremony together with a minister in a church on the memorial day of Tishah B'Av. In his interview Prime Minister Rabin mistakenly identified the rabbi as one of the heads of the Reform movement in New York. On the basis of this information, he referred to the advertisement with the contention that the Reform movement violates Jewish tradition and therefore had no right to oppose the proposal to amend the Law of Return.

I was upset, because I had hoped that during his extended sojourn as an ambassador to the United States, he would have learned to understand the critical role played by Reform Judaism in preventing assimilation and keeping the Jewish heritage alive.

Since the prime minister's remarks were made on Israeli television, I decided that I should issue a public rebuttal. I sent the *Jerusalem Post* an open letter to the prime minister, which was published the following Friday, September 6, 1974, under the bold headline "Keep Religion out of Politics." Extracts from this letter follow:

Dear Mr. Prime Minister,

May I respectfully call to your attention an inaccuracy in a statement you made before the nation in an interview you gave during a television broadcast on September 20 and 21. You stated that "one of the heads of the Reform movement in New York who contacted me in order to oppose the current proposal for the entry of the National Religious Party into the government, officiated at a marriage ceremony on the eve of Tishah B'Av, with a Christian minister in a church."

The description does not fit any leader who approached you or communicated with you officially on behalf of any of our American or international Reform Jewish organizations. We are aware of an advertisement placed in the Israeli press by an organization calling itself "The Movement for Unity of the Nation" that features a photocopy of a notice in the *New York Times* of a rabbi who did so officiate. There is no rabbi of that name in the Reform movement.

In our experience the problem of intermarriage is unrelated to such questions as who performs marriage or conversion ceremonies. Unfortunately, intermarriage is a problem that plagues the Jewish world, including Orthodox Jewry. No movement or group of Jews is immune from its contagion and no group has a sure-fire preventative.

Nothing is gained, therefore, by recrimination and unfounded generalizations. Everything is to be gained by recognizing our common responsibility and by having all responsible Jewish groups join together in mutual respect and in the conviction that differences in approach and emphasis are salutary in attacking a problem common to all.

Over and above the specific statements in your interview, I should like to call to your attention again our firm conviction that these most weighty issues affecting Jewish survival in the Diaspora should be discussed by religious movements themselves and by Jewish leaders in Israel and the Diaspora in an atmosphere removed from the controversies of Israeli politics. To make religion the basis for negotiations between Israeli political parties is to distort both Judaism and the democratic process. It is inconceivable that a minority branch of Judaism should use the political process as a tool to achieve religious objectives that it cannot achieve through education and persuasion. And it is inconceivable that political leaders use Judaism as a tool to achieve political objectives unrelated to Jewish religious concern.

Because of these factors we have been and continue to be opposed to the politicization of religion and the religionization of politics.

That Friday afternoon I was home. Bella and I were setting the Shabbat table and preparing to go to synagogue. The telephone rang. The voice on the other line said, "Dick, it's Yitzchak Rabin. I am sitting here in my office going over the day's press clippings. I see your open letter to me. It is outrageous. I thought you came on *aliyah* to be a religious leader. Why are you interfering in politics? Make up your mind what you want to do here in Israel. Do you want to be a rabbi or a politician?" He carried on in this vein for some fifteen minutes. From time to time, I tried to interject words of explanation. He was not prepared to listen to anything I said and ended the diatribe by saying, "Again, I repeat, make up your mind, Dick. Decide whether you want to be a religious leader or a political leader and act accordingly." He hung up the phone. Two minutes later Mordechai Gazit, a good friend, who was the director general of the prime minister's office at the time, called me back and informed me that he had heard the entire conversation. He apologized profusely and said that I should know by now that the prime minister was prone to sudden eruptions and that I should not be offended. He would calm down shortly and would reestablish normal relations with me.

But I was anxious that the prime minister would not have the last word on this matter, and on Sunday, September 8, 1974, I sent him a letter, excerpts of which follow:

Dear Mr. Prime Minister,

I am very disturbed by the nature of our telephone conversation on September 6, and out of personal friendship for you and respect for your office, I am writing this letter to present some thoughts for your consideration.

Our movement has been opposed in principle to all efforts to impose halachah on the State of Israel. In 1970, following the Shalit decision, we issued statements opposing the revision of the Law of Return, because we realized, as did the majority of the High Court, that once a halachic definition of a Jew is injected into civic legislation, the State of Israel would be embroiled in continuing conflict over divergent interpretations of halachah. During the high-level Knesset debate on the law in February 1970, many members of the Knesset, including members of your own party, expressed views similar to ours. We continue to believe that the revision of the Law of Return in 1970 was a serious mistake, because it opened a Pandora's box that gave Orthodox groups in Israel and around the world a base from which constantly to seek further imposition of their beliefs and practices on the state, and through the influence of the state, on world Jewry.

During the course of the deliberations in 1970, representatives of the Reform and Conservative movements met with government leaders and were given assurance by Prime Minister Meir and Minister of Justice Shapira that the revision of the Law of Return would recognize the conversions performed by any rabbi abroad. Mrs. Meir, despite great pressures from Orthodox groups around the world, maintained the government commitment. When the crisis rose again in your premiership, we continued to express our views in Israel, and around the world.

In light of the extended history of the "Who is a Jew?" controversy, I find it difficult to comprehend your contention that our opposition at this time represents the injection of religion into politics. If there is any issue that symbolizes the unfortunate politicization of religion and the religionization of politics, it is the "Who is a Jew?" issue. Our opposition to

your proposal is based on a fundamental *religious* conviction
that it is against the spirit of Jewish tradition to discriminate
between converts and Jews by birth (see Leviticus 19:33–34).
It is also based in large measure on our conviction that the
integrity of both Judaism and the state is diminished when
a clear-cut religious issue becomes the base for negotiations
between political parties. We reject the notion that Orthodox
Jewish groups representing a minority of the Jewish world
can use the state as an instrument to impose through the
political process what they cannot achieve through the legitimate vehicles available—religious education, and moral and
spiritual persuasion.

Since the current controversy revolves around conversions
performed abroad, we believe that the issue can be resolved
only through discussions between the respective religious
movements and not through decisions made by the secular
instrumentality of the Knesset under the pressure of party
politics and specific time limits. On the basis of the past
record, we are fearful that the government and the Labor
Party will continue the unfortunate process of acceding to
the pressures of the religious parties, thus only encouraging
further encroachments in the future.

In the light of the above we believe that we have not only
the right but the obligation to articulate our views through
the democratic political process. We believe that in so doing
we are not only expressing the needs of our movement, but
above all, that we are helping to shape the Israeli society with
which all Jews will be proud to identify.

Our movement has come a long way. Within the last year
alone we have transferred our international headquarters to
Jerusalem, voted to affiliate with the World Zionist Organization, established the foundations for a kibbutz, expanded our
activities in Israel, and engaged in a host of activities abroad
resulting in increased political and financial support of the

state. In sum, we are committed to an ever more intensive participation in the upbuilding of the country.

I hope that after reflection you will agree that the irritation resulting from a more activist role of the Progressive movement is indeed a welcome price to pay for a more dedicated involvement of a major movement in Jewish life.

When Prime Minister Yitzchak Rabin was assassinated in November 1995, it was my sad duty to attend his funeral. When I was in Washington in 1963, I had attended the funeral of President John F. Kennedy and participated in deliberations on its impact on American society. Many people drew a comparison between the two events. I wrote an article for the Hebrew daily *Maariv*, in which I stressed the fundamental differences. The following are translated extracts from that article:

> The assassination of Prime Minister Yitzchak Rabin has been compared to that of President John F. Kennedy. As one who attended both funerals, thirty-two years apart, I can state that the differences are far greater than the similarities. Indeed, to compare Yigal Amir to Lee Harvey Oswald is to diminish the tragedy of Rabin's murder and to prevent the corrective healing process that Israeli society must now pursue.
>
> To be sure there were elements of déjà vu in the Rabin murder. Both assassinations induced a sustained overwhelming response of public mourning, enshrining the two heads of state as martyrs who in death became even greater than in life. Both men became symbols of hope, proving that effective political leaders can redirect national policy and national mood. Indeed, it was their capacity to project hope within their own societies that propelled Kennedy and Rabin to the center stage of international leadership.
>
> But here the comparison ends. In the Kennedy assassination, no controversial American public policy was at stake.

Oswald was a maladjusted loner whose motivation and political agenda are still shrouded in mystery. In contrast, Amir was an intelligent, well-adjusted law student whose objective was clear: to derail the peace process in the Middle East.

Amir's passion to assassinate the Prime Minister was reinforced by his knowing that a significant percentage of the public and the Knesset opposed Rabin's policies. Furthermore, Amir's peers among religious Zionists proclaimed that settling the whole of the Land of Israel was a prime principle of faith. They were encouraged by their rabbis who indoctrinated them with the conviction that their extremist political positions were sanctioned by divine mandate. In the halachic verdict rendered by leading rabbis several months ago, religious soldiers were informed that halachah superseded the orders of their officers and the policies of a democratically elected government. And now it has become clear that even the assassination of the head of the Jewish state received some rabbinical approval.

Let all teachers of Torah confront the painful reality. In His name, some have defamed God. In fact, *k'dushat hachayim*, "holiness of life," should take precedence over *k'dushat haaretz*, "holiness of the land." To render any other judgment is to pervert halachah and to distort Jewish values. The democratic state of Israel cannot survive if the Torah becomes a weapon in the hands of political extremists.

What is true for religious leadership is true for the political leaders of all parties. Let us all face the truth. The Likud and other right wing parties too easily condoned political extremism, because it enhanced their political strength. Even the Labor Party and its parties to the left were complacent, as Rabin became a sacrificial lamb to the peace effort. The majority kept silent, in the face of demonstrations against Rabin and placards that demonized him and the elected government.

Therefore, it is essential to distinguish between the Kennedy and Rabin assassinations. Oswald's act was without political purpose. Kennedy's removal from the political stage, tragic as it was, did not usher in a major change in the direction of American society.

Amir's political aim has boomeranged. Rabin's assassination ironically has the capacity to transform Israel. The silent majority found its voice. The youth of the nation will not permit Israel's soul to be despoiled. The response to Rabin's murder is more than an affirmation of love and respect for a fallen leader. It is a commitment to pursue his vision of peace, to shape a society of tolerance and respect for diversity, and thereby to ensure that his death ennobles his goals. In the words of the Bible, "Justice, justice shalt thou pursue, so that you may live, and inherit the land which the Lord your God gave to you" (Deuteronomy 16:20).

Chapter Seven

The Jewish State and Christian-Jewish Relations

The failure to mobilize support for Israel among the Christian establishment in Washington prior to the Six-Day War of
1967 became a traumatic experience for me. From the very
beginning of my rabbinic career, I had helped organize interreligious dialogues. In those days it was expected that Reform
rabbis would initiate interfaith programs, often under the
auspices of the National Conference of Christian and Jews.
My congregations participated in an event known as "Brotherhood Week" and held joint religious services with neighboring churches on Thanksgiving. Our programs were generally
built around our common biblical heritage and our shared
views on the social issues confronting American society.

When I came to Washington in 1962, I initiated discussions
with my counterparts in the various Protestant denominations
who had similar social action offices—Methodists, Baptists,
Episcopalians, Presbyterians, Quakers, Unitarian-Univer-
salists, and others. The National Council of Churches, an
umbrella group for the main Protestant denominations, had
recruited a fine professional staff. The Catholics, under the
auspices of the U.S. Catholic Conference, were represented
by priests enjoying high status in the church who were expert
in diverse areas of social action. I established close working

relations with many of these clergymen and in some instances developed lifelong friendships.

My Christian colleagues and I had worked as a team. I had testified jointly before congressional committees with Protestant and Catholic leaders on issues concerning civil rights and anti-poverty legislation. We had organized conferences on a host of social concerns, but after the Six-Day War, I began to question my perspicacity. Why had I not placed the subject of Israel on our common agenda? Why had I not foreseen that these representatives of religious conscience would not necessarily be supportive of Israel's position? How was it possible that they could not see that the survival of Israel was a clear-cut moral issue?

The more I considered the matter, the more I came to realize that it was not just a question of differences on policy or tactics. The fundamental issue was the nature of Jewish identity. I had never conveyed to my colleagues what being a Jew meant personally to me. Even more significant, I had never even fully defined Jewish identity for myself. I saw that my failure to grasp the essence of being Jewish and my inability to transmit that to others was in part responsible for the failure of the Christian community to react in the way I would have wished.

For most American Jews the definition of their Jewish identity has changed dramatically. When Jews immigrated from Europe to America, they were considered one of many national ethnic groups. Take, for example, my grandfathers, who immigrated at the turn of the twentieth century. One came from Hungary, the other from Ukraine. At the port of entry, Ellis Island, the immigration officer might have asked, "What are you?" Most would not have replied, "I am a Hungarian" or "I am Ukrainian," but "I am a Jew." For them "Jew" was a national identity, just as it was for the Greeks, Italians, Irish, Germans, Swedes, and Norwegians who stood beside them in line. However, today, more than one hundred years later, if their descendants were to be asked, "What are you?" many would not answer "Jew," because they no longer identify themselves as such. Almost all of them would define Jews as parallel to Protestants, Catholics, and Muslims. In other words, their self-identify and the identity that society would ascribe to them is as a member of a religious and not an ethnic group. The fact that many if not most of these persons do not belong to a synagogue or lead a religious life is considered irrelevant.

Why do Jewish communal organizations enjoy an excellent relationship with their Christian counterparts? Because Jews and Christians are differentiated only by their theological beliefs. They have their theology; we have ours. They believe that Jesus was the Messiah. We believe that the Messiah has yet to come. They have their churches and their Christian festivals. We have our synagogues and our Jewish festivals. However, when it comes to citizen participation, by and large Jews and Christians share the same social concerns. With regard to voting patterns, the average American Jew tends to be more liberal than his Christian counterpart. Nevertheless, in the American environment, the differences are muted and find legitimacy in debates over public policy in a democratic milieu.

The basis for collaboration among the religious organizations in Washington was a social agenda, predicated on the moral imperative of common religious beliefs. The religious groups were united by their commitment to the social justice values of the Judeo-Christian heritage.

The relations between Jewish and Christian leadership in Washington were so strained after the Six-Day War that it was decided to convene a conference to try to reconcile the differences. I was asked to deliver a paper presenting the Jewish perspective. In the discussion following my presentation, a distinguished Protestant clergyman, a close personal friend, reacted with astonishment to the sharpness of my criticism: "Dick, I am shocked. I always thought you Jews were the prototype of the universal man. After hearing you, I see you are merely tribalists."

The remark of my friend testifies to the gap between Jews and mainline Christians. When Jews are defined as an established religious group, we are seen as authentic partners in the tri-faith lineup. However, as they see it, during the Six-Day War, we Jews reacted with the atavistic impulses of a people. That phenomenon was something mainline church groups found hard to comprehend. For them, religion and ethnicity are completely separate. A Christian can be any nationality, even as any Italian, Frenchman, or German can profess any religion or no religion at all. Who ever heard of a religious group aspiring to create a state? A state by definition is a political entity. A state's character and destiny are determined through a political process. Religious groups are obligated to affect the moral dimensions of politics, but the attempt to mix religion and politics is contrary to the principles of separation of church and state. It is bad for the state and bad for religion.

The fundamental premise of equal rights in America is that each person should be judged irrespective of national origin, race, or creed. Indeed, it is the secular, nonsectarian character of America that guarantees equal opportunity for Jews, as all other peoples, to strive for their goals as individual citizens. Therefore, many non-Jews, including those who enjoy a warm and respectful association with Jews, find the commitment to a Jewish state to be intellectually inconsistent. One senior Christian clergyman even declared that in his eyes the term "Jewish state" was an oxymoron.

It is the mainline Protestant groups with whom the liberal religious Jewish organizations share a common social agenda.

Yet, it is people from these groups, including the National Council of Churches, the World Council of Churches, and their counterparts in the United Kingdom who persistently articulate anti-Israel positions.

Paradoxically, those Christian groups with whom liberal Jews have no common social agenda and, until recently, minimal contact have proved to be among the most fervent supporters of Israel today. Whereas the peoplehood component contributed to the misunderstandings with mainline Protestants, it is precisely that dimension of Jewish identity that has won the support of evangelical and fundamentalist Christians. For them, their enthusiastic commitment to Israel is grounded in their Christian theology. For them, the Bible and its prophecies are to be taken literally. The Jews are God's Chosen People. They believe that the ingathering of the Jews to the Land of Israel is the first wave of the process by which the Messiah will return (the Second Coming). As a consequence, they enthusiastically and unreservedly support Israel as a Jewish state and have become generous contributors to Zionist causes.

Christian evangelism takes many forms. Not all are to be welcomed indiscriminately. In some instances, their ministers identify with the most right-wing elements in Israel. They oppose the two-state solution that the Israeli government has accepted as its political stance. Some of them lobby against any territorial compromise, on the grounds that God granted the entire Land of Israel to the Jewish people for eternity. There are others who engage in intensive missionary efforts to convert Jews to Christianity. However, the majority of fundamentalist Christian sects should be welcomed today as allies in the continued struggle to win universal recognition for the Jewish state.

In any discussion on Christian relations with Israel, special attention should be given to the Catholic Church. Unlike the

Protestant world, with its multiplicity of theologies and organizations, the Catholic Church has one unified framework, in
which the pope sets the tone and policy of the church. From
the very beginnings of political Zionism, the Catholic Church
was ambivalent to the concept of a Jewish state. Even after
the establishment of Israel in 1948, the Vatican did not recognize it. When Pope Paul VI visited Israel in 1964, he could
not bring himself to pronounce the name of the state and
instead referred to it as "the Holy Land." He also refrained
from meeting with any Israeli government official.

Finally, in 1993, the Vatican recognized the State of Israel, and formal diplomatic relations were established. Subsequently, official visits were made by Pope John Paul II in
2000 and Pope Benedict XVI in 2009. In these visits and in
statements by Pope John XXIII (known as "The Blessed")
and since the ecumenical councils on the Jews, the Catholic
Church has made intense efforts to modify its public stance
toward the Jewish people. It has absolved contemporary Jews
of complicity in the account of the crucifixion as related in the
Gospels and has advocated the correcting of church liturgy
and educational materials that were blatantly anti-Semitic in
content. Occasionally there have been instances of regres-
sion, such as the reintroduction of a Good Friday prayer with
clearly anti-Semitic content or a call for the traditional mandate to convert Jews to Christianity. However, in general the
Catholic Church should be credited with valiant initiatives to
change its attitude toward the Jewish people.

Zionism is the movement that has restored the Jews as a
people to the Land of Israel. We Jews have earned the right
to define ourselves. We have chosen to define ourselves as a
people. The Jewish people, in turn, has created a Jewish state.
The state has become our symbol of hope.

For me, the ultimate test in Christian-Jewish relations goes
beyond the issue of how the Catholic and Protestant world

relate to their history of persecution of Jews, to overtly anti-Semitic passages in the New Testament, or to traditional Christian theology concerning Jews. It is not enough for Christians to act without discrimination or prejudice toward individual Jews. The Christian world and especially the official church institutions have to relate to the Jews as a unified people. The ultimate test, therefore, is how the Protestant world and the Catholic Church relate to the State of Israel.

More than forty years have elapsed since the Six-Day War. In reviewing the relations between the Christian world and the State of Israel, I conclude that the wounds have not yet healed. If anything, relationships have retrogressed. In 1967 I wrote an article addressed to Christian friends that was circulated widely among the Christian leadership of the United States. In my judgment it is still relevant, and some edited extracts follow:

An Open Letter to Christian Friends of Israel

There is a Chasidic story that recounts a conversation between two peasants. The first said, "You do not love me," to which the second replied, "How can you say that? I certainly love you." "No," said the first, "if you truly loved me, you would be able to tell what gives me pain." The second mused for awhile and then said, "If you truly loved me, you would not have to wait for me. You yourself would tell me what gives you pain."

The American Jewish community is in pain. In the spirit of true friendship, I address these words to my Christian friends, especially to those who are in positions of leadership in the churches. Events in the Middle East during the last May and June were a traumatic experience for American Jews. We Jews have always taken seriously the calls of Arab leaders for *jihad*, a "holy war," of extermination against the State of Israel. Since the days when Pharaoh of Egypt

undertook to destroy the Jewish people, we have learned that
dictators' illusions of glory and conquest inevitably lead them
to attempt to fulfill their goals. We have learned through
bitter experience that political leaders often mean what they
say. In our lifetime, six million murdered Jews bear witness
to the world's failure to heed the threats of a dictator. We
were not able to regard dispassionately a renewed call by a
latter-day Egyptian Pharaoh for the destruction of the rem-
nant of our people. We could not agree with foreign affairs
experts who for years maintained that Gamal Abdel Nasser's
actions would never carry out his threats.

In May, our fears intensified as his actions began to match
his words. The withdrawal of the United Nations Emergency
Force, the blockading of the Gulf of Aqaba, the signing of
military pacts between Arab nations who had heretofore
been bitter enemies, the massing of Arab troops, and the
calls for a holy war signaled another putative experiment
in genocide. Jews in the Diaspora were confronted with
existential questions: Was the ingathering of the exiles in the
State of Israel to become a convenient method of achieving a
"final solution"? Would the world once again "stand idly by a
neighbor's blood"?

The American Jewish community became united in a
display of spontaneous support for Israel in its hour of need.
The fate of all Jews wherever they lived seemed to us to be
inextricable from the fate of Israel. And, as had been our
wont to do in pluralistic America, we turned to our Christian
brethren with whom we had worked closely on issues such
as civil rights, poverty, and foreign affairs. Protestant, Catholic, and Jewish leaders on both the national and local levels
had developed a joint approach to what are considered to be
moral questions.

What could be a more clear-cut moral issue than the right
of the State of Israel to exist? we thought. And who would

respond to the issue with greater empathy than the Christian churches who had in recent years become so sensitized
to moral issues in general, and to the sin of anti-Semitism
in particular. But to our dismay, the Christian leadership
responded with silence or expressions of neutrality. There
were some outstanding individual exceptions, but the major
Protestant denominations, the National Council of Churches,
and the U.S. Conference of Bishops, long accustomed to
issuing forthright pronouncements, instead issued pallid calls
of impartial objectivity and prayers for peace. An editorial
in the *Christian Century* of June 21, 1967, expressed the
predominant view of the organized Christian institutions in
the United States:

> "Whatever the merits and demerits in the current dispute,
> the National Council of Churches, as well as the World
> Council of Churches, has to take the long view, has to be
> impartial in disputes between Arabs and Jews and has to
> press for peace with justice to all in the Middle East as
> elsewhere. . . . Whatever the loyalties of individual staff,
> members of the NCC, the organization's neutrality in the
> present crisis, is for it the only just and wise position."

The many letters to newspaper editors written by Christian
professors of religion and philosophy, the recurring themes
in editorial opinion in Christian journals, the resolutions
adopted by Christian groups concerning the Middle East
situation, and personal conversations with Christian leaders
offer a clear insight into the dominant presuppositions behind the "objectivity" and "neutrality." These presuppositions
boil down to four contentions: first, establishing the State of
Israel was an unfortunate political compromise, devised as a
haven for persecuted Jews, but generating injustice to Arabs
by its very establishment; second, the war waged by the Arab
states immediately after the creation of the State of Israel,

and the continued state of belligerence for twenty years, is viewed as an understandable, albeit regrettable, reaction to the "political compromise" inherent in the creation of the state; third, for those liberals who saw the outcome of World War II as an opportunity for deemphasizing nationalism and taking a universalistic approach to world politics, the creation of the new state seemed to be a reversion to outmoded nationalism; and fourth, solutions to conflict between nation-states must be sought only through the United Nations. The latter point proved to be most misleading during the crisis in May when the delegates in the Security Council proved that the Arab states and the USSR opposed any UN action to lift the Egyptian blockade of the Gulf of Aqaba.

Beyond these presuppositions, which underlay much of the Christian reaction to the Middle East crisis, was the fact that the churches have numerous programs and institutional interests in the Middle East. Many Christian groups provide relief and assistance to Arab refugees. These programs may be more well-intentioned than well-informed, for while all of us express sympathy for the plight of the refugees as a human problem, the Arab states see the refugees primarily as a political problem. The Arabs steadfastly oppose attempts at resettlement and instead maintain the refugee camps as a political weapon. The Protestant and Catholic churches maintain substantial investments of personnel and funds in missionary activity and religious institutions throughout the Middle East. These investments have a great impact on the American churches. The numerous contacts established have convinced many American Christians of the validity of Arab claims against Israel. Just as Catholic prelates from the Middle East influenced the Vatican Council's deliberations on the Jewish people, so Christian institutions in the Middle East impact upon the judgments of the churches.

These premises tended to obscure the core issue: a sovereign state and a member of the United Nations, pursuing a peaceful and progressive existence, was being threatened with annihilation because of the very fact that it existed. Whether by economic strangulation or by force of arms, clear notice was served by the Arabs, for all the world to heed, that the Jews were to be "driven into the sea." Was there not, in this situation, a moral issue that transcends all other considerations? To Jews, it seemed as simple as that. All other issues could be discussed, debated, and negotiated. But the issue of existence is central and basic. For us, no moral issue could be clearer than that.

The churches view the Middle East crisis as just another political conflict between belligerent states. No Christian is expected to accept the Israeli position on all issues, any more than every Jew accepts it. Specific recommendations for the resolution of the refugee problem, the status of the holy places, and the determination of boundaries are all political issues over which there are legitimate differences of opinion. Jewish criticism of Christian leaders stems not from the church's reluctance to support Israeli positions, but from its inability to discern the clear-cut moral issue underlying the Arab threat to exterminate the State of Israel.

When the UN approved the partition plan in 1947, all the Arab nations rejected it, and seven of them declared war on Israel. Why, at that time, when the United Nations' decision was brazenly repudiated, did the authoritative voices of Christendom keep silent? Since then, the Arab nations, in open violation of the UN Charter, have waged a war of infiltration, terror, and sabotage, continually declaring the intent to destroy Israel. Why were the voices of Christendom silent?

Why have the churches with influence in Arab lands not used that influence to change the cries of *jihad* into calls for peace? Why have Christian personnel in Palestinian refugee

camps not embarked on campaigns to discourage the Arab
hate propaganda that only nourishes the illusions that prevent rehabilitation? Why cannot at least some churches in the
Middle East have the courage of churches in the southern
United States, just five decades ago, to confront those they
serve with the immorality of their beliefs and practices? In
short, how can Christian leadership, so accustomed to taking
unequivocal moral positions on issues, equivocate on the one
simple moral issue of Israel's right to exist?

The silence or neutrality of Christian leadership indicates
that perhaps they are still ambivalent about that right to exist.
If there was no ambivalence, their involvement in the Middle
East could serve as a unique opportunity to promote peace
between Israel and her neighbors.

If Christian leaders truly believe that the State of Israel has
a right to exist, they should agree that it also has the right to
exist in peace. Since Israel was the first nation established by
fiat of the UN, the world has looked upon Israel as a problem child. In the fraternity of nations, is Israel to be considered in a separate category, as Jews have been considered
within nations? If justice demands Israel's right to exist, does
it not demand Israel's right to have interests that are judged
by the same standards applied to all other nations? One cannot help speculating on whether world opinion would expect
the United States to tolerate a blockade of its coast or accept
within its borders refugees nourished for twenty years on a
meal of hate and a promised dessert of conquest. If Buffalo,
New York, were facing repeated acts of sabotage, would the
world expect the United States of America to rest its defense
on the UN?

To understand fully Israel's position among the nations, another issue should be explored. There is general recognition
that at least some of the hostility elicited by the United States
stems from envy. In the Middle East conflict, little recognition

has been given to the role that envy has played in isolating Israel. When Nasser declared a *jihad* against Israel, he was not alone. Not only the thirteen Arab nations with populations outnumbering that of Israel by fifty to one, but nations all over the world—Russia, China, India, Malaysia, Indonesia— together representing more than half the world population, united in condemning it.

What explanation is there for this irrational enmity on the part of nations thousands of miles away? How to explain the enmity of nations that themselves could learn much from Israel's experiences as a developing country and for whom Israel could serve as a model of self-help? Certainly, these nations do not fear military conquest, economic competition, or sinister influences. Evidently, there is a fear greater than all of these. Israel is the only nation created since World War II that is a true democracy and that has proved that democracy can be successful for all developing nations—and that is something those who line up against Israel cannot accept. That is what arouses the fear at the root of their hatred.

If Israel, with a population of just 640,000 Jews in 1948, successfully absorbed by 1967 three times as many refugees as its total population in 1948, what excuse is there for 100 million Arabs to have kept a million refugees cooped up in camps ever since? If Israel managed to shape a democratic society out of the remnants of concentration camps, what excuse is there for other people to tolerate corrupt and unstable government? If Israel was able to create a verdant and flourishing agriculture out of the desert, what excuse is there for the Arab nations not to develop their own, much more abundant, natural resources for the welfare of their citizens? If Israel could send its scientists, farmers, and technicians around the world, bringing knowledge and assistance to developing countries, what excuse is there for some nations to be so insensitive to the needs of others?

Israel is under attack by governments that have failed to provide security and freedom for their own people. Many of the Arab nations have yet to recognize that Israel has a right to exist. For merely to recognize its existence is for them to admit failure. Its very existence proves that democracy works without repression of civil liberties.

Thus, the struggle to preserve Israel is not a struggle, as in World War I, to save the world for democracy, but rather to save democracy for the world. America's support of Israel is not motivated by domestic political factors, meaning the Jewish vote, as some critics contend. America's commitment to Israel is a commitment that should be held as firmly if there were not one Jew living in the United States. Ultimately, it is not a commitment to Israel, but a commitment to America itself.

The diverging response of Christian and Jewish leadership to the ongoing Middle East crisis reveals some fundamental theological differences that in the past have been glossed over but now should be expressed forthrightly. Under no circumstances do I suggest that interreligious dialogue should be dependent on agreement between Christians and Jews concerning Israel. On the contrary, true interreligious harmony should require honesty in the exercise of conscience. There may be some Jews, opposed to interreligious dialogue to begin with, who may use differences of opinion on Israel as corroboration of their opposition to dialogue. But most Jews reject a quid pro quo relationship, which would deprecate Christians and demean Jews.

For both Jews and Christians, the concept of Jewish peoplehood, an area hitherto unexplored between them, should become a major item on the agenda of future dialogue. Christian friends have often said they did not realize, and in some instances could not understand, the American Jew's close identification with fellow Jews in Israel. As one colleague of

French ancestry said, "I never responded with such a sense of passionate personal involvement when France was conquered by the Nazis."

The bond implicit in Jewish peoplehood may not be articulated in theological terminology by all Jews, but the Middle East crisis reveals ties that are felt by the great majority of Jews in the Diaspora. For most contemporary Jews, the fate of the Jewish people is reflected in what might happen in the Land of Israel. Many evangelical Christian believers understand this phenomenon better than other Christians, for as we have seen, they view the return of Jews to the Land of Israel as fulfillment of the biblical promise and a prerequisite step toward the Second Coming. On the other hand, most liberal Christians view the establishment of the State of Israel as a purely political event, unrelated to theology.

For Jews, Israel is the symbolic home of the Jewish spirit. That spirit is both universalist and particularist at the same time. According to Jewish tradition, the return of the Jews to their homeland is an essential precondition for the coming of the messianic era of peace and brotherhood for all mankind.

The destiny of the people of Israel is inseparable from the destiny of all humanity. An Israel redeemed is not an end in itself, but rather the symbol of the redemption of humankind. The upbuilding of the Land of Israel is seen as a step toward the ultimate salvation of the world. The Land of Israel is thus a symbol of Jewish faith in humanity. Wars, injustice, poverty are not inevitable.

To this day, Jews living in Jerusalem pray on the festival of Passover, *L'shanah habaah birushalayim*, "Next Year in Jerusalem." Why would the Jew pray to be in Jerusalem if he or she already lives there? Because Jerusalem is more than a physical entity, just as Israel is more than another country. To the Jew, Jerusalem is an ideal, a glorious spiritual adventure, an eternal messianic dream of a perfect society for all humankind.

Surely it is not too much to hope that Christians will gain a
greater understanding of their own as well as the Jewish faith,
giving new meaning to the words of the Psalmist:

> Pray for the well-being of Jerusalem;
>> "May those who love you be at peace.
>> May there be well-being within your ramparts,
>>> Peace in your citadels."

(Psalm 122:6–9)

Chapter Eight

"Who Is a Jew?":
The Crisis over Conversion

"Who is a Jew?" The very question in itself reflects the uniqueness of the Jewish people. No other ethnic or religious group engages in such a vitriolic debate over self-definition. In Paris, no one asks, "Who is a Frenchman?" In Madrid, the question "Who is a Spaniard?" is never raised. In Rome, the Vatican is not wracked by conflict over "Who is a Catholic?"

If truth be told, the question "Who is a Jew?" does not concern non-Jews. The anti-Semite has no doubts. For Hitler and the Nazis, you could be a devout practicing Christian, but if you had one Jewish grandparent, you would be cast into a concentration camp. The non-Jews have always known who we are. So why do we Jews have such difficulty in defining ourselves?

The answer lies in the history of the last 225 years. Until the Emancipation of the Jews at the end of the eighteenth century, the question "Who is a Jew?" was not an issue. Jews were a homogeneous and easily definable people. They observed Jewish law as prescribed by tradition. Whether they lived in Britain, France, Germany, Poland, or Russia, or indeed Morocco, Egypt, Iraq, or Yemen, they were distinguished from the population among whom they lived by belief, customs, garb, and most important of all, by status. They were not considered citizens and generally did not consider themselves citizens of the societies in which they lived. They were a separate and separated people.

When Jews began to be granted citizenship rights, ghetto walls came tumbling down. For the first time, Jews were free to enter the surrounding society as individuals. New vistas of opportunity permitted and even encouraged the evolution of new and divergent forms of religious belief and practice. No longer did Jews have to remain strictly Orthodox in practice. They were now free to reinterpret their Judaism in the light of their own contemporary views and needs. They could become Reform or Conservative or secular. They were free to reject the Jewish faith altogether if they so chose.

Nevertheless, one fundamental element of the pre-Emancipation period remains. For the Jew, peoplehood and religion are inseparable. A person who is born a Jew remains a Jew. A German can be a Catholic or a Lutheran. An Englishman can be an Anglican or a Muslim. But a Jew can have only one faith—Judaism. If a non-Jew wants to become a Jew, there is only one way—conversion. The way to become a part of the Jewish people is to accept the Jewish faith.

In modern democracies, where freedom of worship is a basic elementary right, religion is not a factor in determining citizenship status. In the United States, for example, the principle of separation of church and state prohibits the state from intervening in matters concerning religion. No American law would ever sanction, let alone mandate, government action to define Jewish identity. Indeed, the United States census, conducted every ten years, does not even permit a question concerning a person's religion.

There is only one modern democracy where Jewish identity is an issue for discussion by the state. That is the State of Israel. Israel was established as a Jewish state. It was recognized as such by the United Nations, in great measure as a response to the decimation of European Jewry in the Holocaust. One of the first basic laws enacted by the new state, in July 1950, was the Law of Return. This law represents the pinnacle of the Zionist enterprise. To counter Jewish homelessness, the State of Israel grants entry to every Jew.* The moment a Jew sets foot on Israeli soil, he or she is entitled to the rights of full citizenship. On the other hand, for a non-Jew, citizenship is not automatic and a process of naturalization similar to that in the United States and other countries is required. Related to the Law of Return is the Law of Population Registration, enacted in 1949, which requires every resident of Israel over sixteen years old to carry an identity card noting nationality, religion, and citizenship.

The adoption of these two basic laws has generated frequent and often acrimonious controversy within Israel, and between Israel and the Diaspora. Initially, it was up to each individual to decide how to define him- or herself. In accordance with this simple practice, the minister of interior, Israel Bar-Yehuda, issued a directive in 1958 that stated, "Any person declaring in good faith that he is a Jew shall be registered as a Jew and no additional proof shall be required." Regarding children, the directive stated, "If both parents declare that the child is Jewish, the declaration shall be regarded as if it were the legal declaration of the child itself." The Bar-Yehuda directive provoked the first major controversy over the question "Who is a Jew?" The National Religious Party, speaking on behalf of the Orthodox Chief Rabbinate, contended that the minister's action was in contravention of Jewish law. According to halachah, a Jew is a person whose mother is Jewish or who has converted to Judaism. In protest, the National Religious Party resigned from the government coalition.

---

*The only exceptions are those with a criminal record or a communicable disease.

In an attempt to resolve any disputes that might arise concerning registration, Prime Minister David Ben-Gurion established a special ministerial committee. At the same time, recognizing that the issue was of intense concern to Diaspora Jewry, Ben-Gurion sent a letter to forty-five of the preeminent scholars in the Jewish world, requesting that they offer their counsel as to how to deal with the problem. More than half of the recipients of the letter lived in the Diaspora, in itself an implicit recognition that Jews outside Israel have a legitimate concern for actions taken by Israel affecting the personal status of Jews outside the borders of the state. While the responses to Ben-Gurion's questions were varied, the vast majority were opposed to separating Jewish national identity from Jewish religion. The government decided, therefore, that it was premature to pass legislation on the subject. Instead, a compromise was arrived at with the National Religious Party. It rejoined the coalition, and new administrative directives were issued that were not at variance with halachic interpretation.

In 1962, the "Who is a Jew?" issue erupted again in the famous Brother Daniel case. Brother Daniel, a Carmelite monk living in a monastery on Mount Carmel in Haifa, petitioned the High Court of Justice to become a citizen of Israel under the Law of Return. He had been born Daniel Rufeisen in Poland in 1922 to Jewish parents, and at his circumcision he was given the first name Oswald. He was raised and educated as a Jew in every respect and was active in a Zionist youth movement in preparation for immigration to Israel. In 1941, he was captured and imprisoned by the Gestapo. He managed to escape, and in order to stay alive, he obtained forged papers certifying that he was a German Christian. Exploiting his assumed Christian identity, he was able to warn Jews of Nazi extermination plans and was responsible for saving many lives. He joined a group of Polish partisans and was later decorated for his courage in the anti-Nazi underground. In 1942, to escape the Nazis, he entered a convent and while there converted to Christianity. Following the Second World War, he became a monk and entered the Carmelite order, because he knew they had a monastery in Palestine, and he had never forsaken his aspiration to live in the Land of Israel.

In 1958, Brother Daniel applied for Israeli citizenship under the Law of Return, on grounds that according to Jewish law, a person born a Jew always remains a Jew. His lawyer cited a Talmudic dictum: "A Jew, even if he has sinned, remains a Jew" (*Sanhedrin* 44a). Therefore, he contended that even the most Orthodox Jew could not deny that Brother Daniel was a Jew. However, the High Court of Justice ruled that the term "Jew" in the Law of Return has a secular meaning: "As it is understood by the ordinary plain and simple Jew . . . a Jew who has become a Christian cannot be called a Jew." In refusing to accept the halachic definition of Jew, the High Court thus gave it a nationalistic definition, reflecting "the healthy instinct of the Jewish people and its thirst for survival."

Another landmark decision of the High Court led to the first legislative amendment to the Law of Return. A lieutenant-commander in the Israel Navy, Benjamin Shalit, born in Israel, married a non-Jewish woman in Scotland. After the marriage they settled in Israel, and Shalit's wife became a naturalized citizen. Though Mrs. Shalit never converted to Judaism, the Shalits reared their two children like any other Israeli child, inculcating in them loyalty to the Jewish people and its homeland. When Commander Shalit filled out the questionnaire for the Population Registry for his firstborn child, in the space for nationality he entered the word "Jewish," and he left the space for religion blank. The Ministry of Interior registrar struck out the entry for nationality and in the space for religion wrote, "Father Jewish, mother non-Jewish." When their second child was born, Shalit did not fill in the spaces for religion or nationality. This time the registrar wrote in the space for nationality, "Father Jewish, mother non-Jewish." In the space for religion he wrote, "Not registered."

Shalit petitioned the High Court of Justice, demanding that the nationality of his children be registered as Jews and, since both he and his wife regarded themselves as atheists, that in the space for religion the children be registered as having no religion. The High Court, understanding the explosive character of the issue, initially recommended to the government that it abrogate the law requiring a citizen to enter his nationality and suggested that only two questions be asked: citizenship and religion. But the government, concerned about internal security problems regarding Arab citizens of Israel, rejected the court's recommendation. The court had no choice but to deliver a judgment. On January 23, 1970, in a historic decision, and by a five to four majority, the High Court ruled that the children should be registered as Jewish by nationality, even though their mother was not Jewish.

The decision caused a furor in Orthodox circles. Once again, the National Religious Party threatened to withdraw from the coalition. Prime Minister Golda Meir was besieged by demands to pass legislation nullifying the High Court decision. Even many non-Orthodox Jews feared that the decision could be seen as sanctioning intermarriage. At the time, the country was engaged in the War of Attrition with Egypt, and a broad coalition government of national unity had been established. Concerned about the stability of the government and the unity of the Jewish people, Prime Minister Meir moved quickly to arrive at a compromise. After a major debate in the Knesset, an amendment to the Law of Return was enacted on March 10, 1970, which for the first time accepted the halachic definition of the term "Jew," with the words "A Jew is a person born to a Jewish mother or who has converted to Judaism and is not a member of another religion." The last phrase was to ensure that people like Brother Daniel could not be considered as Jews for purposes of the Law of Return.

During the course of the debate some Orthodox leaders had proposed that the words "according to halachah" be inserted after the words "converted to Judaism." The addition was intended to disqualify recognition of conversions performed by non-Orthodox rabbis outside of Israel. (As we have noted, the established Orthodox Rabbinate has a monopoly in Israel, and conversions performed in Israel are registered only if they are performed under Orthodox auspices.) But the Knesset refused to insert the additional words because it was understood that the majority of conversions in the Diaspora are performed by Reform and Conservative rabbis. Neither the Knesset nor the government saw fit to pass judgment on the religious practices of the major non-Orthodox Diaspora movements abroad, nor did they want to jeopardize the close and interdependent relationship between Jews abroad and Israel. Furthermore, they were anxious to keep the gates of Israel open to all potential immigrants, including converts and the progeny of converts from all branches of Judaism.

It was thought that the amendment to the Law of Return would settle once and for all the issue of "Who is a Jew?" at least from a legal perspective. In effect, the Orthodox view had prevailed against those who preferred a more secular, liberal, and nationalistic definition of the term "Jew." Indeed, the National Religious Party and the right-wing Herut party voted for the amendment. Those who voted against the amendment were the parties on the left—Mapam, the Independent Liberals, and most of the Liberals whose party later merged with Herut. The only religious parties to oppose the compromise legislation were the small ultra-Orthodox Agudat Israel, joined by the even smaller Poalei Agudat Israel.

However, the State of Israel was to have no respite from the issue. Encouraged by the highly influential Lubavitch rebbe Menachem Mendel Schneerson, who lived in New York and had never visited Israel, some Orthodox elements have kept up a steady barrage against the alleged peril of Reform and Conservative conversions. Ever since 1970, the issue of "Who is a Jew?" has come to the fore after every national election. Why after the election and not before? Because no political party has ever won an absolute majority in the Knesset elections. In order to form a government, the party with the largest plurality needs to seek the support of the smaller parties. In almost every case, the easiest potential coalition partners are the religious parties. Cognizant of the fact that the major party blocs are willing to compromise to gain their support, the religious parties make demands far beyond what is warranted by their electoral strength. High on the list of demands is inevitably the Law of Return.

Despite the heavy political pressures exercised by Orthodox Jewry both in Israel and abroad, the Knesset has to this day continued to reject all efforts to amend the legislation. Reform, Liberal, Progressive, and Conservative Jews in Israel and around the world have led the opposition to amendment. Among the major reasons for opposing any change are the following:

1. Countless numbers of converts to Judaism and their progeny, now considered fully Jewish in every respect, would discover that their Jewish identity would be called into question. This could have a major deleterious effect on immigration to Israel.
2. The Knesset is a secular political body the members of which also include those who are not Jewish, as well as secular Jews. For the Knesset to pass judgment on the authenticity of Jewish religious acts performed abroad is

an unacceptable intervention in the affairs of Diaspora Jewry.

3. The right of defining Israeli citizenship would be transferred from the state—a civil, democratic body—to the Chief Rabbinate, which does not recognize the legitimacy of non-Orthodox rabbis. If the state were also to refuse to recognize the legitimacy of non-Orthodox rabbis, the overwhelming majority of Diaspora Jews would feel alienated and would inevitably become estranged from Israel.

4. The major objective of the Orthodox establishment is to preserve its monopolistic control over the interpretation of halachah. Not "Who is a Jew?" is their concern, but "Who is a rabbi?" The leaders of Orthodoxy in Israel are using their political power in the Knesset to achieve objectives that they have been unable to achieve through accepted religious means—education and moral guidance. As a consequence Orthodox Judaism has been severely damaged. When religion becomes politicized, it loses its integrity.

For the Knesset to pass legislation in Israel will not change the reality of Jewish life abroad, nor will it affect the practices of the various religious movements. No political body has the moral right or the ability to impose a particular religious practice.

Until the day comes when Jewish religious leaders are able to reconcile their differences outside the Knesset, Progressive Jews the world over will continue to oppose any change in the "Who is a Jew?" legislation. A growing number of Israeli and Diaspora legislators and leaders have begun to understand the harmful ramifications of Orthodox agitation.

If Israel is not a society where all Jews feel at home, then it cannot remain the spiritual home for all Jews. What is at stake in the "Who is a Jew?" issue is the very character of the Jewish state and its relationship to the Diaspora. The struggle is to maintain Israel as an open and pluralistic society with which all Jews will be proud to identify.

Shortly after Benjamin Netanyahu became prime minister for the first time in 1996, the "Who is a Jew?" issue rose again in full force. Led by the Orthodox members of the Knesset, the religious parties were determined to nullify Knesset legislation that permitted state recognition of non-Orthodox conversions performed abroad. The proposed legislation led to a major crisis in Israel-Diaspora relations. Concurrently, the Reform and Conservative movements presented cases to the High Court of Justice that would have validated Reform and Conservative conversions performed in Israel. Some Diaspora Jews threatened to reduce, or eliminate altogether, their contributions to Israel, and delegations of leading non-Orthodox religious leaders came to Israel to protest the proposed legislation.

In response, the prime minister decided to appoint a commission to try to resolve the crisis. As chairman of the conversion commission, Netanyahu appointed Yaakov Ne'eman, a highly respected and distinguished professor of law who was a partner in Herzog, Fox, Ne'eman, one of the largest law firms in Israel. Ne'eman fully subscribes to the Orthodox way of life but is liberal in his ideological perspectives. Subsequently, the prime minister appointed Ne'eman to be minister of finance. Even though this was a demanding position with heavy responsibilities, Ne'eman accepted the appointment on condition that he could continue to chair the conversion commission.

At this time, I was contacted by Bobby Brown, the advisor to the prime minister on Israel-Diaspora relations. He urged me to agree to serve as the representative of the Reform movement on the conversion commission. I told him that I did not think it would be wise for me to accept the appointment. I understood that if the commission were able to arrive at some kind of acceptable proposal, it would represent a compromise among the Orthodox, Conservative, and Reform movements. I knew that my Reform colleagues considered me to be "soft on Orthodoxy." I had expressed my views many times that the issue of conversion in Israel was not exclusively related to the issue of the right for Reform rabbis to officiate at conversion ceremonies. Rather it was an issue that affected the totality of Israeli society.

I informed Bobby Brown of my concerns and recommended the appointment of Rabbi Uri Regev, who in addition to being a rabbi was also a lawyer and the most knowledgeable person on the issue of religion and state in our movement. Should the Ne'eman Commission be successful in arriving at a compromise formulation, the knowledge that Regev had been our representative would expedite the approval of the Reform movement for the commission's recommendations. Rabbi Regev was duly appointed to be our representative on the commission. At the same time, in my many meetings with Professor Ne'eman, I indicated that I would give the commission my full support. During the course of its hearings, which lasted many months, I kept my commitment to try to be a positive factor and to keep the Ne'eman Commission on an even keel.

In 1997 it was estimated that of the nearly one million immigrants who had come to Israel from the former Soviet Union (FSU) under the Law of Return, approximately 225,000 were not halachically Jewish. As we have seen, the Law of Return defines who is eligible for Israeli citizenship, namely a person born of a Jewish mother, or who has converted, or one of whose parents or grandparents was Jewish. This definition was a counterpoint to the Nazi Nuremberg Laws of 1935, which categorized as Jewish a person one of whose grandparents was Jewish. When the State of Israel was established, it passed laws that stated categorically that a person who had one Jewish grandparent was eligible to immigrate (*aliyah*) under the Law of Return. However, in the eyes of the Chief Rabbinate, Israeli citizenship did not automatically define such a person as Jewish.

As co-chairman of the Jewish Agency's FSU Department, I was in constant contact with Soviet Jews who were coming to Israel on *aliyah*. I was also aware of the high rate of intermarriage in the FSU. The figures that my department had compiled indicated that by 2000 there were at least three hundred thousand new immigrants who were not Jewish according to halachah. This represented a very high percentage of new immigrants and is likely to be even higher in the future. According to the studies carried out by my department, at least 80 percent of Jews in the FSU were intermarried. A high percentage of the new immigrants were young women whose children would be recognized as Israeli citizens, but not as Jews. This represented a profound and potentially disruptive force in the demographic structure of Israel. It meant that a growing percentage of Israel's citizens would not be legally defined as Jewish, with all the ensuing complications beginning with marriage and childbirth. Of even greater consequence was the possibility that eventually some might not even consider themselves to be Jews. Therefore, in my view, the fundamental objective was to find a way for as many new immigrants to convert as soon as possible.

As far as the Reform movement was concerned, I had always maintained that the movement should fight for its rights to convert on grounds that a religious movement that does not convert is not a full-fledged religious movement. However, I was aware that with our limited staff and financial resources, we could not even begin to solve this massive problem. I therefore maintained that conversion of the FSU immigrants should be seen as a national objective. We had to think in terms of ten or twenty thousand converts a year. It would have been impossible for the Reform movement to presume to solve the problem, even if we were recognized to do so. Therefore, I saw my primary objective to be to fight for a more liberal attitude that would be conducive to encouraging FSU immigrants to seek conversion. This goal could not possibly be achieved under the anachronistic and unrealistic authority of the Chief Rabbinate.

The Ne'eman Report, adopted by the commission, recommended that the Institute for Jewish Studies be established under the auspices of the Jewish Agency and the government of Israel, which would fund the Institute. Its purpose would be to teach Judaism to Israeli citizens and new immigrants who were not registered as Jews to prepare them for conversion. The curriculum was to emphasize the unique character of the Jewish people and the Torah and to inculcate knowledge of the different movements and religious streams in Jewish life. Representatives of Reform and Conservative Judaism would serve on the board and teach on the faculty. It was understood that upon successful completion of the course of studies, conversions would be authorized by the Chief Rabbinate, which would establish special conversion courts for the purpose. Professor Benjamin Ish-Shalom, a distinguished scholar renowned for his liberal attitudes toward all streams of Judaism, was appointed chairman of the Institute for Jewish Studies.

The government approved the Ne'eman Report at its cabinet meeting of April 7, 1998. However, the Chief Rabbinate refused to accept the report and its recommendations. We were fully aware that it would be highly unlikely for the official Orthodox rabbinical establishment to accept any compromise. Conversion was the ultimate cause célèbre for the Chief Rabbinate, and its obduracy led to heated internal discussions within the Reform movement. The overwhelming majority of

our leadership believed that our continued participation in
the Ne'eman Commission weakened our petition before the
High Court of Justice in the cause of recognizing conversions
performed by Reform rabbis in Israel.

The conflict within the Reform movement is best reflected
in an exchange of correspondence between Rabbi Eric Yoffie,
the president of the Union of American Hebrew Congregations (now the Union for Reform Judaism), in a letter written
on March 3, 2000, and my response to him three days later.

From: Rabbi Eric Yoffie
March 3, 2000

To: The Leadership of Reform Judaism

I returned from my recent trip to Israel feeling very positive
about many aspects of our work there but very discouraged
about our battle for religious rights. I fear that we have lost
our direction and lost our nerve. I fear that we are making
decisions now that may hinder us for years to come in our
struggle for equal rights in Israel and around the world.

There is no need to review at length the history of the
Ne'eman Commission. We made painful compromises,
but in return for leaving final authority over conversion in
Orthodox hands, we at least were promised recognition and
cooperation by the Chief Rabbinate. What happened instead
is that the Chief Rabbinate retains full authority over conversion without agreeing to recognize us or cooperate with
us in any way. We have a minority voice in a Jewish Studies
Institute that has no official standing with the Rabbinate at
all. Perhaps the Rabbinate will convert its graduates; perhaps
not. But even if they do so the first time, there is no guarantee that they will do so in the future. We are completely
at their mercy. And whatever happens, the Rabbinate will
loudly proclaim that their decisions were not influenced in

any way by the presence of Reform rabbis on the Institute board. The bottom line: the Chief Rabbis have sole authority to convert and we have an insignificant role in the process— so insignificant that our standing is not enhanced in any real way.

I believe that if a bill endorsing the current conversion arrangements were to come before the Knesset, we would be unable to generate any substantial opposition to it in the United States, even though it would in essence be the Conversion Bill in another form. We would be unable to convince American Jewish leaders why they should oppose something that we ourselves have apparently accepted.

The cases calling for recognition of Reform and Conservative conversions in Israel came before the Israel Supreme Court in April. In his brief to the court arguing against recognition of our conversions, Natan Sharansky, the Minister of the Interior, argued that the existence of the Jewish Studies Institute proved that non-Orthodox conversions were not necessary; after all, both the Reform and Conservative movements were joining in the Ne'eman approach. The Reform and Conservative movements seemed to be shocked and angered by this response, but this of course is exactly what Sharansky and many others have been saying for the last two years.

A proud, assertive, self-respecting religious movement is one that never relinquishes its right to bring converts into the Jewish people. But I fear that, unwittingly, that is exactly what we have done. I fear that the precedent we have established will undermine our struggle in Israel and for Reform rights everywhere in the world.

Dick Hirsch is a dear friend, but he and I have very different views on this subject. In arguing that we should remain part of the Institute, he asked me: "Are we better off today than we would be if we had not joined the Institute?" My

answer is: clearly not. I think that we are far worse off today
than we were several years ago. The religious issue has essentially disappeared from consciousness. There is a widespread
and mistaken assumption that a solution has been found to
the conversion issue and that we have endorsed the solution.
The Chief Rabbinate is the biggest winner of all. It has managed to attack us, reject the Ne'eman proposals, retain complete authority over conversions, and still give the impression
that what is now happening is in fact the Ne'eman approach.
Let me be very blunt: we have been outmaneuvered by
professional politicians who are smarter than we are when it
comes to these political games.

   In the final analysis, the Israel Movement must decide
whether or not to proceed with the Institute. But I hope that
in making this decision, you will consult with the leaders of
our world movement.

This was my reply:

From: Rabbi Richard G. Hirsch
March 6, 2000

To: Rabbi Eric Yoffie and the leaders of Reform Judaism

I welcome your memo, because it initiates a process of
responsible discussion. I appreciate your trying to condense
my views to a sentence or two, but in all fairness, in order to
place the issue in perspective, I am obliged to state my position in somewhat greater detail.

To summarize my position:

Points of Agreement:
1. Under no circumstances should we agree to abrogate our
   right in principle to conduct conversions any place in the
   Diaspora or in Israel. In fact, there is no greater symbol
   of our significant progress in Israel than the new reality of

conversion. Until the crisis that resulted in the establishment of the Ne'eman Commission, the "Who is a Jew?" controversy was over conversions performed abroad; today the controversy is over conversions performed in Israel. Because of the controversy, the Israeli public, the Israeli government, the Israeli Rabbinate now know that we are an Israeli movement, not only a movement in the Diaspora. This is a major achievement that has enhanced the significance of our movement both here and abroad.

2. The Chief Rabbinate has not learned its lesson, nor has it changed its colors. It is more concerned about defending halachah than it is concerned about the problems of social integration of *olim* [immigrants] to Israel and to a Jewish society. For them, retention of its monopolistic control takes precedence over the well-being of new immigrants. Therefore, it is questionable whether over the long haul the Rabbinate will encourage a liberal, tolerant attitude toward *olim* who are halachically non-Jews. Again, this is all the more reason for our insisting on our right, in principle, to convert.

Points of Disagreement:

1. The Ne'eman process was not a defeat, but a victory for Conservative and Reform Judaism. It prevented the passage of legislation. There is no question that had we not participated affirmatively in the Ne'eman process, the Knesset would have passed legislation that would have mandated conversions by the Orthodox establishment only. It was our agreement to extend the deadline several times and our willingness to seek a compromise that enabled the majority in the Knesset to resist pressure from the Orthodox and right-wing parties to pass the legislation. Because of our willingness to extend the process, it was the Chief Rabbinate that was blamed for its obstinacy

and anachronistic views, whereas the Conservative and Reform movements were credited with statesmanship and a sense of responsibility for *K'lal Yisrael*. Therefore, the Knesset resolution approved by 80 MKs was a victory. It also enabled us to continue with our court cases. We are far better off with no legislation. A de facto situation is always better for us than a de jure situation. Why? It is far easier for us and our allies to prevent Knesset legislation *against* our interests than to get the Knesset to enact legislation *in favor* of our interests. Given the present and future composition of the Knesset, the latter is an almost insuperable political task.

2. The Ne'eman process enabled the Reform and Conservative movements for the first time to be appointed officially to an Israel government commission—a clear recognition of our right to status as a religious movement in Israel. It gave us credibility in the eyes of the Israeli public as an authentic and legitimate Israeli movement.

3. The Institute for Jewish Studies is a fact—it exists. The first graduates will be eligible for conversion within two to five months. We have representation on the policy-making board and in the faculty. It is a pilot program. If it is successful and if its graduates will be converted, it is beneficial for Israeli society and for the individuals converted, who will be identified as Jews. As a consequence they and their progeny are more likely to have a successful integration into Israel's society. Do we oppose that? Should we project the image that we oppose that?

4. Neither in your memo, nor in the discussions that I have held with our colleagues in Israel, is there mention of the human and humane problems confronting the individual *olim* and the problems confronting Israeli society. If we criticize the Orthodox for permitting halachah to take precedence over the human factor, how about criticizing

ourselves for allowing the issue of rights for our movement to take precedence over the human dimensions
and the demographic time bomb ticking away in Israeli
society? Whereas in 1990, 25 percent of the *olim* were
halachically non-Jewish, in 2000 the number is probably
over 50 percent. In some of the programs for high school
students, the number is approaching 70 percent. One
striking fact: of the children born in the FSU, 85 percent
were born in households of mixed parentage. A high
percent of the persons coming are young females. What
will happen to them and their progeny over the course of
a generation? Do we want hundreds of thousands of non-
Jews who feel alienated from their Jewish heritage and
who have a weak identity with the State of Israel and who
are not integrated into society at large?

5. Where do we as a movement come in? If our ultimate
   objective is, as I believe it should be, the encouragement
   of Jewish identity on behalf of the masses of Jews who are
   already here and those who we hope will come, then we in
   our movement do not have the funds, the staff, the human
   and material resources to begin to deal with the program
   in the full magnitude of its scope and challenges. Do we
   seriously think that we can duplicate or set up an independent program that will fulfill the vital needs of the entire
   Jewish people? Are we not better to insist on having an
   equal participatory role?

6. Because of the increasing number of non-Jewish *olim*
   there is growing pressure, not only among the religious
   parties, but among all parties, who are beginning to talk
   about eliminating the clause in the Law of Return that
   permits the grandchildren of Jews to come on *aliyah* with
   full rights. To even raise the issue of amendments to the
   Law of Return would inject renewed divisiveness in the
   Diaspora and between Israel and the Diaspora. Nothing

would be more disastrous than a renewed fight over the Law of Return. One way of preventing passage of amendments to the Law of Return is to proceed as quickly as possible with the program for Jewish identity and to keep the spirit of the Ne'eman process going.

7. Your stated reason for announcing that we are withdrawing from the Institute is to remove the argument that its very existence makes it unnecessary for the High Court to deal with the issue. In my judgment, this argument makes no sense. Most of the cases before the High Court arose before the establishment of the Institute and are unrelated to it in any way. By withdrawing from the Institute, the Court could conclude that the Reform and Conservative movements are not interested in any form of compromise and that the case in court is more important in our eyes than the well-being of the Jewish identity of *olim*. The vast majority of the Conservative and Reform leadership wanted us to break with the Ne'eman Commission. A few of us prevailed upon the majority not to do so. If we were right then, at least give credit to the possibility that our position now has some justification. We are eyeball-to-eyeball with the Orthodox Rabbinate. Let us stand firm and if anybody blinks, let it be the Rabbinate.

In this exchange of letters the major issues on both sides were elucidated. The vast majority of the Reform leadership wanted us to withdraw from the Ne'eman Commission. I was in a minority. We agreed that at a forthcoming meeting of the Central Conference of American Rabbis, the entire leadership of the major institutions of Reform Judaism—the Union of American Hebrew Congregations, the Hebrew Union College, the Central Conference of American Rabbis, and the World Union for Progressive Judaism—would be represented and that at this meeting we would strive to formulate an agreed resolution. The discussions were intense. Had a vote been taken then, it would undoubtedly have been fifteen to one against my position. However, I persuaded my colleagues that in the final analysis this issue should be decided by the movement in Israel, on the grounds that the key issue was not recognition of conversions performed abroad, but recognition of conversions performed in Israel. Therefore, I argued, the Israel movement should be the framework in which continued participation in the Ne'eman Commission should be discussed. Not only did I believe that my position was correct in theory, but also I felt that pragmatically, I would be able to persuade the Israel movement of the validity of my position and that they would be more cognizant of the Israeli political realities than would be the leadership in America.

In my private discussions with Professor Ne'eman, he maintained that the Chief Rabbinate would never agree to recognize conversions performed by non-Orthodox rabbis. He did acknowledge the possibility of the High Court of Justice ruling in our favor, but he also pointed out that should it do so, there would be an immediate danger that the Knesset would reverse the High Court decision by legislation and that this would prove to be more detrimental than maintaining the status quo.

I stressed to Professor Ne'eman that Progressive Jews needed recognition of the legitimacy of our equal participation in Israeli society. In our view, such recognition was essential in the eyes of Diaspora Jewry. Since the majority of Diaspora Jews were non-Orthodox, it was essential for them to realize that the government of Israel gives full recognition to the non-Orthodox movements; otherwise, Israel could not be considered the spiritual home for all Jews. I contended that without the full integration of the Reform and Conservative movements, Israel would be incomplete, just as without Israel, the two movements would be incomplete.

Evidently impressed by this contention, Ne'eman committed himself to making a valiant effort to try to win recognition of the rights of Reform and Conservative rabbis to officiate at marriages in Israel. Even under current conditions, some 20 percent of Israeli marriages are not performed by the official rabbinic authorities. Many secular couples deeply oppose the process they are forced to undergo, in which rabbis who have had no contact with the couple before the wedding officiate at marriage ceremonies. Often the ceremonies are conducted in a perfunctory way without any meaningful or aesthetic content.

I urged Ne'eman to press for approval for non-Orthodox rabbis to officiate at marriage ceremonies. Thousands of young couples prefer to go to Cyprus and get married by a Greek municipal official. When they return to Israel, the marriage is registered in the Ministry of Interior. Following the registration, a "real" wedding takes place: a religious ceremony performed by a Conservative or Reform rabbi. In other words, in the eyes of the state, the marriage abroad has the status of a civil marriage. If it were possible to regularize this process, that would be a significant achievement.

According to Jewish law the participation or even the presence of a rabbi is not a prerequisite for the authentication of a marriage. A marriage is sanctioned by two witnesses who witness the groom's offer of marriage and the bride's willing acceptance of the offer, symbolized by the groom's giving a coin or a ring, or a *p'rutah*—a coin of very little value. Since a rabbi is not required to perform the ceremony, theoretically this would facilitate the Chief Rabbinate accepting the proposal that non-Orthodox rabbis could perform marriage ceremonies.

The practice of having non-Orthodox rabbis officiate at wedding ceremonies would very quickly spread to a broad authentication of the non-Orthodox movements. Ne'eman

"Who Is a Jew?": The Crisis over Conversion   **115**

committed himself to work on this proposal. However, to my great disappointment, no progress has yet been made. On July 15, 1997, I accepted the invitation of Professor Ne'eman to present my views to the commission. The following are excerpts from my presentation:

> I have participated in two previous discussions on this issue. The first was with Prime Minister Menachem Begin in 1977. We had two full-day discussions. The participants from the government, in addition to Prime Minister Begin, were Yosef Burg, the minister for the interior, and Aharon Abuhazera, the minister of religious affairs.
>
> Again in 1988 and 1989, there was a major effort to resolve this issue. Now it is 1997. It appears that the issue arises once every decade. It is my hope that somehow or other we can make some progress by the year 2007. However, as I look back at the last twenty years, I think we have retrogressed.
>
> I want to point out five major differences between the issue this time and the previous efforts to arrive at a solution.
>
> 1. The nature of the relationship between Israel and Diaspora has undergone a radical change. Today there is a much more tenuous relationship. The Jews of Israel and of the Diaspora are more distant from each other than was previously the case, and therefore, the circumstances are different.
> 2. The composition of this commission: This is a much more serious process than in the two previous rounds. The nature of the discussion leading up to the establishment of the commission, the appointment of its members, and especially the appointment of the chairman, Professor Yaakov Ne'eman, all recognize that the situation is more serious than ever before.
> 3. The relationship among the major Jewish streams has deteriorated significantly. There is a certain militancy, one

might say extremism, leading to verbal violence, which is
perhaps characteristic of our society. This is a phenomenon that did not exist before. For example, in the United
States, for many years there was an organization called
the Synagogue Council of America, which represented
the leadership of Orthodox, Conservative, and Reform
national organizations. Before coming on *aliyah*, I was the
founding director of the Religious Action Center, established by the Union of American Hebrew Congregations
and the Central Conference of American Rabbis. In that
capacity I testified before the Senate and the Congress on
behalf of the Union of Orthodox Jewish Congregations,
the Rabbinical Council of America, and the Rabbinical
Assembly, the major institutions of Orthodox, Conservative, and Reform Judaism. That could not happen today,
because the Synagogue Council of America is defunct, the
Orthodox having pulled out on grounds that they refused
to be identified with Conservative and Reform Judaism.
I am sure that the commission is aware of the extremist
statements made by right-wing Orthodox rabbis in the
United States who refuse to recognize the legitimacy or
authenticity of the non-Orthodox movements. The dete-
rioration in relationships between the Orthodox on the
one hand and the non-Orthodox movements on the other
is in great measure a consequence of the religion-state
relationship in Israel.

4. In the past, the issue before meetings such as this was
conversion abroad. Today we are talking about conversion
within Israel itself. I speak to you, not only as a Reform
rabbi, but as one who was responsible for advocating
the move of the international headquarters of the World
Union for Progressive Judaism to Jerusalem and was the
prime mover in having the Reform movement join the
World Zionist Organization and the Jewish Agency. When,

after the Six-Day War, it was first proposed that we should move our international headquarters to Israel, the idea caused considerable controversy within the movement. Many of our leadership asked the question, "Why should we move to Israel, where our movement is not recognized and we do not receive government support?" Yet after years of debate there was a decision to move to Israel. Why? Because we recognized that unless we are in Israel, unless we are rooted in the soil of the Jewish people, we will never be authentic—not in the eyes of other Jews, and ultimately not even in our own eyes. Our move to Israel was a declaration of our Jewish authenticity. We began to build our institutions, we established kibbutzim, kindergartens, schools, and cultural centers, and we began to train rabbis, one of whom was ordained here in Jerusalem and is a member of this commission.

I would like to ask you, Orthodox members of the commission, what would you have preferred? That we should stay in the Diaspora and complain about our lack of rights? Would you have preferred to accuse us with the allegation that we are not really a religious movement? That we are a sociological movement, good for the Jews of the Diaspora because, in any case, they do not need too much Judaism. Would you have preferred us to remain totally separate from the State of Israel?

If I were a committed Orthodox Zionist Jew, I would look upon the evolutionary development of the Reform and Conservative movements in Israel as a great victory for Zionism.

The Conservative and Reform movements represent the vast majority of religious Jews in the world. Do you really want us to be isolated from the State of Israel? We cannot accept that view, because by not coming to Israel, and not building our institutions here, and not fighting for our rights,

we would not be preserving the Jews of the Diaspora, and we
would not be participating in what I consider to be the greatest drama on the surface of the globe today: *binyan haaretz*,
the upbuilding of the Jewish state.

5. We are confronted with evolving divergent, conflicting
    definitions of Jewish identity. In the Diaspora increasingly,
    the Jews are defined as a religion. The truth is that more
    and more Jewish identity is based on the synagogue. It is
    a religious identity, in contrast to the ethnic identity that
    pertained until twenty to twenty-five years ago. In Israel,
    we are witness to a contrary process. This is the nation-
    alization of Jewish identity. An example is the National
    Religious Party, which is stressing more and more its
    nationalist character and less and less its Jewish religious
    dimension. As a consequence, the secular Jews in Israel
    believe that the only authentic form of Judaism is Ortho-
    doxy. Then they say, if that is the authentic formulation of
    Judaism, they want no part of it. This is not the genera-
    tion of Ben-Gurion. Ben-Gurion loved the Land of Israel;
    he loved the Bible. His generation knew that the God in
    whom they claimed not to believe was the God of Israel.
    They envisaged Israeli society as evolving into a renewal of
    the Jewish people and of Jewish peoplehood in a renewal
    of Judaism. Today's secular Jews do not have that aspira-
    tion. Why? Because they have been alienated by Ortho-
    doxy as they perceive it.

Many years ago, flying back to Israel from South Africa,
I found myself seated beside Chief Rabbi Shlomo Goren.
In those days, the Chief Rabbinate used to insert a notice
in the newspapers every year before the New Year, in which
it advised Jews not to approach a Reform or Conservative
synagogue on Rosh HaShanah and Yom Kippur. The notice
stated that you cannot fulfill the injunction of *t'kiah bashofar*,

"to hear the blast of the shofar," in a Conservative or Reform synagogue.

I asked Rabbi Goren, what he would prefer? That the Jews in Tel Aviv attend a Reform or Conservative synagogue on Rosh HaShanah or that they go to the beach? Without hesitating, Rabbi Goren replied, "I prefer that they go to the beach." I asked why? His response was, "If they are on the beach, someday they, and if not they, then their children, and if not their children, then their grandchildren may come back to true authentic Judaism. But if they are in a Conservative or Reform synagogue, they are on the way to apostasy."

It is essential that Israeli Jews understand the perspective of Diaspora Jewry. Whether we like it or not, in the Diaspora religion is the vehicle for Jewish identity. Therefore, when the State of Israel does not recognize the non-Orthodox movements, and here I stress the state, not the Rabbinate, this means that the Jewish state is rejecting the vast majority of Jews in the world. For the Diaspora Jew, the State of Israel is the symbol of Jewish peoplehood. If the state delegitimizes their religious movements in Israel, then they are, in effect, delegitimizing them in the Diaspora.

Statistics show that just 6 to 10 percent of Diaspora Jews are Orthodox. So what do you think will happen with the rest of World Jewry? Are you prepared to alienate them? Are you going to cast doubt on their Jewish authenticity? Can Orthodox Judaism exclude them? Can the State of Israel exclude them?

We have to make up our minds. Are we going to raise money from world Jewry for an Operation Exodus, for an Operation Moses, to bring the Jews of the world here, and then when they get here, exclude them? Thousands of these people risked their livelihoods, their careers, their very lives, to identify as Jews. And when they finally arrive here, are they to discover they are not considered Jews?

Do you want to continue insisting that we are second-class Jews? We want authenticity, we demand respect by the state. Because the state belongs to the entire Jewish people. We are not asking the Chief Rabbinate to read us in and we are not going to let you read us out. We cannot permit this situation to continue.

I appreciate that it is easier for us to consider Orthodoxy as an integral part of our Jewish being than it is for the Orthodox to consider Reform or Conservative Judaism as an integral part of theirs. But if you want to preserve the Jewish people, you have to understand that we are the instrument for keeping hundreds of thousands of Jews Jewish. If you want to reduce the Jewish people to a million people or so in the world, keep on doing what you are doing. But I would hope that you want to expand the Jewish people, not diminish it.

Our movement requires that all first-year rabbinical students spend their first year in Israel. I tell them, "If you leave Israel and you do not feel at home in an Orthodox synagogue, you cannot be a good Reform rabbi." I know there is much in Reform and Conservative Judaism that is alien to Orthodox Jews. But nothing Jewish is alien to us. Do you really want to exclude us from the Jewish people? But you will not succeed. It is wrong for Zionism, it is anti-Zionist, it is anti-Jewish, it is the antithesis of preservation of the Jewish people.

Somehow this commission must arrive at a compromise. We have to compromise, because otherwise we are putting a burden on the state that will destroy it as the spiritual and cultural center of world Jewry. We will destroy the purpose for which the state was created: that of being the homeland for all Jews.

Despite the heavy political pressures exerted by Orthodox Jewry both in Israel and abroad, the Knesset has up until now continued to reject all efforts to amend the Law of Return. Reform, Liberal, Progressive, and Conservative Jews in Israel and throughout the world have led the opposition to amendment.

Reform Jews understand that some Orthodox rabbis are sincerely concerned about the differences in practice that have arisen among the various strands of Judaism. However, these differences should be resolved by religious leaders conferring with each other in a dialogue founded on mutual respect and recognition of a shared Jewish destiny.

Were the Knesset to pass legislation, it would not change the reality of Jewish life abroad, nor would it affect the practices of the various religious movements. No political body has the right or the capacity to impose a political solution in the area of religious practices.

Until the day comes when Jewish religious leaders will be able to reconcile their differences, Progressive Jews the world over will continue to oppose any change in the "Who is a Jew?" legislation. The struggle is not for the vested interests of Progressive Jews alone. If Israel is not a country where all Jews feel at home, then it cannot remain the spiritual home for all Jews. What is at stake in the "Who is a Jew?" issue is the very nature of the Jewish state and its relationship to the Diaspora. Through this struggle Progressive Jews are helping to maintain Israel as an open and pluralistic society with which all Jews will be proud to identify.

The ongoing crisis over conversion reflects the paradox of Israeli politics. The Knesset is not the proper forum in which to resolve controversial issues among Jewish religious movements. Knesset members, most of whom define themselves as secular, have neither the expertise nor the knowledge to legislate on Jewish religious issues. The Knesset has become a tool of the Orthodox religious parties to maintain their monopolistic control over Jewish religious practices. But world Jewry is pluralistic. Less than 10 percent of world Jewry and less than 20 percent of Israeli Jewry is Orthodox. Yet, because of the unique character of Israeli politics, established Orthodox Jewry wields political influence far beyond their proportion of the population. They have exploited this political influence to impose religious coercion in the public sector and to extract government funds for their educational and religious institutions. The official position of the Chief Rabbinate is to deny eligibility for conversion to any persons who do not commit themselves in advance to live an Orthodox way of life. Thus, most potential converts are automatically excluded from candidacy. The harsh policies of the Rabbinate have led to numerous instances of personal anguish and ill-treatment. In the case of immigrants from the former Soviet Union, persons who were discriminated against as Jews in their countries of origin have fulfilled the Zionist dream by coming on *aliyah*, only to find that the moment they enter the Jewish state, they are treated as non-Jews.

The damage to the reputation of Orthodox Judaism itself is irreparable. Most Israelis do not even expect high standards of integrity from the Orthodox Rabbinate. An increasing number of Israelis recognize that the autocratic Orthodox control of personal status issues infringes on civil liberties, the rights of women, and other fundamental principles essential to a democratic society.

Tens of thousands of non-Jews living in the Jewish state are eager to cast their lot with the Jewish people but are refused the opportunity to do so because of the stringent policies of the rabbinic authorities. Not to be Jewish in Israel creates unnecessary hardships on issues of personal status, marriage, divorce, burial, education, and participation in society. In many instances, these persons have turned to Reform and Conservative rabbis. Knowing full well that their conversions will not necessarily be recognized, they have nonetheless undertaken intensive study courses and undergone conversion, including commitment to lead a Jewish life, circumcision for males, and immersion (fulfillment of the halachic requirements for conversion). They are sincere in their desire to live as Jews. The state cannot forever remain oblivious to the present narrow, exclusivistic practices of the official Rabbinate. If the system is not corrected, it will cause continuing personal hardship, fracture Israeli society, and jeopardize future immigration.

Contrary to the image projected in the Knesset and in the media, this is not only a struggle for vested interests to win rights for Reform and Conservative rabbis. It is above all a struggle to create an open, inclusive, democratic society in Israel to welcome all who wish to participate in the upbuilding of the Jewish state.

The controversy over conversion rights in Israel must be viewed not as an isolated issue, but as a symbol of the larger issue: is there only one valid form of Judaism or does Judaism encourage divergent interpretations, varying theological perceptions, and different forms of organizations? In the long run, the Jews of Israel and the Jews of the Diaspora must respond as one. The non-Orthodox forms of Judaism cannot be legitimate in the Diaspora and delegitimized in the Jewish state. No geographical boundaries or theological barriers can divide the Jewish people and Jewish destiny.

PART TWO

Getting Things Done

Chapter Nine

To Build and to Be Built

In my lectures advocating Reform Zionism, I was wont to sing an old Zionist song *Anu banu artza livnot ul'hibanot ba* ("We have come to Israel to build and to be built up"). I contended that by our building the movement in Israel, the entire world Reform movement would be transformed. Reform Judaism would be strengthened and enriched ideologically, institutionally, and programmatically. We would become an integral part of *K'lal Yisrael* and would be considered as equal partners in the most exhilarating drama on the face of the globe, the upbuilding of a Jewish and democratic society in Israel. But, I argued, if we continued on the path of noninvolvement, Reform Judaism as a movement would become marginalized and eventually inconsequential within world Jewry.

When in the late 1960s the French left Algeria, Charles de Gaulle declared, "The French people have become married to history." In the same way, when the World Union for Progressive Judaism (WUPJ) moved to Jerusalem in 1973, we became married to Jewish history.

We were committing our movement to a mission: that of building the Jewish state by establishing our own institutions and programs that would enrich Israeli society. No less important was the consequence: in the process of building, we too would be built up. The experiences of Jewish peoplehood would enhance the identity of Reform Jews all over the world and have an impact on the ideology and observance patterns of the entire movement.

Furthermore, the WUPJ as an organization would become a major force. In 1973, the WUPJ occupied one and a half rooms in the New York headquarters of the Union of American Hebrew Congregations (UAHC, now Union for Reform Judaism), and its annual budget was $78,000. By now, the WUPJ has built its world center and synagogues throughout Israel and has expanded programs in Russia, Germany, Latin America, and elsewhere.

A fundamental premise of Judaism is that ideas and deeds are inseparable. Our Rabbinic Sages were adamant about this precept. They stressed that "one who studies without implementing his knowledge, it would have been better had he not been born" (Jerusalem Talmud, *Shabbat* 1:2).

In Judaism, a blessing is incomplete if it is not followed by action. When we pronounce the blessing over bread, we need to eat the bread immediately, otherwise it is considered to be a "blessing in vain."

In essence, the message I tried to convey in 1967 was that our movement had to apply this basic premise of Judaism to our efforts to promote Zionism. Over the years all the organizations within our movement had adopted resolutions supporting Zionism and Israel, but where were the deeds? In order to give meaning and purpose to the ideology of Reform Zionism, I believed that we needed more than resolutions. We should not limit our efforts to conveying messages from abroad. The message had to be delivered by Israeli messengers, who would convey the values of Progressive Judaism through participation in Israeli society in their daily lives and deeds. It was incumbent on us to build synagogues, schools, camps, and educational and cultural programs for all ages and for as many sectors of society as we could attract. This required local Israeli leadership. It required support for financial and cooperative ventures from the movement abroad. It required educational exchanges for Diaspora Jews who would realize that Israel is today the central creative campus for the Jewish learning experience. It required winning allies within all sectors of Israeli society—political, educational, cultural, and the media. We were aware that, to begin with, we would not attract large segments in Israel to affiliate with our movement, but it was essential for the Israeli public to realize that without Progressive Judaism, Israeli society would be incomplete, just as it was essential for us to understand that without a dynamic movement in Israel, we would be marginalized and unfulfilled.

It was comparatively easy to formulate the goals and objectives for the WUPJ and our Reform and Progressive institutions around the world. But how were we to implement them?

Until the Six-Day War, the WUPJ had defined as its main mission the spreading of Progressive Judaism around the world. Prior to the Second World War, after the Nazis came to power, the WUPJ was instrumental in rescuing rabbis and rabbinical students from Fascist Germany. Funds were raised in order to send rabbis of German origin to far-flung countries to help develop progressive and liberal congregations. Because most of these men were exceptionally learned and capable, they succeeded in establishing major Reform congregations and movements. Rabbis were sent by the WUPJ to São Paulo and Rio de Janeiro in Brazil, to Buenos Aires in Argentina, to Melbourne and Sydney in Australia. Others were sent to Britain, where they infused both the Union of Liberal and Progressive Synagogues and the Reform Synagogues of Great Britain with new vitality. Two rabbis who had studied at the Hebrew Union College were sent to Johannesburg and Cape Town in South Africa. The sums of money required for establishing these movements were comparatively modest, because the rabbis were able to

expand their congregations and to make them self-sufficient
financially. In addition, after the war, the WUPJ convened international conferences every two years in Europe. The conferences dealt primarily with theological issues of concern to
the Reform rabbinate. The operating budgets were minimal
because the WUPJ considered itself a coordinating umbrella
group. Half the budget came from a comparatively small number of individual contributions; the other half came from the
National Federation of Temple Sisterhoods (NFTS, today
Women of Reform Judaism [WRJ]). Over the years they had
dedicated themselves to supporting the WUPJ and had always
raised funds for special projects. They were effective advocates
and a constant source for educating the movement as a whole
on the needs of the WUPJ.

Again it was the Six-Day War that ignited the revolutionary
change. The Biennial Conference of the WUPJ in 1968 was
scheduled to take place in Amsterdam. However, a few of us
contended that it was inconceivable that the conference be
held anywhere but in Jerusalem. We felt a great compulsion
to express solidarity with Israel in the aftermath of the war
and also to begin laying the groundwork for a significant Progressive movement in Israel.

The conference, which duly took place in Jerusalem with
four hundred delegates in attendance, was the best attended
of all WUPJ conferences until that time. The convention adopted a strong statement calling for equal rights for Progressive Judaism.

The enthusiastic response to the conference provided the
background that spurred me to recommend a redefinition of
the goals of the WUPJ. It was insufficient for us to limit our
role to that of an umbrella agency. I maintained that we had to
become an active operating agency. We had to build religious,
educational, and cultural institutions in Israel. I also began
to advocate that eventually the headquarters of the WUPJ

should be transferred to Israel. I used as the precedent the transfer of the UAHC headquarters to New York. The UAHC had since its inception been headquartered in Cincinnati, but under the inspiring leadership of its president Rabbi Maurice Eisendrath, it had moved to New York in 1951 in order to be at the center of American Jewish life. This move had encouraged the reinvigoration of Reform Judaism in America. Similarly, I advocated, the WUPJ had to move to Jerusalem "in order to be in the pulsating heart of Jewish destiny."

I recognized that for many of our leaders these objectives would seem to be distant, far-fetched, and impossible to attain. The very first question generally asked was, "Even if we agree on the objective, where are we going to obtain the funds?" My response was, "In my whole career, I never permitted the first question to be 'Where is the money?' Instead I always insisted that other questions take precedence. Is the proposal a good idea? Does it make sense? Is it attractive? Does it enhance our goals? Do we have someone who is capable of leading the effort and will devote his life and career to achieving it?" Then, and only then, does the money factor enter. In my experience, if all the answers to the previous questions are answered positively and enthusiastically, then we should seriously consider the project, irrespective of the money issue. I have always told my colleagues who worked with me, "If the first question asked about any new idea is, 'Where is the money?' the probability is we will never manage to raise it, but if we are convinced that the project is a worthy one, then we should go with it. If we have people who will sell the idea, we'll manage to get the money together."

From the very beginning of my assuming office with the WUPJ, I began to advocate the idea that it was incumbent upon us to transform the WUPJ into an operating agency. To achieve this objective we needed a lay board including a significant number of people of means. I told my colleagues that

when rabbis head institutions and make all the decisions, it is
difficult to develop effective lay leadership. In order for the
WUPJ to achieve its new objectives, we needed to attract a
board of wealthy and generous lay leaders.

That was not the case when I became active in the WUPJ
and was appointed by the president, Rabbi Jacob Shankman, to be chairman of the WUPJ's Commission on Israel.
Shankman, a rabbi of rare integrity and commitment, was
the active leader of a congregation in New Rochelle, New
York. He was a Zionist but was not active in a Zionist organization. He predicted that our efforts to make significant
progress as a movement in Israel would be frustrated by the
political machinations of Knesset politics. Among colleagues
around the leadership table were Rabbi Maurice Eisendrath; Rabbi Harold Saperstein, a committed Zionist who was
still active as the spiritual leader of his congregation; and
Jane Evans, executive director of NFTS, an articulate and
dedicated leader but with no previous active involvement
with Israel. When Rabbi Shankman's term ended in 1970,
Rabbi Bernard Bamberger, a distinguished biblical scholar
and the rabbi of a congregation in Manhattan, was elected
president of the WUPJ.

When the proposal to move the WUPJ headquarters to Israel was initiated, Bamberger, who was not an ardent Zionist,
strongly disapproved and refused to run for a second term as
president. Alexander Schindler (at the time the vice president of the UAHC) and I discussed whom we could find who
would be more attuned to the move of the WUPJ to Israel
and to the development of the movement there. Schindler
suggested that Rabbi Maurice Eisendrath, who was due to
retire from the presidency of the UAHC in 1973, might be
willing to serve as president of the WUPJ. Eisendrath had
always been supportive of the WUPJ and had traveled around
the world on its behalf. Rabbi Eisendrath was duly elected

president at the WUPJ conference in Geneva, Switzerland, in 1972.

Tragically however, Rabbi Eisendrath died while attending the UAHC Biennial in November 1973. He was replaced by Rabbi David Wice, who had been chairman of the Executive Committee of the WUPJ. Although Wice was a dedicated person who had raised some funds for the WUPJ, he was not an ardent Zionist and had even written a chapter describing Reform Judaism's non-Zionist approach in a book published by the Central Conference of American Rabbis (CCAR) in 1940. However, to his credit, Wice went along with the decision to move the WUPJ to Israel.

As Rabbi Wice's second term was coming to a close, the leadership of the WUPJ began to think about selecting its next president. The leading candidate was Rabbi Gunther Plaut from the Holy Blossom Temple of Toronto, Canada. He had been born in Germany, was fluent in German, French, Hebrew, and English, and was a recognized leader, having been elected president of the Canadian Jewish Congress. He was an outstanding scholar who was writing a commentary on the Torah, subsequently published by the UAHC. Rabbi Joseph Glaser, executive vice president of the CCAR, who was a member of the nominating committee, informed me that Rabbi Plaut was the choice of the CCAR. However, he also intimated that Rabbi Plaut was not a good fund-raiser and that the WUPJ would have to budget a substantial sum to support Rabbi Plaut's travels around the Jewish world.

As I have said, I was totally committed to enlist lay leaders who would help change the character of the WUPJ. Gerard and Ruth Daniel had become active in the WUPJ. They spoke Hebrew fluently, loved Jewish culture, and recognized the importance of building a Progressive movement in Israel. I was particularly impressed by the phenomenon of two people who had once lived in Palestine, had left the country, and were still positive about it. They had left Israel penniless in 1946 and had since built a considerable fortune. In addition to English and Hebrew, they were fluent in German and French and traveled extensively. I therefore began to raise the idea of Gerard Daniel as a potential president to a few of our leaders.

My initiative was no secret nor had I any intention that it should be. Early in my discussions with the lay leadership and the members of the nominating committee, I initiated a conversation with Rabbi Plaut. I was pleased that I did so, because he of course had already heard of my interventions. He indicated that he was surprised, and I told him how much I respected his scholarship, leadership qualities, and dedication. I explained that under normal circumstances, the professional head of an organization should not intervene as directly as I had done to influence the appointment of the president of the organization. Furthermore, if we were to follow the accepted pattern of selecting the leadership on the basis of previous qualifications, he would be the ideal candidate. However, in order to transform the WUPJ into an effective organization, it was essential that we attract to leadership roles dedicated laypeople of means who would be so dedicated that they would contribute their own funds and mobilize funds from others for our organizational expansion, primarily in Israel. To his credit Rabbi Plaut said that even though he was not happy, he understood my motivations and respected them.

Immediately thereafter, I met with Gerry and Ruth Daniel and asked Gerry if he would be prepared to become president of the WUPJ. He responded that he would be happy to take on the task and would agree to make a significant capital contribution. There were two building projects we had in mind: the new world center in Jerusalem and the synagogue in Tel Aviv. As we still did not have the plans developed for Jerusalem, we recommended the synagogue in Tel Aviv as the first objective. In any case, Ruth loved Tel Aviv, and they both felt that this was where the potential for developing Progressive Judaism in Israel had the greatest potential. Most of the population was secular, whereas in Jerusalem a high percentage was Orthodox and we had already established some institutions there. Therefore, after the election at the WUPJ Conference in 1980 in Jerusalem, we announced that the Daniels had given a major gift to build the Kedem Synagogue and Cultural Center in Tel Aviv.

The rabbi of the Kedem Synagogue, Rabbi Moshe Zemer, had struggled for years with the city to acquire a piece of land and to develop the architectural plans for the building. The city council was reluctant to grant the plot, even though the mayor, Shlomo Lahat, supported the project. There was a substantial group of religious members on the city council who were ideologically opposed to granting land for a Reform synagogue, although the plans for the building had already been accepted by the local planning authority. When I reviewed the plans, I told Rabbi Zemer and his committee that from my perspective the plans were inadequate. My concept of a physical facility was that it should serve not only as a synagogue but also as a cultural and educational center. The planned facilities were limited. The kitchen was too small and there were too few classrooms. I recommended that we try to upgrade the plans to house the multifaceted activities I visualized. Rabbi Zemer and I met with Mayor Lahat and explained that we wanted to make major changes to the plans. He advised us not to submit any changes, because there had already been considerable difficulty in getting the plans approved. To open up the subject again, he warned, would jeopardize approval. His recommendations were that we build the building according to the plans that had been approved and then subsequently make whatever changes we could. This is what we were eventually forced to do.

The Daniels had made it clear that they did not want their name to be associated with the building. I spent many hours over a period of years trying to persuade them to call the building "Beit Daniel." But they steadfastly refused.

In 1988, at a conference of the WUPJ in Jerusalem, we had scheduled one of several dedications of the building. I decided to make a last-ditch effort about the name issue when Bella and I drove Ruth and Gerry Daniel to Tel Aviv for the ceremony. Accompanying us in the car was Meir Azari, director-general of the Israel Movement for Progressive Judaism, who later became the charismatic rabbi of Beit Daniel and who led its development as a synagogue and community center. As soon as we left Jerusalem, I said to the Daniels, "I am making one last effort. I have come to know you very well. I know that you would love nothing more than to bring your children and grandchildren closer to Israel. By giving the name Beit Daniel to the facility, they will be much more likely to identify with it and its programs, and with Israel in general. I urge you, for the sake of your family, to permit us to designate the facility Beit Daniel." Ruth said, "But you expect us to give significantly more money as a naming gift." I responded, "Yes, I do, but I hope you do not think it presumptuous of me to say that I think it will be money well spent." Ruth reacted negatively to my remarks. She answered, "You presume too much. We are very good friends and we respect each other, but no one is going to tell us what to do. You are imposing on our friendship; you are exploiting our relationship. Stop the car. We are getting out." I said, "Ruth, I can't stop the car. We are in the middle of the highway, it would be dangerous to let you out here. Let us continue the journey and see how the conversation goes."

By the time we arrived in Tel Aviv, I had managed to persuade them that the building should be called "Beit Daniel" and that they would give a significant additional sum of money as a naming gift.

In July 2006, Ruth Daniel died. The Jewish Federation of Sarasota, Florida, together with the Reform Synagogue of Longboat Key, in both of which Ruth and Gerry had been active, planned a memorial meeting in January 2007. I agreed to deliver the major address at the event, which was to be attended by some 350 people.

When I arrived at the hotel, there was a note from Gerry: "Dick, I am very anxious to talk to you. Please give me a ring as soon as you arrive and I will come right over." When Gerry arrived be began to cry. He said, "I want you to know that Ruth and I often talked about that trip from Jerusalem to Tel Aviv when you persuaded us to name the facility Beit Daniel. We consider it to have been a very important moment in our lives. Had you not convinced us to give it our name, I don't know what our relationship would have been to the synagogue and to the construction of the new hostel–cultural center facility in Jaffa. Now that Ruth has died, I would not have had a facility—called Mishkenot Ruth Daniel—to perpetuate her memory, nor would the children and grandchildren have felt so close to Israel. What you predicted has indeed come to pass. I will be grateful to you until my last day." We hugged and cried. For me it was a moment of great gratification and confirmation of my belief that those who give so generously of their material resources receive back more than they contribute.

During his term as president Gerard Daniel set a new standard of leadership, a standard that was maintained by Donald Day. I had known Donald Day when he was chairman of the board of the UAHC. He was universally respected for his intelligence, perspicacity, and judgment, and he had the capacity to advocate new initiatives.

I sought an opportunity to try to involve him in the WUPJ, knowing that in a short time he would leave his position as chairman of the UAHC. Martin Strelzer, director of the North

American board of the WUPJ, and I asked him to serve as chairman of the Biennial to be held in Toronto in 1986. He accepted and we worked very closely with him on a highly successful program.

I believed that given Don's status and character, he would be able to become a major leader of the WUPJ and that through his person we would reinforce the bonds of common destiny and shared interest between the UAHC and WUPJ.

Don was elected president unanimously and was a constant source of support and good counsel. When his term of office ended, we asked him to serve as the chairman of the Mercaz Shimshon project. Once again he put his knowledge and skills at our disposal and was of enormous help to us.

Austin Beutel succeeded Donald Day as president of the WUPJ. Here too, we had considered him long before we offered him the position. We had first met Austin and his wife, Nani, when they joined the first WUPJ mission to the Soviet Union. Following the mission, we organized an international commission for the development of Progressive Judaism in the Soviet Union. We convened a meeting in London at the West London Synagogue, which was well attended by representatives from around the world. Austin and Nani Beutel had been among the most committed people on the mission, and we immediately saw in them potential leadership. Following the mission, we involved them in many activities. They brought intelligence, commitment, and their own financial resources to our programs. When the time came to choose a new president to succeed Donald Day, we informed Austin that he was the unanimous choice to serve as the next president.

Chapter Ten

Hebrew Union College Campus–World Education Center for Progressive Judaism

My involvement in helping to create an additional campus on the grounds of the Hebrew Union College–Jewish Institute of Religion in Jerusalem began during my sabbatical year in Israel in 1969–70. I had come to know Dr. Nelson Glueck well because he had asked me to serve as a visiting lecturer in social ethics at HUC-JIR while I was director of the Religious Action Center in Washington. From 1964 until 1969 I taught at HUC-JIR both in Cincinnati and New York. During the course of those weekly visits I had many occasions to meet with Dr. Glueck and discuss both social issues and the future development of the Reform movement in Israel.

The Hebrew Union College had been granted a plot of land by Prime Minister David Ben-Gurion, on which Glueck, who had been the director of the American School of Oriental Research in East Jerusalem, planned to construct a comparable institution in West Jerusalem under the auspices of HUC-JIR. After the War of Independence in 1948, East Jerusalem was occupied by the Jordanians and he no longer had access to the American School. Glueck anticipated that the primary purpose of the West Jerusalem building would be for archeological research. At the time of construction Glueck had no perception of obligating students to study in Israel. In fact he had no real interest in doing so, nor was he particularly interested in establishing a Progressive movement in Israel. However, he did insist on including a chapel in the building. To his credit, Dr. Glueck had waged a courageous battle against bigoted members of the Jerusalem municipal council who had refused to grant a building permit for the building because there was going to be a chapel in which Reform Jewish religious services would be held. Despite the opposition, which forced long and costly delays, Glueck prevailed, establishing the principle that Reform Jews have a right to build their own place of worship in Jerusalem. In 1963, the impressive new building designated as the Hebrew Union College Biblical and Archaeological School was dedicated. It was both a personal triumph for Glueck and a source of institutional pride.

In part his disinterest in the development of a Progressive movement in Israel was a consequence of his controversy with Rabbi Maurice Eisendrath, the president of the UAHC. Eisendrath was very active in the leadership of the WUPJ and had prevented Glueck from being elected as president of the WUPJ.

In my meetings with Dr. Glueck during my sabbatical year, he asked me if I would be interested in becoming the administrative head of HUC-JIR in Jerusalem. I reminded him of our conversation many years previously when, as an undergraduate, I had decided to spend a year in Israel and he suggested that I should wait until after ordination, at which time the College would give me a fellowship and might even propose that I become a member of the faculty. I told him at the time, and reaffirmed my views yet again, that I had no interest in becoming an academician. I considered myself an activist and did not see myself psychologically oriented to serve as a scholar and faculty member.

However, I did suggest that in my capacity as director of the UAHC-CCAR Commission on Israel and as chairman of the Israel Commission of the WUPJ, I thought it appropriate that we give consideration to close cooperation between HUC-JIR, the UAHC, and the WUPJ and recommended that we should consider acquiring the twelve-*dunam* (three-acre) plot of ground adjacent to the College. I had closely followed the development of Bar Ilan University, which had opened a few years earlier and which already showed promise of being highly successful. I suggested that together, with HUC-JIR playing the lead role, the movement should consider establishing an Academy of Jewish Learning along the lines of Bar Ilan. I told Dr. Glueck that I had always felt that the role of HUC-JIR as an institution that produced rabbis, cantors, Jewish educators, and Jewish communal workers was too limited and that we should expand our horizons so that with time, it would become a major Jewish institution that would synthesize a contemporary form of liberal Judaism with the ideology of Zionism. Dr. Glueck rejected the idea on grounds that (1) the idea was too far-fetched and visionary, (2) the College was having enough difficulty raising funds for its own budget, and (3) he was not particularly interested in working more closely with the WUPJ. In effect, Dr. Glueck obstinately refused to consider the idea.

The idea of acquiring the plot adjacent to HUC-JIR rose again when Professor Ezra Spicehandler, dean of HUC-JIR in Jerusalem, and Dr. Alfred Gottschalk heard that the land was available. It had been suggested that the Sheraton Hotel would be built on the plot; however, the developers thought that it was not sufficiently large, and the hotel was subsequently built in a nearby location. Gottschalk, who had become president of the Hebrew Union College following the death of Nelson Glueck, extended an invitation to the UAHC (and by inference the WUPJ) to share in a mission to see if the plot could be acquired for the use of the College and its affiliated institutions.

For the purpose of negotiations, HUC-JIR was represented by Gottschalk, Spicehandler, Dr. Paul Steinberg, dean of the New York school of HUC-JIR, and Richard J. Scheuer, who was chairman of the administrative committee of the Jerusalem school and subsequently the chairman of the HUC-JIR board. I represented the UAHC and WUPJ. We were accompanied by S. Zalman Abramov, a distinguished member of the Knesset and a good friend of both the College and the movement. In March 1971, the delegation met with Prime Minister Golda Meir and Minister of Finance Pinchas Sapir and appealed to them to lease the land to the HUC and the other institutions belonging to the Reform movement. Sapir agreed to lease the land on the terms of what he referred to as a "package deal," namely that the Reform movement would undertake an extensive building program. He also agreed in principle to a matching fund arrangement in which the government would contribute a dollar for each dollar raised by the Reform movement. (Following the disastrous economic consequences of the Yom Kippur War in 1973, we agreed that this proviso would be canceled.) Sapir stipulated that the land would be leased on condition that the building project be undertaken; otherwise it would be returned to the government. The delegation convened a meeting the following day with Mayor Teddy Kollek, who expressed enthusiasm for the project and offered his own counsel on how to implement it, warning us that it could be a highly complicated process.

The delegation reported back to HUC-JIR and the UAHC-WUPJ with great enthusiasm. It was deemed essential to establish a framework for intra-institutional cooperation. Therefore, in April 1971, a two-day meeting was held in Miami Beach to discuss how the land could be most effectively utilized and to create a framework for institutional cooperation. Representing the College were Gottschalk and Steinberg; representing the UAHC-WUPJ were Alexander Schindler and myself.

A policy decision had been made in Jerusalem that the formal request for the land grant should be made in the name of the HUC-JIR, because the government was more likely to lease the land to an academic institution than to a Reform religious movement. It was agreed that the College, in turn, would make land available to the movement.

It was also agreed that each institution would develop its own facilities, since the function and character of each were different. However, wherever possible there were to be shared use of facilities and common programming. It was agreed to engage an architect to develop a master plan that would be in architectural harmony with the existing campus. It was agreed that the UAHC-WUPJ would assume responsibility for raising its own capital and that all prospective donors would be cleared with the ollege prior to solicitation.

On my return to Washington, I sent a memorandum of understanding to Gottschalk, Schindler, and Steinberg. The memo was to be discussed and approved by each institution. It makes no mention of the World Union for Progressive Judaism, because at the time I was functioning only as chairman of the Commission on Israel of the WUPJ and no discussion had been held with the leadership of the WUPJ itself. Furthermore, it was understood that the WUPJ was not structured to assume responsibility for the building project. (It was not until June 1973, more than two years later, that I officially accepted responsibility for the WUPJ.)

But subsequent to the meetings held in Jerusalem in March, the Israel Land Authority and the Ministry of Finance had second thoughts. They came to the conclusion that the land was too valuable. They decided that instead of granting a lease to HUC-JIR for the entire twelve-*dunam* plot, they would grant only five and a half *dunams*. During a meeting in June 1971, in which the College was represented by Professor Spicehandler and MK Abramov, the matter was again discussed at length. The Israel Land Authority and the Ministry of Finance also demanded that we pay 1.7 million Israeli pounds in land-clearing costs. Spicehandler and Abramov negotiated with the ministry officials, who were chaired by Arnon Gafni, the director-general of the ministry. During the discussions they indicated that HUC-JIR might agree to accept half the plot but would not agree to the land-clearing charges under any circumstances.

When Professor Gottschalk and I received the report, I objected strenuously, on the grounds that we could not erect the kind of facilities on the campus that we deemed necessary if we were only to receive less than half of the plot envisaged. Gottschalk and I agreed that I should return to Jerusalem to try and reverse the decision and to return to the original grant of twelve *dunams*. Gottschalk wrote a letter to Minister of Finance Sapir indicating to him that though the College was pleased to receive official confirmation of the land lease for an area of five and a half *dunams*, nevertheless, the curtailment of the original lease would severely restrict the scope of our long-range development program. I flew to Israel at the suggestion of Dr. Gottschalk to meet with Minister Pinchas Sapir and Director-General Arnon Gafni. Professor Spicehandler and I did meet again with them and were able to persuade them to revert to the original plan, so that the entire plot was granted to HUC-JIR for the development of our World Education Center for Progressive Judaism.

In retrospect, the allocation of the full 12.8-*dunam* plot made it possible to build the campus as it is today. Had we accepted the government's insistence on only half the area, the beautiful campus would not have been realized.

The key lay leader in the process of building the campus was Richard Scheuer, who was chairman of the Jerusalem Committee of the HUC-JIR board and subsequently became chairman of its board of trustees. He had four passions: Jerusalem, HUC-JIR, Reform Judaism, and architecture.

Immediately after our meetings Scheuer agreed to advance the funds to engage an architect to draw up preliminary designs. All of us were disappointed with the first architectural proposals. It was Scheuer who then suggested that we approach Moshe Safdie, a young and brilliant Israeli-born architect, who had already won the admiration of the mayor of Jerusalem, Teddy Kollek, and who had redesigned the plaza facing the Western Wall in the Jewish Quarter of the Old City. Safdie had become world famous when his master's thesis "Habitat" had been accepted as the revolutionary keynote feature of the Montreal Exposition of 1967.

We agreed that the HUC-JIR and the WUPJ would work together in planning the entire campus. The major participants were Richard Scheuer, Alfred Gottschalk, and myself. Even though at times we had disagreements, we established a remarkable degree of harmony, because all of us were totally dedicated to the project.

Gottschalk and I had assumed a tremendous responsibility. As heads of our respective institutions, each of us was committed to raising funds to sustain existing programs as well as embarking on new creative projects. And now we were undertaking responsibility for raising vast sums for the new buildings. We knew, particularly after the Yom Kippur War, that mobilizing capital funds for new buildings would be difficult, but we undertook the challenge willingly.

One incident will illustrate some of the issues with which we dealt. When Safdie presented his initial drawings to us, Gottschalk and I spent hours going over the plans with a fine-tooth comb to see how it would be possible to cut costs. We

saw that one of Safdie's major architectural themes was a series of arches that made up the walkways alongside each building. We appreciated the aesthetic value of the arches, but we
could not see their functional purpose. We investigated what
the cost of the arches would be, and we were given an approx-
imate cost of $3 million. We carefully prepared for a meeting
with Scheuer in order to try to convince him and Safdie to
modify the plans. But when we met him we stood no chance.
In his own inimitable, gentle manner Scheuer told us, "We
are not building this campus for ten years or even fifty years.
This project is a hundred-year undertaking. We are making
a statement to Israel and the Jewish world that Progressive
Judaism is here to stay. Besides, if you take $3 million and
amortize it over one hundred years, we are not talking about
much money at all."

In our early discussions we had agreed that HUC-JIR would
erect three buildings: an academic center, a library, and a museum of archeology; the WUPJ would erect three buildings: a
youth hostel, a synagogue at the end of the plot facing the Old
City, and an office building at the front on King David Street
that would also be a tourist center.

From the time we had our first meetings with Golda Meir
and Pinchas Sapir, I had begun to plan the three buildings the
WUPJ was assigned to construct. For me the most important
of the facilities was Beit Shmuel, the youth hostel and cultural and educational center. I was motivated by many factors.
The first was to demonstrate that Judaism is a culture and a
civilization and not just a religion. I also felt it important to
attract Israelis to our campus. Until the establishment of Beit
Shmuel, the HUC-JIR campus was primarily a place of quiet
contemplation where American rabbinical students came to
spend their first year of studies. I felt that in order to bring life
to the campus, it had to become a center for Israelis and not
just for students from abroad or for tourists. The center was

also designed to make a statement. It was essential that Jews in Israel as well as world Jewry recognize that the Reform movement was in Israel to stay and that we undertook to contribute to the educational and cultural dimensions of Israel as well as to build the movement. Finally, it was essential to demonstrate that we intended to serve Jews of all religious persuasions. Therefore, I went to great efforts to make sure that the kitchen would be kosher and all food served there would observe the dietary laws. We had to struggle to get a kashrut license and to have a *mashgiach* (kashrut supervisor). I also insisted that the architect design an attractive place for *n'tilat yadayim* (the ritual washing of hands) and that the appropriate blessing in Hebrew be engraved in the marble at the entrance to the dining hall. This was in contrast to almost all of the places in Israeli hotels, yeshivot, and synagogues, where the *n'tilat yadayim* is usually a simple metal container with tin cups.

After the building was complete and in operation, I took great pride that the rabbi in charge of kashrut supervision told me and everyone else under his jurisdiction that the kashrut at Beit Shmuel was *m'had'rin min ham'had'rin* (an especially high level of kashrut). Indeed, to prove his point, he asked if he could hold the regular meetings of his supervisors at Beit Shmuel. I invited him and his colleagues to come and provided them with lunch. It gave me great pleasure to know that even the most Orthodox rabbis considered our standards to meet the highest demands.

With regard to the construction phase of the buildings, the remarkable support of Joy Ungerleider should be mentioned. I had come to know her because of her friendship with Richard Scheuer and other mutual friends involved with archeology. Decades earlier, her father, Sam Gottesman, had provided Professor Eliezer Sukenik with the sum needed to acquire the Dead Sea Scrolls from an Arab antiquities dealer. Joy and her family had subsequently contributed the funds to erect the Shrine of the Book, housing the Dead Sea scrolls, the most notable and precious treasure in the Israel Museum.

It had come to my attention that Joy was seeking to find a project worthy of perpetuating the memory of her late husband, Samuel Ungerleider. I contacted her and suggested that she might like to consider making a contribution to our youth hostel and cultural and educational center. She informed me that she was coming to Israel for five days with her children and invited me to make a presentation to the entire family. She cautioned that they were considering many projects and that in order to win their support our project would have to be especially creative and appealing. Our staff immediately set to work to prepare a dramatic proposal. I sensed that we had made an impact when after our initial presentation, the family extended the allocated time from one to three hours of questions and discussion. Toward the end of their visit, Joy called me to announce that they had decided that our project had won their support.

The original commitment letter stipulated that the sign on the building should read "The Samuel J. Ungerleider Youth Center Hostel of the World Union for Progressive Judaism." However, when it came time to prepare the sign, I suggested that we call the institution by the simpler name Beit Shmuel, thus perpetuating the Hebrew name of her husband, and that it would be preferable if all our institutions would carry Hebrew names. The Ungerleider family readily agreed.

As the construction of Beit Shmuel neared completion, we began to search for the staff to administer the facility. I knew the kind of person I wanted as director. I sought someone who would be knowledgeable about Judaism, would identify with Progressive Judaism, and would have the creative skills to develop the programmatic ideas we envisaged.

We established a high-level committee to search for a director, recognizing that it was essential that the director be hired at least six months before the completion of the building, so that he would have ample opportunity to develop his own ideas and engage additional staff. One of the candidates, Menachem Leibovic, had been eliminated by the committee because he had told them that he was not willing to accept the precondition that the person selected needed to live on the campus. When the committee met with him they were impressed, but he was eliminated because he had told them, "I am very anxious to have this position, but I don't think that the campus is a place to rear my four children, and therefore, if you insist on that condition, I am reluctantly removing myself from your consideration." When the committee reported to me that Leibovic would have been favorably considered except for his refusal to live on campus, I reacted positively to his candidacy. I told the committee, "That is precisely the sort of man we want, someone whose family takes precedence over everything else." I requested the committee to interview him again, and this time he was offered the position. I consider that decision one of the most important in terms of developing the movement. Menachem Leibovic began working in May 1986, some eight months before Beit Shmuel actually opened. He was most helpful in the completion of the project and later in developing its outstanding and creative cultural and educational programs. Subsequently he assumed many leadership roles in the movement, including a period as director-general of the Israel Movement for Progressive Judaism. Throughout all the years we worked together, he was my trusted ally and confidant.

As an additional bonus, Menachem's wife, Maya, a teacher by profession, decided to study for the rabbinate and become the first Israeli-born woman in history to be ordained as a rabbi. She developed the congregation of Mevasseret Zion, near Jerusalem, which, under her leadership, has constructed a beautiful building and become a dynamic educational and cultural center.

As the program of Beit Shmuel developed and expanded, thousands of people of all ages from all walks of life and of all ideological and religious persuasions participated in our educational courses, tours, cultural, and educational events. Once we recognized that Beit Shmuel had become the major cultural center for Jerusalem, we began to plan for the adjacent building, which subsequently came to be called "Mercaz Shimshon," for a reason that will become apparent.

We had originally planned to include a synagogue, but in the light of our experience, we decided to build another multipurpose facility with a large hall (which could also be used for worship) overlooking the Old City of Jerusalem, an auditorium, classrooms, conference rooms, and a residential section.

In the construction of this facility, the cost of which exceeded $16 million, we were confronted with numerous problems, including opposition from neighbors and an attempt by the Jerusalem Municipal Planning Committee, controlled by ultra-Orthodox council members, to halt construction. However, we finally prevailed.

The construction of Mercaz Shimshon corroborated some of my theories in terms of institution building. I am convinced that there are many people in the Jewish community who are eager to donate funds for projects with which they identify. Persons of means who have guaranteed their own and their family's financial future are in search of causes that can reflect their values. I never hesitated to ask potential donors for a contribution, because I always firmly believed that our projects offered them an opportunity to find personal fulfillment. The challenge is to conceive of the right projects. As I contemplated the construction of Mercaz Shimshon, I knew that if we had engaged an architect other than Moshe Safdie, the building would have been less costly. Perhaps we could have saved as much as 30 percent of the construction costs. However, I also knew that a building designed by Moshe Safdie would inspire people to contribute funds on a higher level and that the privilege of working with such a world-renowned architect would attract a different caliber of donors. Therefore, in a way, it may have been easier to raise $16 million for a building designed by Safdie than to raise less money for a lesser-known architect.

Many donors contributed to the construction of Mercaz Shimshon, and we remain grateful to all who participated. We are especially proud that the major donors head foundations that are renowned in the world of Jewish philanthropy for their insistence on worthy creative programming.

I first met Charles and Lynn Schusterman when I addressed a meeting commemorating the eightieth anniversary of the synagogue in Tulsa, Oklahoma. I had heard about the Schusterman family and their many sophisticated and caring philanthropic activities. I asked Rabbi Charles Sherman to arrange a meeting with the Schustermans, because I wanted an opportunity to present the concept of Beit Shmuel and the building that eventually became Mercaz Shimshon to them. I found a receptive ear and an immediate bond of common interest with Lynn and Charles Schusterman. On a visit to Israel several months later, I took Charles to the top of Beit Shmuel and showed him the magnificent view from the roof garden, overlooking the walls of the Old City. I told him what I had told others: "We have the rare privilege of being able to acquire this land, which is on the seam of the old and the new, Arab and Jewish. Our tradition projects the concept of two Jerusalems: heavenly Jerusalem and earthly Jerusalem. Our challenge is to bring the heavenly Jerusalem down to meet earthly Jerusalem." Charlie, who was a very practical man, said to me, "Dick, I appreciate the theory, but let's talk straight to the point. What do you expect of me?" I said, "I hope you and Lynn will contribute the naming gift." He asked, "How much do you want?" I told him $5 million. He replied, "Dick, I have to tell you the truth, I am a wealthy man, but no one has ever asked me for a gift of $5 million." I responded, "Charlie, I'll also tell you the truth. I have never asked anybody for $5 million before, but I believe it is very much worth it, because this will become a dynamic facility that will be a center of inspiration for youth and adults from Israel and all over the Diaspora." In due course they agreed to give the designated naming gift.

The director of the Schusterman Foundation, Sandy Cardin, was most helpful in the negotiations. When the time came to name the building, I suggested to Lynn and Charlie that we call the building "Mercaz Shimshon." I had thought of Shimshon because when I had been in Tulsa I had noted that the headquarters of the Schusterman company were in the Samson Building. When I asked them where the name Samson came from, Charlie responded that his father's name was Sam and that he had decided to name his company Samson because he had such wonderful recollections of his father. Shimshon is the Hebrew name for the biblical Samson.

Over the years I had become friendly with the children of Jacob and Hilda Blaustein, especially Barbara and David Hirshhorn and Betty and Arthur Roswell. I had approached them for a contribution to the construction of Beit Shmuel. They made a tentative commitment to underwrite the large conference room, which we had designated as a $200,000 gift. David Hirshhorn, the head of the family foundation, asked me to call him following the scheduled meeting of the foundation's board. When I spoke to him he said, "You asked for $200,000 for the conference room. We have decided not to give you that. Our foundation believes in contributing for program as well as physical facilities, so we are adding another $50,000."

Over the course of the years, Bella and I became close friends with Jacob and Hilda Blaustein's youngest daughter, Betty, and her husband, Dr. Arthur Roswell. During the construction of Mercaz Shimshon, Betty and Arthur Rosewell, Nani and Austin Beutel, then the president of the WUPJ, and Donald Day, past president of the WUPJ and chairman of the construction committee, and Bella and I went to Ottowa to visit the National Museum of Art of Canada, which had been designed by Moshe Safdie. I suggested to Betty and Arthur that the Blaustein Foundation donate the great hall at the top of the building. The family agreed to make a contribution of $1.5 million. Arthur was active on the building committee and, as an engineer, was knowledgeable about the acoustics and played a key role in ensuring that they were of a high level. After the building was constructed, I mentioned that the hall, now called the Blaustein Hall, had cost considerably more than we had anticipated. To my great pleasure, the family added another $250,000. They have since made many contributions to our programs and always in their characteristically modest manner.

Once after a trip abroad, I returned to Jerusalem and found on my desk a note from Bernard Rapoport, a well-known insurance magnate and philanthropist: "Dick, it has been many years since we have seen each other. I have followed your career in Israel and am proud to hear about your successes. If you ever get to Waco, Texas, be sure to look me up." I respected Bernard Rapoport for his many contributions to liberal causes and soon found an opportunity to visit him in Waco. For the first phase of construction of the campus, we and HUC-JIR had produced a professional movie and an expensive brochure. It had been my experience that the movie, which lasted thirteen and a half minutes, and the brochure were not particularly effective in fund-raising, so when it came time to raise the money for Mercaz Shimshon,

I decided not to produce a brochure, but just to take pictures of the model with me when I solicited funds from potential donors. I started to show the pictures to Bernard Rapoport. He said, "Dick that won't be necessary. When you entered the room, how much money did you hope to receive?" I said, "I hoped you would consider a naming gift of $2.5 million." He said, "You have it. Now let's work out the details."

Two months before the dedication of the building, the Intifada of 2000 broke out. Arab laborers from the West Bank were unable get to work, and we were forced to rely on foreign workers from Asia. Because of the violence, many of our world leaders and major donors canceled their plans to attend. Despite calls to postpone the ceremony, we refused to allow the violence to postpone our plans. My address at the dedication ceremony reflected our firm identity with the State of Israel:

> We hereby declare that we are not only dedicating Mercaz Shimshon. No Intifada can deter us from reaffirming our solidarity with the Jewish state. We declare our enduring commitment to help shape the cultural and spiritual character of Israel. We aspire to make our contribution toward the creation of a Jewish, democratic, and just society, a nation that will live in harmony within its borders and be at peace with its neighbors.
>
> When our architect Moshe Safdie first showed me his plans for this hall with its glass wall and ceiling gazing over the majestic view of the Old City of Jerusalem, I was overwhelmed. I immediately thought of a midrash in Leviticus Rabbah (31:6). The midrash teaches that when a human king decides to build a palace, he constructs the windows so that they are narrow on the outside and become wider toward the interior. The reason? So as to allow the light to enter inside. But when the King of Kings ordained the construction of the

First Temple in Jerusalem, the windows were built so that they were narrow on the inside and grew wider toward the outside. Why? The midrash teaches us, "In order to send forth a great light."

The windows in Mercaz Shimshon are wide on both the inside and the outside. We are not kings, nor do we presume to speak in the divine name of the King of Kings. We do not believe we have all the answers. We do not believe that our way is the only way, but we do believe that we have discovered one way to search for Jewish meaning and purpose and that this way is authentically Jewish and deserving of proper respect and full rights in the State of Israel.

We are critical of ourselves and we invite criticism from others. We declare that we aspire to have the light of the Land of Israel and the People of Israel shine in to illuminate our path. At the same time, we also declare that we wish "to send forth a great light to the Jewish people." We welcome all Jews to use our facilities and to participate in our programs: Orthodox, ultra-Orthodox, Conservative, Reform, Reconstructionist, Liberal, secular—all are welcome. Moreover, we invite all non-Jews, some of whom are here today—Christians, Muslims, people of all faiths and all ethnic identities—to join with us. As I said at the cornerstone laying ceremony, "All the food in this center is kosher, but no food for thought is *t'reif* [unkosher]."

Please join with us in the sacred quest for eternal light. "May a new light shine on Zion and may we all be privileged to bask in its radiance" [from the daily prayer book].

Chapter Eleven

The Reform Kibbutz Movement

I had always been fascinated by the kibbutz movement in Israel. Throughout my teen years and during the course of my rabbinical studies I read extensively about the Labor Zionist movement and its attempt to blend social idealism with the economic and political realities of Israeli life. I was impressed with the social justice concepts underlying the Labor Zionist movement and its passionate commitment to all workers. I had read the writings of pioneer socialist theoreticians such as A. D. Gordon and Berl Katznelson and believed that the Labor movement in Israel represented the best possible synthesis of Jewish tradition and the demands of Israeli life.

In 1949 I had spent the summer working on two kibbutzim, Hazorea and Ginegar. I performed a variety of tasks: laying irrigation pipes, washing dishes, waiting on tables, cleaning out the dairy barns and chicken coops, working in the fields and the orchards, and spreading manure on the fields (an especially good preparation for a life of public service).

In those days, many of the leaders of Israeli society, including members of the cabinet and the Knesset, were kibbutz members. Many other political leaders had been kibbutz members and were advocates of the socialist labor ideology.

In addition, a high percentage of senior army officers were from the kibbutzim.

During the course of my year's sojourn in Israel I would take advantage of holiday periods to visit different kibbutzim. When there was a break in university studies, I worked on archeological excavations at Khirbet Kerach and lived in Kvutzat Kinneret, where I also experienced at firsthand the social idealism of the pioneering movement.

During my mission to Israel in the fall of 1967, I met with a number of leaders of the Israel Labor movement and the Histadrut and the leadership of the kibbutz movements (today there is one united movement, but then there were three). In discussing potential programmatic objectives for the Reform movement during that trip, I raised the idea of trying to establish a Reform kibbutz. The Labor movement leaders discouraged me. They said that to establish a kibbutz was a complicated and arduous process. They asked me what I thought would distinguish a Reform kibbutz from any other. Among the persons I met was Aryeh Ben-Gurion, a nephew of David Ben-Gurion and a member of Kibbutz Beit Hashita, who was an expert on new and creative programs in the kibbutz movement. Every kibbutz had a Passover seder and prepared their own Haggadah with some reference to tradition, but with the addition of creative writings. They were not conventional prayers but readings, often produced by either the kibbutz movement as a whole or by individual kibbutz members. The Labor movement leaders were far from enthusiastic about the notion of a Reform kibbutz. They asked, why not strengthen the existing kibbutzim by encouraging young Diaspora Jews to join? Why separate yourselves from the others? I responded that I aspired to forge dramatic new programs that would capture the imagination of the Reform movement as a whole.

During my trip I began to develop a formula that I suggested should be our Reform movement objective, namely, "Unless we root ourselves in the soil of the Jewish people, we cannot root ourselves in its soul." It was my contention that the best way to root ourselves in the soil of Israel was to establish a kibbutz. A book by Gidon Elad, *Light of the Arava*, edited by Michael Livni, includes the following letter of mine,* which explains my rationale for wanting to establish a kibbutz:

> When I originally conceived the idea of establishing a Reform kibbutz, I had a number of objectives in mind. One of my objectives was to root Reform Judaism literally in the soil of Israel. I considered the development of the Kibbutz Movement to be a magnificent blending of the social ideals and traditional values of Judaism. For us as a movement, to develop kibbutzim would literally put us on the map of Israel, not only geographically, but also intellectually and spiritually.
>
> I had another objective. I thought it was essential to create a new form of Israeli religious expression. The kibbutz environment was conducive to experimentation of religious observance and ritual innovation. A new kind of indigenous Israeli Judaism could emerge in a Reform kibbutz. That expression of Judaism would impact on other kibbutzim, on Israeli society in general, and on our movement abroad.
>
> After we began the process of establishing the first kibbutz, Yahel, we began to talk about establishing a second kibbutz and even began to dream about establishing a third one. I had initially believed that if we could establish a distinctive lifestyle with an emphasis on a liberal expression of Judaism in one Reform kibbutz, then that distinctive lifestyle would impact on other kibbutzim. In other words, the way to influence the kibbutz movement as a whole was not only by establishing Reform kibbutzim, but by bringing to bear the influence of the lifestyle on many other existing kibbutzim.

°Gidon Elad, *Light of the Arava* (Tzell Hatamar, 1997), 312–13.

Without necessarily identifying as Reform kibbutzim, other kibbutzim could adopt a progressive Jewish lifestyle, which would reflect a rich blend of Jewish tradition and contemporary social idealism.

Several colleagues and I formulated a resolution for the UAHC Biennial in 1967. The resolution that was adopted contains the phrase "to encourage the development of adult programs, including, if feasible, settlements under the auspices of Progressive Judaism." In the summer of 1971 we convened a conference at Oranim, a kibbutz education center, together with leaders of the Labor movement and the Israel Labor Party. The purpose was to encourage joint activities and to establish a working relationship. During the course of the discussions, the idea of establishing a Reform kibbutz rose anew. In my address at the conference, I clarified my views of the relationship between Reform Judaism and the kibbutz movement. Some excerpts follow:

> We need to lay the groundwork for collaboration between our two movements. To enumerate some premises on which both the Reform movement and the kibbutz movement can reach consensus:
>
> 1. *The mission of the people of Israel may be fulfilled through the State of Israel and its institutions.*
>
> The traditional concept of the messianic era is still relevant. The return to Zion was never the ultimate goal of the Jewish people, but rather it was a step toward the salvation of all mankind. Jewish tradition understands that no group can be religious or righteous in the abstract. In order to have a just society, men must do more than preach about it, but must strive to create it in a specific place and time. Our forefathers believed that the return to Zion would provide the opportunity for the Jewish people to create a just society. The

restoration of the people to its land was a symbol of Jewish faith in man as well as in the Almighty. War, injustice, hatred are not inevitable. If the Jew, the most oppressed of peoples, could be redeemed, then was there not hope for all nations? The Jew in his own land would serve as the example, leading mankind to everlasting peace.

If there is any institution in Israel that bears the unique stamp of Jewish social idealism it is the kibbutz. We point with pride to the kibbutz as the noblest contemporary fulfillment of Jewish values.

2. *We must resist artificial distinctions between religious and secular Jews.*

Many aspects of kibbutz life, with its stress on social idealism rooted in Jewish needs and loyalties, may be considered "religious," even without the formality of prayer, just as many of the activities of an American synagogue may be considered "secular," even if accompanied by prayers.

The renewal of Jewish ritual observance in kibbutzim, both in traditional and creative forms, the reintroduction of study, and a creative effort to present Judaism in positive terms, all reflect a search to reconcile the ritual and moral, the religious and secular dimensions of Judaism.

3. *To be authentic, a Jewish movement must contain a moral dimension.*

A Jewish religious movement must insist on adherence to personal and public morality with as much fervor as it insists on ritual observance. The kibbutz movement has been a pioneer in the search for authentic Judaism. However, because of misconceptions of the nature of Judaism, the kibbutz has sometimes considered its search as a rebellion rather than as a reform of Judaism. The early pioneers were in the forefront of return of the People of Israel to the Land of Israel. Now

they have an opportunity to pioneer in returning the faith of
Israel to the State of Israel.

After the conference at Oranim, representatives of the two
movements began to meet with greater frequency to discuss
the possible establishment of a Reform kibbutz. We were very
much aware of the difficulties. In order to recruit Americans
for a Reform kibbutz, it was essential to send an emissary to
New York to seek out and organize potential candidates. In
the meantime, we sent two American rabbis, Allan Levine and
Henry (Hank) Skirball to Israel. Levine worked as a counselor
at the Ben Shemen youth village and Skirball worked with
NFTY (the National Federation of Temple Youth) and was
instrumental in organizing an Israeli youth movement (Noar
Telem). The two rabbis played a key role in locating Israeli participants in the framework of Nahal (an Israel Defense Forces
unit that combines military service with work on the land; the
Hebrew acronym stands for Noar Halutzi Lochem, "Fighting Pioneer Youth"). Rabbi Steve Schafer, who was director
of NFTY, encouraged Michael Livni, an emissary from Israel,
to organize the American group. The five of us—Schafer and
Livni in New York, Levine, Skirball, and I in Israel—were the
key activists in the efforts to develop a Reform kibbutz.

We felt it was important to gain the support of the leadership of the Israel Movement for Progressive Judaism as well
as MARAM, the Council of Israel Progressive Rabbis. We
made a presentation to both groups, explaining what a historic
move it would be to establish a Reform kibbutz, enumerating
the difficulties and the potential problems, but nevertheless
explaining that in our view, it was urgent to make an affirmative decision.

To our great disappointment, the two leadership groups rejected the proposal. They did not consider the establishment
of a kibbutz to be within the purview of Progressive Judaism in

Israel. Furthermore, they were concerned that if the attempt to establish a kibbutz failed, it would harm our reputation. This, of course, ran contrary to my ideological views and activist approach with regard to institution building: if we have a worthy idea and people who will commit their lives, livelihoods, and careers to implementing the idea, then we should go ahead and run with it. Consequently, we decided that if we could not advance the kibbutz idea within the framework of the Israel Movement for Progessive Judasim, we would do so within the framework of the World Union for Progressive Judaism. On other issues as well we used the framework of the WUPJ to further institution building. We knew that there were many potential complications.

It was relatively easy to articulate the ideological rationale for a kibbutz but the bureaucracy involved was complex and arduous. We discovered the hard way that it involved a multiplicity of bodies: the army, the Ministry of Agriculture, the kibbutz movements, the Jewish Agency Settlement Department, the Jewish National Fund, local governments, and numerous departments within each of them. Each entity had its own regulations, and extensive negotiations were required in order to conform to all the requirements and procedures. Furthermore, young people entering the Nahal program had to commit themselves to an additional year of army service (four years instead of three years for boys; three years instead of two for girls). Unfortunately, the majority of soldiers in the Nahal program left immediately or shortly after their basic term of service finished. Even when the kibbutz movement was in its prime, no more than 10 to 15 percent of the young people ended up actually living on a kibbutz.

The selection of the site was of paramount importance to us. We had decided that for ideological reasons, we could not contemplate a site over the Green Line. We narrowed the possibilities to a site in the Arava Valley, seventy-five kilometers

north of Eilat, knowing full well that there were certain dis-
advantages, such as oppressive heat, the desert environment
and soil, and distance from the center of the country. Nevertheless, this is where we established Kibbutz Yahel, the first
Reform kibbutz.

We had scheduled the dedication of Yahel for November
1976, to coincide with the biennial conference of the World
Union for Progressive Judaism. Despite all the promises and
undertakings, on a visit to the site two months before the dedication date, it seemed that virtually nothing was ready. The
director-general of the Ministry of Housing asked me to delay
the dedication for at least six months. I therefore asked for an
emergency meeting with Avraham Ofer, the minister of housing. I told him that one thousand people were coming from
abroad for the convention and that the scheduled highlight was
to be the dedication of Kibbutz Yahel. We could not change
the date of either the convention or the kibbutz dedication.
Ofer said, "Rabbi, we have at least eight months' work ahead
of us. We'll never be able to make it." I replied, "The entire
State of Israel itself is one big miracle. Can you not condense
eight months' work into two and make one more little miracle
happen?" He promised to make every effort, and I prevailed
on him to deliver the main address. Less than a month after
the dedication, Ofer died, and his speech at Yahel was his last
public address. Our movement is deeply indebted to him.

One of the most memorable moments of my life was the
dedication day. We started the drive from Jerusalem in a long
convoy of buses, conveying the eager Reform Jewish leaders from all over the world. I still meet friends who recall
that they planted a tree or affixed a mezuzah on a building
that day. For me the nail-biting uncertainties contributed to
the exhilaration of the dedication. The road into the kibbutz
from the main highway was paved the day before, and the
sign pointing to Kibbutz Yahel was set up on the morning of

the dedication. At long last, Progressive Judaism was also on the physical map of Israel.

Following the establishment of Yahel we repeated the process all over again when we established a second kibbutz, Lotan, located twelve kilometers south of Yahel and dedicated in 1983. The movement proudly nurtured the two kibbutzim. At Yahel we constructed a conference center and library-synagogue, the funds for which were contributed by NFTS. We established a fund the proceeds of which were used to enrich the educational and cultural dimensions of kibbutz life.

The two kibbutzim have since developed in divergent directions. Yahel has adopted the process of privatization that has evolved in most of the kibbutzim in the country. Lotan has preferred to retain the traditional socioeconomic principles of the kibbutz movement. It has also become well-known for its innovative experimentation with ecological living and a world-renowned center for bird-watching. In addition to the two kibbutzim, in 1985 the movement established Har Halutz, a communal settlement in the Galilee combining a blend of collective and free enterprise principles.

In reviewing nearly four decades of activity to advance the cause of collective settlements in Israel, we as a movement have much of which to be proud. All three settlements are flourishing. Hundreds of people have passed through the settlement framework. For some new immigrants the kibbutz was a first stop to ease the first stages of life in Israel and to learn Hebrew. For others, kibbutz life represented an experience in social idealism that had a great impact on their personal value system. Nevertheless, and despite the feelings of personal satisfaction, my original aspiration to affect the lifestyle of other kibbutzim was not fulfilled. Perhaps the modern developments within the kibbutz movement as a whole were not conducive to an injection of Reform

Judaism. Perhaps there were other factors. Nevertheless, I consider it a great privilege to have been involved with the establishment of the kibbutz movement and to have developed enduring friendships with people who reflect the original kibbutz ideals.

Chapter Twelve

The Israel Movement for Progressive Judaism

When I went on my first exploratory mission to Israel in 1967, the fledgling Israeli Progressive movement was served by just three rabbis: Rabbi Moshe Zemer, who had started congregations in Kfar Shmariyahu and Tel Aviv; Rabbi Robert Samuels, who was the assistant to Rabbi Meir Elk, the principal of the Leo Baeck School in Haifa and who had also organized a congregation there; and Rabbi Toviah Ben-Chorin, who was serving a congregation in Ramat Gan. The World Union for Progressive Judaism had raised only meager funds to support these rabbis and their congregations. When I met them, two of them informed me that they were so disappointed in their minimal salaries and lack of support for their programs that they were seriously considering leaving Israel. I promised that on my return to the United States I would make an effort to raise their salaries and to mobilize additional funds for programming. I kept my promise to them. All three of them were talented, knowledgeable, and dedicated to their task, and it is they who should be recognized as the true rabbinical pioneers of the Israel Movement for Progressive Judaism.

The oldest Progressive congregation in Israel, Har El, had been established in Jerusalem in 1958 by a small group of learned Jews led by Dr. Shalom Ben-Chorin, a scholar and journalist (and father of Rabbi Toviah Ben-Chorin mentioned above). It was my privilege to organize and head the first mission of the National Federation of Temple Youth to Israel in 1958, and during that visit, I brought the first Torah scroll to the Har El congregation from the United States. Subsequently, Rabbi Jay Kaufman, vice president of the UAHC, was instrumental in raising funds to purchase the building that houses the congregation to this day. In 2008, the congregation celebrated its fiftieth anniversary.

By 1968, the six congregations that had been established by then formed a national organization known as the Israel Movement for Progressive Judaism (IMPJ). During the summer of 1968 and subsequently during a sabbatical year of 1969–70, I worked with the leadership to formulate a plan for the establishment of new congregations and the expansion of the movement in Israel. Until then WUPJ funds were distributed to each congregation directly from New York. However, in order to encourage independent initiatives and a sense of responsibility, the WUPJ agreed to funnel its funds through a national budget to be administered by the IMPJ itself.

From the beginning we recognized that it was essential for the movement to be led by local Israeli rabbis trained in the country. Just as the Reform movement in America, which was originally served by rabbis ordained in Germany, had to establish the Hebrew Union College in order to train American rabbis for the movement in the United States, so was it understood that the Israeli Progressive movement required the training of local rabbis. It was natural that we should approach our own rabbinical school for help. HUC-JIR, however, was at first reluctant to initiate the program. From where was the funding to come? Where were the students to be trained? Leading members of the College faculty insisted that the students should be trained in Cincinnati, at least for a year or two of their studies. After considerable debate, it was finally agreed that a rabbi could be ordained in Israel without studying in Cincinnati.

The first Israeli student, Rabbi Mordechai Rotem, was ordained by Professor Alfred Gottschalk, the president of HUC-JIR, in 1980. To his credit, Rabbi Rotem insisted that his entire rabbinical training should take place in Israel. The curriculum specified that a student would earn a master's degree at an Israeli university and study concurrently at HUC-JIR. The program has been markedly successful, and as of 2010, over sixty-five Israeli rabbis have been ordained. A growing percentage of our rabbis are female, which, although vehemently opposed by the Orthodox Rabbinate, reflects a primary principle of Progressive Judaism—equal status for women in all aspects of religious observance, rights, and obligations. Accepting our stand on egalitarianism, the Masorti movement has now also followed suit in giving equal status to women.

In moving the WUPJ to Israel, my primary focus was to build an indigenous Israeli movement. In those early days, I recognized that sooner or later Israel would become the demographic center as well as the ideological and spiritual center of world Jewry. Therefore, it was essential for the Reform movement to become established in Israel in as vital and dynamic a way as possible.

I did not see the movement that I aspired to establish purely as a religious movement in the narrow connotation of the term. I foresaw it as a broad spiritual, cultural, and educational movement with religion as a crucial element, but not the sole one. In that sense, I aspired to see the Israeli movement be much broader in scope and perception than its counterpart in America. I was very much influenced by the views of Mordecai M. Kaplan, which became the foundation for the Reconstructionist movement. The Jews are a separate people with a distinct civilization. A major component of

Jewish civilization and Jewish culture is religion, but it is not the only one.

A major area of concern for me was that both the rabbis and lay leaders involved in Israel were limited in their ideological perspective. In defining the nature of the Reform synagogue, they accepted the basic framework of the Orthodox synagogue. They did, however, want to introduce the distinguishing characteristics of Reform, such as that women should be equal participants in worship and should sit together with the men; the liturgy should be relevant and should reflect the theological changes that had been made in Reform Judaism. I visualized a movement that would concern itself not only with the synagogue as a framework for ritual and prayer, but also as an institution encouraging Jewish education, culture, and social action.

In order to develop the IMPJ, it was essential to encourage the leadership to undertake new initiatives. I made sure that everyone knew that I personally was committed to back all innovative endeavors. We needed creative ideas leading to development of new programs and new institutions. I had developed the reputation of being a good fund-raiser, but I rejected the ostensible compliment. Instead, I defined myself as a Jewish educator. In order to raise funds, one has to educate and inspire potential donors.

What new strategies are required in order to achieve our ultimate objectives? What new programs can we initiate that are considered necessary, enlightening, attractive, impactful? How can we make a difference in society and in the lives of individuals? And perhaps the most important question: Is there one qualified person who will commit him- or herself to develop the program and sell it to potential participants and potential donors? I called this a policy of "one-person mission." To illustrate the implementation of my "one-person mission," I present a few examples.

"Heart to Heart" Camps for Arab-Jewish Youth: Bruria Bar-ish, a former chairperson of the IMPJ and a prime figure in the development of Beit Daniel, was an exemplary social activist. In 1980 she conceived a program for sponsoring camps where Jewish and Arab youth of high school age would learn to live, study, and engage together in sports and recreation. I viewed her idea as a splendid example of *tikkun olam*. She single-handedly recruited the participants and the joint Arab-Jewish staff, who in turn planned and implemented the program. Given her total commitment to the project, I became an ardent backer and helped her raise funds, primarily in the United States and Great Britain. During the 1980s the Heart to Heart camps served as a model of Arab-Jewish harmony and received much coverage in the public media. Unfortunately, after the first Intifada, the political tensions between Jews and Arabs forced us to discontinue the program.

The Establishment of Kol HaNeshama: I greatly respected Rabbi Felix Levy when I served as his assistant from 1951 to 1953. Felix Levy's youngest daughter, Jacky, married Rabbi Wolfe Kelman, who served his entire career as the executive vice president of the Rabbinical Assembly of America, the Conservative rabbinical organization. While in Washington at the Religious Action Center, Rabbi Kelman and I shared a close personal and working relationship of mutual esteem.

Levi Kelman, Jacky and Wolfe's son, after being ordained as a Conservative rabbi at the Jewish Theological Seminary, immigrated to Israel to live at Kibbuz Gezer. One day Levi came into my office to inform me that he and his wife Paula had decided to leave the kibbutz. He had thought of starting a congregation in the Baka area of Jerusalem, an area of town that was rapidly being gentrified and had a large percentage of English-speaking immigrants. He had approached the Masorti movement (the Israeli Conservative movement) to solicit their help. He had been questioned about his personal pattern of observance of Jewish tradition (such as if he drove on the Sabbath) and what siddur and liturgy he would use in the congregation. He was told that unless he submitted to the discipline expected of Conservative rabbis, he would not be offered any assistance.

Levi was in a quandary. I said to him, "Levi, I will help you. In my career I have helped start many new congregations. Let us together set out a plan of action and a budget. We'll find a hall, put advertisements in the paper, and hire chairs. You can use our movement's siddur and *machzor*. If you want to add or subtract from the liturgy, feel free to do so. Knowing you as I do, I am sure you will be successful. If you prove yourself, we'll engage you as one of our rabbis."

He began to remonstrate with me. "But I am a Conservative rabbi." I responded, "That is fine. In any case, I don't believe that there is justification for two separate liberal movements in Israel." I called our bookkeeper and asked her to prepare a check, which I gave to him.

Kol HaNeshama with Rabbi Levi Kelman became an overnight sensation. Its notoriety was amplified when on Simchat Torah the rabbi of a neighboring Orthodox synagogue led an incursion into the synagogue. The Orthodox Jews objected to the scene of young women dancing with the Torah scrolls. They tried to rip the scrolls from their hands and a melée ensued. A few days later the Israel Movement for Progressive Judaism convened an emergency demonstration in the center of Jerusalem advocating freedom of religious observance. Three thousand people joined the demonstration, and the media gave it full coverage. I was so fascinated by the potential that I brought Joy Ungerleider to the congregation. She fell in love with the congregation and her Dorot Foundation became the major donor of the building. Today, more than a quarter of a century later, Kol HaNeshama is one of Jerusalem's larger and most dynamic congregations.

Levi Kelman's sister, Naamah, also immigrated to Israel. She expressed an interest in studying for the rabbinate. Since 1972 the HUC-JIR in the United States had been ordaining women, but the College had reservations about introducing ordination for women in Israel. I became Naamah's advocate. Appreciating her talents as I did, I concluded that Naamah would be the forerunner of women rabbis in Israel. Indeed, she became the first of many women ordained in Israel and was instrumental in founding our kindergartens, the TALI school, and many other programs. Today she serves as the dean of HUC-JIR in Jerusalem.

Once Beit Shmuel began to function, the staffs of HUC-JIR, the WUPJ, and the IMPJ took the initiative to start kindergartens. We offered space for the kindergartens in the College and Beit Shmuel, and they developed a distinctive curriculum based on the observance pattern of liberal Judaism. They quickly gained such a splendid reputation that parents throughout the city enrolled their children. In some instances, parents applied for entrance when the child was born to ensure a place. The parents and staff established an independent board and foundation. The first chairman was Rabbi Joel Oseran, a key member of our WUPJ staff who is today the vice president for international development of the WUPJ.

As the children advanced in age, we started an elementary school. For the first few years we carved out space in Beit Shmuel. We began to pressure the Jerusalem municipality's Department of Education for official recognition as a TALI (the Hebrew acronym for "augmented Jewish studies") school. We also began to pressure for a physical facility to house the school.

The IMPJ provides congregations with subsidies for rabbis' salaries and some programming. However, each congregation establishes its own policies and aspires to achieve financial independence. Some of the congregations have managed to construct their own facilities, funds for which were raised through the efforts of both the world movement and congregational leaders. In recent years some congregations have even received buildings through Israel government allocations.

In 1999, a historic event took place. Over fifty thousand people participated in a public demonstration against a perceived ultra-Orthodox assault on the authority of the Supreme Court, a bastion of Israeli democracy. In conjunction with the demonstration, Amos Oz, A. B. Yehoshua, David Grossman, and other leading Israeli writers and public figures signed a manifesto. They declared that in the Reform and Conservative movements they see the potential for "a new dynamic Israeli Judaism which will renew our spiritual and cultural landscape." They called on Israelis to affiliate with the Reform and Conservative movements in the hundreds of thousands. In the words of A. B. Yehoshua, "To stand with the Reform and Conservative movements is to defend ourselves."

When Israelis support rights for liberal Judaism, Israelis are not doing Progressive Judaism any favors. Israel needs liberal Judaism. Just as the struggle on behalf of Soviet Jewry accelerated the attainment of democratic rights for all peoples in the USSR, just as the struggle for racial equality in America advanced the pursuit of democratic rights for all citizens, so support of liberal Judaism is essential for the well-being of Israeli society. To guarantee rights for all streams of Judaism is to guarantee the preservation of Israel democracy for the entire society, just as to deprive liberal Judaism of its fundamental rights will inevitably weaken the democratic institutions of Israeli society. Liberal Judaism in Israel is an idea whose time has come. But not only for liberal Jews—for all society.

A popular Israeli television personality, Yair Lapid, the son of the maverick past minister of justice and editor of the *Maariv* newspaper Yosef Lapid, was the featured speaker at the annual convention of the Israel Movement for Progressive Judaism at Kibbutz Shefayim in 2006. On that occasion, he declared that "all of us secular Jews are really Reform Jews—except that we don't know it."

What should be the vision of the Israel movement, and by extension Reform Zionism, for the future? In my view, there are seven major goals:

1. *To create a Jewish society in Israel reflecting authentic Jewish values.* This requires social action on a much broader scale than hitherto undertaken. It is understandable why we have concentrated on the struggle for rights for our movement. However, as we become stronger, our social agenda needs to be expanded. We need to become more active on the major issues confronting Israeli society, such as minority rights, poverty, education, and absorption of new immigrants. In contrast to our social action agenda in the United States, which is limited to issues we define as being of Jewish concern, here in Israel *every* social issue is of Jewish concern. Every cause is a Jewish cause, and every socioeconomic situation reflects on the Jewish condition.

2. *To broaden the definition of Judaism.* The tragedy of Orthodoxy in Israel is that its brand of Judaism has concentrated on prayer, ritual observance, and Talmudic study. Interpersonal issues have been neglected. The definition of Judaism as practiced by the Orthodox distorts the character of Judaism by diminishing Jewish culture and civilization. The multifaceted cultural and educational programs that we administer need to be expanded. Every congregation should become a center of Jewish culture and education. An increasing number of Israelis are in search of greater Jewish spiritual meaning

in their lives. We have the obligation and the capacity to
offer programs of spiritual inspiration and intellectual
purpose for such people.

3. *To strengthen and expand our institutions of Jewish
   learning on every level.* This includes the training of rabbis and Jewish professionals, teacher training, adult education, study groups, high schools, and early childhood
   programs. In the winter of 1969–70, I was in Israel on a
   sabbatical and spent hours talking with Nelson Glueck
   about, among other topics, the future of the Progressive
   movement in Israel. Among the proposals, I advocated
   that the HUC in Jerusalem should be transformed into
   an academy of Jewish learning, a comprehensive institution for adult Jewish studies for both Israelis and world
   Jewry, based on what had taken place at Bar Ilan University. The Leo Baeck School in Haifa, the TALI schools
   with their curriculum of augmented Jewish studies, and
   our early childhood programs are creating new liberal
   educational opportunities. We should aspire to expand
   all our educational institutions throughout the country.

4. *To serve as the bridge between Israel and the Diaspora.*
   In recent years North American Jewry has undergone
   radical changes. Whereas at the turn of the twentieth
   century Jews were identified as an ethnic group, in the
   twenty-first century Jews are more often identified as
   a religious group. This transformation has resulted in a
   diminution of Jewish ethnicity, dilution of Jewish identity, and a distancing from the Jewish state. At the same
   time, in Israel the nationalistic dimensions of Jewish
   identity have been strengthened, with a consequent distancing from world Jewry.
      On the assumption that Israel will eventually succeed
   in its quest for peace with the Arab world, these trends
   are likely to be reinforced. The lessening of terrorism

and threats of war will be conducive to a condition of greater distancing of Israel and the Diaspora from one another.

The feet of our movement are firmly planted in both worlds. We have the opportunity and the responsibility to serve as a bridge. Identity with Israel can serve as an essential counterbalance to the process of excessive religionization that is characteristic of Diaspora Jewry. A closer affinity between Israel and world Jewry can serve as a vital counterbalance to the radical nationalization process presently at work in Israel.

Why is the People of Israel different from other peoples? Because world Jewry is inevitably linked with the destiny of the Jews of Israel. Why is the State of Israel different from other states? Because we are inevitably linked with the destiny of a worldwide people. The inseparability of a people and land is the distinctive characteristic of both Judaism the faith and Jews the people.

5. *To work toward a closer relationship between Conservative and Progressive Judaism.* Immediately after the Six-Day War, Maurice Eisendrath, president of the UAHC, and I convened a meeting with the leadership of Conservative Judaism in New York and recommended that we merge our efforts in Israel in order to establish one united liberal movement. We did so recognizing that the recommendation would be controversial within our own movement, but in confidence that we could persuade our Reform colleagues to agree. But the proposal was rejected. The Conservative movement contended that their halachically based theology was substantially different from that of Progressive Judaism. They chose not to be identified with us and persisted in the vain hope that they would eventually be recognized as a legitimate movement by the Orthodox.

From time to time, some of us have renewed the proposal—again with no affirmative response from the Conservative movement. However, over the last forty years it should have become obvious to all that the Orthodox will never recognize the Conservative brand of halachah as authentic and that the Israeli public will continue to be unable to distinguish between Reform and Conservative Judaism. In contrast to Orthodox Jewry, Conservative Judaism, like Reform Judaism, continues to respond to the needs of contemporary society on the role of women, homosexuality, and many other issues. Even though some professional Conservative leaders have been turning theologically to the right, almost bordering on Orthodoxy, the vast majority of Conservative Jews are adopting a more liberal approach, even as concurrently Reform Judaism is adopting a more traditional approach. Except for some elements on the fringes of each movement, the majority of the membership of both is moving toward the center. At the same time, the National Religious Party, which previously espoused a modern approach, is becoming indistinguishable from the radical nationalist movement on political issues and almost indistinguishable from the ultra-Orthodox on major religious issues.

The establishment of a strong liberal movement within Israeli society has become ever more urgent and relevant. From both the ideological and pragmatic perspectives, Conservative and Reform are one. The differences within each movement are greater than the differences between them. Our way of life is similar. Our rabbinic-training programs should be similar. In Israeli politics, it is a given that the political parties are in a constant state of flux, realignment, and restructuring in order to respond to current political interests. I predict that the same phenomena will prevail among the various Israeli religious movements. By the middle of the twenty-first century, one strong religious liberal movement will emerge, which will include Progressive (Reform) Judaism, Masorti (Conservative Judaism), and perhaps also components of modern Orthodoxy.

6. *To mobilize the material resources for developing the world movement.* The goals and values of a movement are determined to a large extent by how it raises and expends funds. The major organizations of Jewish life, including the Jewish Federations of North America and the Keren Hayesod countries, the defense organizations, and the American Jewish Joint Distribution Committee all conduct coordinated campaigns seeking funding for both overseas and domestic needs. The successful advance of American Reform Judaism is in great measure due to its percentage plan of funding the national institutions. Despite repeated pleas since the Six-Day War that the obligation to advance the Israeli Progressive movement is no less a vested interest of American Reform Judaism than is the concern for the national movement, the leadership has not responded affirmatively. It is the task of Reform Zionism to continue to exert pressure for the integration of international needs in the national campaigns. When it comes to Jewish needs, no geographical borders should separate Jewish hearts, pockets, and obligations.

7. *From ideology to movement.* The question is, has the ideology of Reform Zionism penetrated the movement as it should have? If a movement is judged by how its ideals are practiced and by its impact on life patterns, goals, motivations, and aspirations of individuals, then we must confess that our impact has been minimal. This is not to deny our achievements, but rather to encourage us to build on the foundations we have laid.

According to studies made in recent years, the American Reform movement is low on the scale of identity with Israel. By all criteria, whether it is tourism to Israel, *aliyah*, identifying with Israel, or sending young people to educational programs in Israel, our movement is low down the list.

In 1995, I made a prediction at the CCAR convention in Jerusalem that has now come true. Today the Reform movement is the largest Jewish religious movement in America. However, I warned against the spirit of triumphalism and urged that if we are serious about our mission, we would ask one fundamental question: "What would American Jewish life be like if we were the only religious movement in America and if the future of American Jewry was exclusively dependent on us?" What institutions would we create? What standards would we advocate? I believe that the question I posed then is all the more relevant today. If Zionism is fundamentally Jewish peoplehood, how do we as a movement relate to our Jewish peoplehood?

I stated that "modernity would no longer be an excuse for minimalism; relevance would no longer be a pretext for irreverence; and autonomy would no longer be a euphemism for license. Reform Jews would be known by what we practice and not by what of Orthodoxy we do not practice; by our Jewish knowledge and not by our Jewish illiteracy; by our commitments and not by our disavowals; by our high standards and not by our low discipline."

What applies to our movement in America applies equally to the movement in Israel. We need to be self-critical. We need to seek to define our ultimate goals in the light of our aspirations. What we do should be judged in the light of what we believe we should be doing.

The nineteenth-century founders of Reform Judaism attempted to transform Jewish identity into a "community of faith." The changes they made in ritual and observance, ostensibly for theological reasons, were in reality an effort to cast off the distinctive signs of Jewish peoplehood. As we have said, abandoning the *kippah*, ignoring the dietary laws, minimizing worship in Hebrew, and many other changes symbolized the attempted transformation.

So why have we in the Israeli version of Progressive Judaism restored the *kippah*, the tallit, kashrut, and a more intensive observance of the Festivals and life-cycle events? Because we are planted solidly in the land where peoplehood has been restored. The challenge of Reform Judaism in America was to "respond to modernity."* The challenge of Reform Zionism is to respond to Jewish peoplehood. This is a twenty-first-century challenge that is no less significant than that initiated by our movement in the nineteenth century.

By the year 2025, the Jews of Israel will constitute the majority of world Jewry. In the final analysis, the destiny of the movement in Israel impacts on the destiny of the Diaspora movement. If we cannot create the message of Progressive Judaism in the Jewish environment of Israel, will world Jewry continue to authenticate our message in the non-Jewish environment of America?

Zion is the expression of hope, our destiny, our eternity. It will be redeemed through the creation of a just, equitable, pluralistic, and peaceful society. This is the Jewish vision. This is the Jewish challenge, and it is to this commitment to which our movement is devoted.

---

*See the definitive book of Michael A. Meyer, *Response to Modernity: A History of the Reform Movement in Judaism* (New York: Oxford University Press, 1988).

PART THREE

Reform Judaism and Jewish Peoplehood: The Marriage

Chapter Thirteen

Tragedy and Triumph:
The Struggle for Soviet Jewry

During the World Zionist Congress of 1997, I was elected co-chairman of the Jewish Agency's Department for the Former Soviet Union (FSU), the Baltic States, and Eastern Europe. I accepted the position knowing that in June 1999, I was due to retire from the leadership of the World Union for Progressive Judaism. I served in that position until the World Zionist Congress of 2006. It was a period of heightened activity in the department. Though the major objective of the Jewish Agency at that time was to encourage as many Jews to immigrate to Israel as possible, it had also become obvious that many thousands would choose to remain in the FSU. The Jewish Agency was determined to help those Jews who would remain to preserve their identity and to deepen their Jewish involvement. These goals were of supreme importance. It was clear that the highest potential of *aliyah* would come from the FSU. It was also a region that was seriously lacking in indigenous leadership and in Jewish educational, religious, and cultural frameworks. The Jews of the FSU needed the stimulus and the support of world Jewry. Since I had been very active in the struggle on behalf of Soviet Jewry and had initiated the development of Progressive Judaism in the FSU, I welcomed the opportunity to continue my efforts.

When I met with the staff of the FSU department for the first time, they asked me when I had first become interested in Soviet Jewry. I responded, "In 1954." Said they, "1954?" Very few people were interested in Soviet Jewry at that time. It was widely assumed that either through anti-Semitic repression or assimilation, there was no future for Soviet Jewry. I answered them that, nevertheless, I had fallen in love with Soviet Jewry in 1954, and I recounted how I had met my wife, Bella, who grew up in a Russian city in the Ural Mountains on the border of Siberia and who to this day is still deeply immersed in Russian language, literature, and culture.

It was in the early 1960s that the American Jewish community first mobilized to demand civil rights for the Jews of the Soviet Union. The National Conference on Soviet Jewry was established, comprising all the major American Jewish organizations. Its leaders asked me to serve as the first professional head of the organization in New York. Even though I refused that position, because I considered the building of the Religious Action Center as my priority, I agreed to represent the organization in Washington and assumed responsibility for organizing lobbying efforts with the American administration and members of Congress.

In 1968, a mass demonstration was held on the Mall in Washington in the same place between the Washington Monument and the Lincoln Memorial where the famous March on Washington on August 28, 1963, led by Martin Luther King, was held. This time, in contrast to the pre–Six-Day War period, we did enlist a broad cross-section of supporters from Christian and interracial groups. I was asked to be a main speaker. Following are some excerpts from my speech:

> Mankind is one. The call for justice rings out in countless
> foreign lands and in countless foreign tongues, but always
> in one voice understood by all. When we muffle our ears to

the call for justice in one part of the world, our consciences are dulled to injustices in every other part of the world. That is the lesson of history for humankind. That is the lesson that this ground on which we stand vividly calls to mind. We see before us the Washington Monument, like the ladder in Jacob's dream from the Book of Genesis, "set firmly on the earth and its top reaches toward heaven" [Genesis 28:12], signifying the ongoing revolution, aspiring toward the fulfillment of America's founding principles. On the other hand, we behold the Lincoln Memorial, its blocks of gleaming stone symbolizing the mission to assure equality and dignity for all citizens. Washington is our symbol of freedom from the tyranny of foreign oppression; Lincoln, our symbol of freedom from the oppression of fellow citizens.

Today we salute yet another symbol. Unlike other religions or nationalities, we Jews have erected no memorials of stone, no cathedrals, no obelisks, no sacraments. What is our symbol? The Jew himself. The Jew is our monument. The Jew is Judaism's living testimonial to God. Who could express it better than the revered Russian author Leo Tolstoy? Writing before the Russian Revolution in the time of pogroms and persecutions against the Jews he declared: "The Jew is the symbol of eternity. He whom neither slaughter nor torture of thousands of years could destroy; he whom neither fire nor sword nor Inquisition was able to wipe off the face of the earth; he who has been for so long the guardian of prophecy and who transmitted it to the rest of the world—such a nation cannot be destroyed. The Jew is everlasting as is eternity itself."

Not only did Tolstoy know that the Jew is "the symbol of eternity." The anti-Semites know it too. Year after year in Germany the Nazis called Jews "Communists." This year in Russia and Poland the Communists call Jews "Nazis." The Russian Revolution advocated a worldwide brotherhood of

the proletariat, under which nationalism would be deemphasized and eventually disappear. Paradoxically, what reason
did Stalin give for his anti-Semitic campaigns? Jews were
"cosmopolitans," literally persons of the world, who could not
be trusted to be loyal to Russia. Today, these same Jews who
yesterday were cosmopolitans have become nationalists.

Jews cannot be trusted to toe the party line. They are too
independent, too individualistic. In the monolithic Soviet
society that is determined to repress every expression of
independence, the Jew is irrepressible. So, say the Soviet
rulers, if we want to eliminate nonconformity, dissent, and
protest, eliminate the Jew together with all expressions of
Jewish identity—the Hebrew and Yiddish languages—Jewish
cultural expression; the observance of the Jewish religion.

We will soon commence the Festival of Passover, commemorating the struggle for freedom. Humanity learned
the lesson of Jewish history as in the Book of Exodus, "The
Egyptians set over them task masters to afflict them . . . but
the more they afflicted them, the more they multiplied and
the more they grew" (Exodus 1:12). So it is with the Soviet
Jews. They take courage and pride in the victory of their
fellow Jews in Israel. During the Six-Day War, they were
strengthened by their fortitude. They are rediscovering their
Jewish identity. Ignorance and indifference are giving way to
curiosity, commitment, and the search for knowledge. Jewish
emotions are being transformed into Jewish acts and creative
Jewish experiences.

God will preserve his monument. The miracle of Passover
is being revivified. God will rescue his people by bringing
them safely through the Red Sea of Communism to the
Promised Land.

During the course of my activities on behalf of Soviet Jewry,
I established a close relationship with Lishkat Hakesher, the

so-called "Liaison Bureau," a special office attached to the office of Israel's prime minister, also known as Nativ ("path"). In effect, Nativ was the center of all efforts to mobilize the worldwide campaign on behalf of Soviet Jewry. I worked closely with it in organizing lobbying efforts with Congress, the administration, the office of the Secretary of State, nongovernment agencies, and the media. Following the Six-Day War, the USSR had severed diplomatic relationships with Israel. Nevertheless, the leaders of Nativ were able to acquire detailed information on the USSR's socioeconomic and political developments and on all activities within the Jewish communities. I became privy to their deliberations and participated in policy discussions. When a few Soviet Jewish dissenters managed to get out of the Soviet Union in the late 1960s and early 1970s, I arranged for them to meet with leading senators and congressmen; I even wrote a talk on Soviet Jewry for Vice President Gerald Ford.

In order to enable me to be more effective in my efforts, the leaders of Nativ deemed it essential for me to have more direct contact with Soviet Jews. Nativ made arrangements for Bella and me to travel to the USSR in the fall of 1969, before the Festival of Sukkot and returning after Simchat Torah. We were an ideal couple. We carried American passports, and Bella was fluent in Russian. We were given extensive briefings in the United States, in Israel (where we were on a sabbatical), and in Vienna. We had to acquire new American passports so that the Russian authorities would not know of our Israeli connections. However, when we asked for information on people we should meet, we were told that Nativ wanted us to make our own contacts. "How are we going to meet the Jews?" we asked. Said they, "Don't worry. With your *Yiddishe punem* [Jewish physiognomy] and your wife's Western clothes and fluency in Russian, the Jews will find you." And find us they did, in dozens and dozens of chance contacts and clandestine meetings. We were inspired to discover that despite decades of anti-Semitic oppression, there were so many people prepared to risk their lives and livelihood to identify as Jews, to study Hebrew in secret locations and in the forests, and to begin to observe the Sabbath and Jewish Festivals.

When we were briefed in advance we were warned not to discuss our experiences in private conversations in taxis, on the metro, or even in hotel rooms. In the hotel we were instructed to write notes to each other and to tear up, burn, and throw the notes down the toilet. Fortunately, I have an excellent memory for names and numbers, and we returned with the details and addresses of the many Jews we came across. One of those we met and whose name we transmitted to Nativ, Eli Valk, was given permission to leave for Israel several years later. He was eventually appointed as Israel's first ambassador to Belarus. At his farewell party I was asked to speak and told the story of how we had met and established the initial contact with him and his family. During the following years, we continued to maintain our contacts with many such individuals in the USSR and with the key leaders of the struggle, both in the USSR itself and in Israel.

On our return to Israel, I was debriefed by the key staff of Nativ and was asked to report on our trip to Prime Minister Golda Meir. I was also debriefed by Shaul Avigur, the legendary founder of Nativ. I was interviewed on television and radio, and a censored version of our experiences was printed in the daily newspaper *Maariv* as well as in the American magazine *Jewish Frontier*.

The following excerpts from these articles will give a graphic idea of the circumstances of the time and the experiences we encountered.

> Tears were streaming down the old man's face. He led me
> by the arm through the mass of worshippers, down the

steps. We stood outside the synagogue in Moscow's Archipov Street. The street was filled with tension in anticipation of the event. It was Sabbath morning. Simchat Torah would not begin until later in the evening. But small knots of people had already gathered outside. The old man whispered, "During the purges in 1937 I stood at this very spot. Then I was sure in view of forced assimilation, imprisonment, exile and the execution of many that in another ten years you would be able to put all the Jews of Moscow inside this one synagogue. But come this evening and you will find this entire street packed with young Jews from one end to the other. It is a *nes min hashomayim*—a miracle from Heaven."

Jewish survival in Russia cannot be explained in terms of logic alone. My wife, who was born in Russia and left when she was 16 years old, had to experience it herself to believe it. Contrary to all expectations, Judaism in Russia is not only surviving; it is reviving. The revival is not a religious one. Young Jews reared in the worship of Communism have not yet discovered the God of Israel. But they have discovered the People of Israel. And, in increasing numbers and with increasing intensity, they want to affirm their Jewishness. After two weeks of touring in Russia and meeting with young Russian Jews in restaurants, elevators, stores, buses, on the street, at the theater, at museums, it is clear that the primary cause of Jewish revival in Russia is the existence of the State of Israel.

The Jews of Russia live in a society whose government is hostile and whose controlled public media incessantly denounce Israeli "aggressors and extremists." Paradoxically this closed society intensifies concern for Israel. Despite or perhaps because of, the oppressive atmosphere, anti-Semitism, and the constant barrage of anti-Israel propaganda, Israel has become a source of sustenance for the Jews of Russia.

In all of Russia there is not one Jewish school for the study of the Hebrew language or of the Jewish heritage. Yet we

conversed in Hebrew with young Jews who gather once a
week, ostensibly to go on a social outing, and who when they
arrive at their destination, in the woods or a private home,
pull out Hebrew readers and teach each other the language.
Leon Uris's book *Exodus*, which is banned in Russia, has
been translated into Russian by hand, photocopied and
widely circulated—one of the many *samizhdat* or clandestine
publications which circulated widely amongst Soviet Jews.

We met young Jews who wear a Star of David on their
lapels and proudly call themselves Zionists, a term which is
anathema in Soviet society. One teenager took out his wal-
let and carefully unfolded what he called his most precious
possession—a tattered Israeli travel brochure.

The Six-Day War was a traumatic experience for the Jews
of Russia, as it was for Jews all over the world. But the plight
of the Russian Jews was especially poignant. For they knew
that their government was in great measure responsible for
the war and had supplied the arms which were being used
against Israel. A number of young people told us that the
Israeli victory marked a historic turning-point for Russian
Jewry, because the Russian people, who still remembered
Jews as weaklings led to mass slaughter by the Nazis, could
now see that Jews could fight courageously and win against
overwhelming odds.

Many Jews we met had one persistent hope—that somehow or other they would be permitted to leave Russia to
immigrate to Israel. We sought to find an answer to the
question so often asked by Jews outside Russia—if the gates
were open, how many Jews would leave? I believe that a
large number of Jews would want to leave, but it is impossible now to estimate the exact number who would actually
file applications. The filing of the application is a step that
marks a person for life. He immediately becomes suspect
as disloyal to his country and is subject to police or secret

service surveillance. Since the management of his place of work is involved in the application process, the employee automatically loses any chance of promotion and risks the possibility of being demoted or fired. If he has children who are of an age where they are ready to apply to an institution of higher learning, the children are automatically barred. The competition for positions in professional schools is stiff, and no institution will give a place to a student whose parents have declared their intention of leaving Russia.

We were privileged to meet some desperate and courageous people. According to regulations, application may be made once a year, in some places twice a year. If it is rejected a new application cannot be filed until the full term has expired. One young man, still in his twenties, had applied five times and was going to file his sixth application shortly. He told us that the last time, the official who had refused his application told him, "Why don't you realize that you have no chance? Do you think we are going to let you go to Israel and give another soldier to Dayan?"

Another young man who had graduated from university five years before told us that he has not taken out his diploma and is employed beneath his professional capacity, because he is fearful that if he is engaged as a professional in his field, his application for exit will be refused on the pretext that he is doing essential work. So he is supporting his wife and child on a much smaller income than he is capable of earning in the hope that their immigration to Israel will eventually be approved.

The refusal of previous applications and the sense of futility in proceeding through normal channels has generated in some of Russia's Jews all kinds of daring measures to draw the attention of the outside world to their plight and to pressure or embarrass the government into acceding to their request for exit permits. We were asked for advice. Should an open letter be written to Prime Minister Kosygin and smuggled to the *New York Times*? Should a plea be made through the UN? An open or a secret letter to U Thant? Should a letter be sent to the president of the United States? To the American ambassador in Moscow? Would it do any good to seek asylum in a foreign embassy?

Second only to developments in Israel, Jews in Russia were eager to hear about Jewish life in America. They judged America by the way Jews were treated, and because they had all heard so many accounts of the flourishing religious and cultural life of Jews in the United States, they appeared to have been unaffected by anti-American propaganda and many were avid listeners to Voice of America broadcasts.

The same questions about American Jewish life were repeated again and again. What is the status of the Jews in America? How many Jews are there? How many live in New York? In Washington? How many synagogues are there? Are there Jewish schools? How many seminaries for rabbinical studies are there? Do Jews hold important positions in the government and in the political parties? What is the average monthly salary in America? Are there Jewish newspapers? Is there a Jewish theater? Are there Jewish libraries? Most of these questions manifested the sense of cultural deprivation experienced by Jews in Russia. For in the Soviet Union there are no Jewish schools, no rabbinical seminaries, few synagogues, no libraries, no Jewish publications (except for one government-controlled magazine in Yiddish) and few Jews in prominent public positions.

The magnetic power of American Jews was brought home in an incident which occurred to us in the synagogue in Leningrad. When we attended the Sabbath evening service, I met a man who made me promise several times that I would come to services the following morning. Next morning, I discovered the reason for his concern. He had brought his 21-year-old son with him to the service. He had evidently tried to persuade the son to come to services many times before, but this was the first time the young man had ever been in a synagogue. He had come because his father had promised him he would be able to meet a Jew from America and, as an added inducement, he could practice speaking English. As I talked with him in English, the father kept whispering instructions in Yiddish in my ear. "Tell him he should marry a Jewish girl." "Tell him to come to the synagogue once in a while. It won't hurt him." "Tell him your children in America know how to read and speak Hebrew."

Simchat Torah, one of the happiest of Jewish festivals, has been transformed by the young Jews of Russia into a symbol of their yearning for freedom of Jewish expression: thousands of them gather around the synagogue in the major cities to sing and dance in the streets. We had planned to be present in Moscow for the occasion.

It had rained intermittently during the day. As we left our hotel we were pelted by hail. We were fearful that the cold drizzle would diminish the number and the enthusiasm of the youth. We were wrong. By the time we arrived, Archipov Street was so packed that we had to force our way through the crowds, thickest around the synagogue. It was impossible to get near the steps, let alone enter the synagogue. We were told that if we had wanted a seat inside, we should have come at 4:00 p.m. (the services were scheduled for around 6:00 p.m.). The street, approximately 500 meters in length, was blocked off at each end by signs prohibiting traffic. As darkness descended, the crowd became still denser. The foreign press corps later estimated that 10,000 people were in attendance, but other estimates reached as high as 20,000. The bulk of the crowd was young—most of them in their teens, twenties or early thirties. But many older people were also present, milling around, waiting for the services to end.

It took us almost an hour to make our way through the crowd to the end of the street. We stopped and talked with dozens of persons along the way. To our question, "Why have you come here?" we received one overwhelming response: "To show the Jewish people still lives." Some told us that they had come to meet other young Jews. One person, in his late twenties, told us that he was anxious to marry a Jewish girl and hoped that he might be able to find someone during the course of the evening. Another said that Simchat Torah was a time for Jews to be happy, and he wanted everyone to know that Jews still knew how to rejoice.

About 7:30, even before the services were over, the crowd could no longer be restrained. Guitars were strummed, dance circles formed, and simultaneously, in about 15 to 20 places along the street, dancing and singing began. The dances were frequently interrupted when the moving circles bumped into a wall of bystanders. Most of the dancers knew only one dance, the *Hora*, and only two Hebrew songs. We wondered how long they could continue singing and dancing the same limited repertoire over and over again.

On the periphery of the crowd we saw four youngsters who had learned the songs of the Six-Day War, evidently from a record. They were teaching the songs to a group of young people who were eagerly and excitedly repeating the words. At another place, someone had set up a tape recorder with Hebrew and Yiddish songs, but so many people had gathered around that we were unable to distinguish which songs were being played.

We heard from several persons that the street was filled with official observers, stooges and other assorted "spies." From time to time we noticed men who were standing alone with no obvious relation to other persons in the crowd, and we assumed that some of them must have been government-appointed agents. But their presence did not appear to daunt the singers.

At about 11:00 p.m. the crowd began to thin out. Almost everyone had come by public transportation. One person apologized as he took leave that he did not want to be stranded there for the entire night. But a surprising number remained. The dampness and cold had begun to penetrate our shoes and we felt chilled through and through. We began to wish that our young fellow Jews would call it a night.

About midnight, police cars arrived and drove through the crowd, the loudspeakers calling on everyone to disband and go home. At first the crowd, reluctant to end the festivities, formed again immediately behind the cars as they drove by, but after a while the street began to empty. By 12:30 a.m. all was back to normal on Archipov Street—whatever normalcy may mean for the street in front of the synagogue in the capital of a country where Judaism as a religion is condemned and where the Jews as a nationality are being forcibly pressured to assimilate.

It would be inaccurate to explain the phenomenon of Simchat Torah in narrow religious terms. The young people did not come to pray. Only a very few even entered the synagogue. For the time being, it is unlikely that the synagogue as an institution of worship will become a moving force of Jewish identification for those who are spoon-fed from birth on an anti-religious diet. But a Jewish ethnic revival is occurring and, paradoxically, the revival is using the forms of the Jewish faith. Perhaps the phenomenon is best described in the words of a participant in the Simchat Torah "happening"—a young man wearing a skull cap and sporting a beard. When I first caught sight of him in the crowd, I thought that I had discovered my first young Orthodox Jew. Are you religious? "No, I don't go to synagogue." Then why the beard and the skull cap? "These are the symbols of a Jew to the outside

world, and I want the world to know that I am a Jew and that
am Yisrael chai—the Jewish people lives."

"The Jewish people lives." We could not help but repeat
that constant refrain while traveling in Russia. Evidence
of that fact is present even in mass-burial grounds. On
the outskirts of Riga, the capital of Latvia, there is a section called Rumbuli. There, at a barren spot in the woods,
17 kilometers from town, the German troops lined up the
Jews of Riga and in two days of operations, on November
30 and December 8, 1941, killed 36,000 men, women and
children. Several kilometers away is a former concentration
camp called Salaspils which the government has established
as a national shrine. Thousands of visitors flock daily to the
imposing memorial to pay their respects to the victims of
persecution.

At Salaspils there is no mention of Jewish victims, and
until 1963 there was nothing at Rumbuli even to mark the
spot, let alone to memorialize the deceased. At the annual
meeting of Jews of Riga commemorating the Warsaw Ghetto
uprising, a woman arose to tell the story of Rumbuli. She had
been shot, wounded and left for dead by the Nazi soldiers.
Moved by the account, the Jews in the community decided
to establish a memorial at Rumbuli. When they approached
the government it refused to co-operate. The Jews decided
to go ahead on their own and with their own hands and at
their own expense began clearing away the brush from the
mass-grave pits. As they dug they uncovered the bones of
bodies and reburied them. The project became the passionate concern of the Jewish community, particularly the young.

After repeated requests, a truck was finally secured.
A road was built from the main highway and paths were
laid. As the memorial neared completion, the community
requested permission to erect a stone monument. The

government permitted only the erection of a simple stone marker engraved with the words "Victims of Fascism" in Russian and Latvian, but prohibited specific reference to Jews. The Jewish community persisted and after many petitions and pressure, the government finally compromised and consented to have the words "Victims of Fascism" engraved in Yiddish. But to this day the word "Jew" does not appear in Rumbuli. Without receiving permission in advance, a wooden relief portraying a Jew breaking his chains was erected, but the government ordered it removed.

Though Rumbuli bears no written reference to the Jews, the burial ground has become a symbol of Jewish determination to live. We visited it on a Tuesday morning. Freshly-cut flowers had been placed on the mass graves, the paths were clean of debris, and the grass was neatly trimmed. Later in the afternoon we met some Jewish teenagers and were told that the local Jewish youth gather every Sunday morning to travel together to Rumbuli and spend three or four hours in upkeep of the grounds.

As a result of their common effort at Rumbuli the youth have been welded into a closely-knit community. They study Hebrew and Jewish history together and teach each other Hebrew songs and dances. Thus, the mass grave of Jews has become the meeting-ground for a new generation committed to the perpetuation of the Jewish heritage.

As we conversed with the young Jews of Riga who had made Rumbuli into a living memorial and as we exalted in the revival of the spirit of Soviet Jewry, the words of the prophet Ezekiel kept coming to mind:

> And He said to me, "O mortal, these bones are the whole House of Israel. They say, 'Our bones are dried up, our hope is gone; we are doomed.' Prophesy, therefore, and say to them: Thus said the Lord God: I am going to open

you graves and lift you out of the graves, O My people,
and bring you to the land of Israel. I will put My breath
into you and you shall live again, and I will set you upon
your own soil. Then you shall know that I the Lord have
spoken and have acted"—declares the Lord.

(Ezekiel 37:11–12, 37:14)

In 1987, one of our closest personal friends, David Bartov, who
had become the head of Nativ, informed us that in Nativ's judgment, under Mikhail Gorbachev, the Jews would eventually be
permitted to emigrate and perhaps also to practice Judaism
openly. The experts conjectured that most of the Jews would
want to leave, but that many would remain. Bartov told us that
even though he and his colleagues were for the most part secular, they recognized that Judaism was a vital factor in preserving Jewish identity. At that time, the major religious movement
committed to working with Soviet Jews was the Chabad movement. It was clear to Nativ that the Orthodox pattern of life,
while acceptable to a small minority, would not appeal to the
vast majority of Soviet Jews, conditioned as they were to the antireligious, secular indoctrination of Communism. Therefore,
he said, "We want to send you and Bella to the USSR again to
explore the possibilities of establishing a liberal Jewish religious
movement that can appeal to the Jews who will remain."

That year Bella and I spent several weeks traveling throughout Russia. Unlike our first visit, this time we were given
names, phone numbers, and addresses of key workers in the
struggle and of leading intellectuals. It was still considered
dangerous for Jews to congregate, so we organized meetings
in homes and led discussions on Israel, on Progressive Judaism, and on how creative Jewish living could enrich people's
lives. At the beginning, I would lecture and Bella would trans-
late after every few sentences. But after a while it became
tedious, so we decided that I would give some introductory

remarks and Bella would make a presentation and lead a discussion in Russian. That method led to much more effective sessions. We found a profound thirst for knowledge and a search for new ways to observe Judaism.

It is of historic significance that the idea of establishing Progressive Judaism in the FSU was first proposed by David Bartov, a senior official in the prime minister's office. It also represented a major shift in policy, for until then the ostensible policy of the Israeli government was to convince all the Jews to immigrate, on the grounds that there was no future for Jews in the USSR. For our part, we in our movement have always contended that the task of the WUPJ is to preserve the Jewish heritage for all Jews wherever they choose to live.

We recognized that in order to develop a Progressive Jewish movement, it was essential to establish a movement-wide support system, to mobilize funds, and to create a staff of Russian-speaking rabbis and leaders. We organized WUPJ missions to Russia in 1988 and 1990 and held a conference in London to establish an international commission on Soviet Jewry. During the 1988 mission we initiated pioneering changes in the rules of the Intourist Travel Agency, the official USSR tourist office. Until that time no Russian citizen could enter a hotel where foreigners were staying. In both Moscow and Leningrad we invited the leaders of the local Jewish community to share a Friday evening Shabbat meal with us, and I managed to persuade the officials of Intourist to permit local Jews to enter our hotel, on the grounds that American Jews were avid tourists and that meeting with Soviet Jews would attract more tourism. At these dinners, we asked each person to stand up and introduce themselves. One young man stood up and started to cry. He stood trembling for a few minutes without uttering a word. Finally, he blurted out, "This is the first time in my life I have ever experienced a Shabbat." And then he sat down. There was not a dry eye in our group.

Until our trip, Intourist tour buses were not allowed to go to synagogues and Jewish cemeteries. Again, after an extended discussion, I persuaded Intourist that to put places of historic Jewish interest on official tours would attract Jewish tourism. When we took another mission to the USSR in 1990, a leading Intourist official thanked us for encouraging them to change the rules.

By the time of the 1990 mission the WUPJ had established its first congregation in Moscow. Our mission participated in the Friday evening Shabbat worship, and we conducted a formal ceremony establishing a Russian region of the WUPJ. Anyone who attended the WUPJ International Convention in London in May 1990 will never forget the inspirational impact of the reading of the Ten Commandments in Russian at the Shabbat morning service by Zinovy Kogan, the president of Hineini, the first Russian congregation to be welcomed into the WUPJ family.

During the following years we expended great efforts in establishing a dynamic movement for Progressive Judaism in the FSU. We encouraged our leading staff and lay leaders from Israel, North America, and Europe to make ongoing visits so as to establish outposts in the major metropolitan areas of Russia, Ukraine, and Belarus. We engaged Russian-speaking staff and began the process of attracting young, dedicated Russian Jews to consider a professional career as rabbis, educators, or communal workers. In order to tool up quickly, we established a leadership training institute in Moscow and developed a two-year work-study program. We produced a Russian newspaper and a prayer book and later a High Holy Day *machzor*. We established camping programs and a youth movement. Our youth program under the auspices of Netzer Olami has become the largest Jewish youth movement in the FSU. Today we are training Russian-speaking rabbis at the Hebrew Union College–Jewish Institute of Religion, Jerusalem, the Leo Baeck

College in London, and the Abraham Geiger College in Berlin. We have acquired buildings for synagogues in Moscow, Minsk, and St. Petersburg and are actively searching for suitable facilities elsewhere. Many people, too numerous to mention here, contributed to the development of the movement including lay leaders, rabbis, and professional staff. Among the prime movers in the development process, the following staff members nevertheless deserve special mention: Rabbi Joel Oseran, Menahem Leibovic, Rabbi Maya Leibovic, and Alex Kagan.

In 2005, the WUPJ convened its first international convention in Moscow to commemorate our achievements and to assess our future in the FSU. At the convention I enumerated several factors of concern:

1. *Socioeconomic-political conditions in the FSU.* The USSR is no more. The FSU describes a geographical territory, but not a political entity. In reality, there are fifteen separate and independent nations, each with its own character and governmental system. Because the conditions of each nation vary, the character of the Jewish community, its status and problems vary. Most of the countries suffer from socioeconomic and political instability. From our historical experience, we know that instability breeds anti-Semitism, which in any case is endemic in most of these countries. The situation in the Russian Federation is of particular concern. Sixty percent of FSU Jewry lives in Russia and the majority of them live in two cities—Moscow and St. Petersburg. We are wary of recent trends toward authoritarian governmental policies and curtailment of many civil liberties so essential to a democratic society. The relationship between government and some leaders of the Jewish community is not the religion-state relationship with which we are familiar in the United States. The Jewish community is much more dependent

on government sanction for its activities. Because the conditions are so tenuous and because of the rising extremism of nationalist groups, we need to be alert to potential radical changes that can impact deleteriously on the status and well-being of Jewish communities.

2. *Demographics of the Jewish community.* As of 2005, we estimated that there were approximately 750,000 Jews (defined as those living in a household where at least one person is halachically Jewish) in the former Soviet Union. The population is aging rapidly. The birthrate is extremely low, and intermarriage is well over 80 percent. Although FSU Jewry must still rely on outside Jewish organizations, they aspire to develop their own independent institutions and are beginning to garner local support for their programs and activities. They are also beginning to develop effective indigenous leadership. FSU Jewry is the second largest community after the United States in the Diaspora and still offers the largest realistic pool of potential new immigrants to Israel, although the rate of immigration has been declining.

3. *The struggle for Jewish rights is a struggle for human rights.* Jewish destiny is inseparable from the human condition. Our Rabbinic Sages taught us, "As the myrtle is sweet to him who smells it, but bitter to him who bites into it, so Israel brings prosperity to the nation that grants them kindness, and depression to the nation that afflicts them with evil" (Esther Rabbah 6:5). The struggle waged on behalf of Soviet Jews became the harbinger of the freedom struggle for all peoples of the USSR. Perhaps the monolithic Soviet regime would have self-destructed eventually, but the fight for Jewish rights precipitated the breakup of the USSR. It highlighted the inequities in Soviet society and demonstrated the injustices of antiquated political structures.

It encouraged other nationalities in the Soviet empire to organize in pursuit of their own national rights. Conversely, when oppressed peoples are released from the shackles of oppression, the Jews benefit. The breakup of the USSR in turn gave legitimacy to the Jewish people's struggle all over the world. Moreover, it is a vital factor in the foreign policy of Russia. The domestic policies of every nation impact on its international policies. The fate of Russian Jews as individuals is interdependent with the fate of the entire Jewish people, and the fate of the Jewish people is interdependent with the fate of the Jewish state. The status of the Jews in Russia affects the relations of Russia with the outside world. The pursuit of justice on the domestic front inevitably leads to the pursuit of peace on the international front. Russia's policies toward its Jewish citizens affects its policies toward the Jewish state, even as Israel's diplomatic ties to Russia are inextricably related to what transpires to the Jewish community in Russia.

4. *Preservation of Jewish identity.* The revival of Jewish identity in the USSR was inspired by events in the Middle East—the Israeli War of Independence in 1948, the arrival of Golda Meir as the first ambassador in 1948, and the Six-Day War in 1967. However, even though affinity for Israel was motivated by a renewed sense of Jewish national consciousness, in order to sustain and enhance Jewish identity, it is essential to observe Judaism as a faith. One of the most exhilarating experiences of our 1969 trip was to experience Simchat Torah on Archipova Street outside the Great Synagogue in Moscow, as related earlier. In Israel, nationalism alone may provide a satisfactory framework to sustain Jewish identity, but not in the Diaspora, and eventually not even in Israel. Ethnicity without faith diminishes Jewish identity

and will eventually lead to assimilation. It is the observance of the Sabbath, the holidays, and the Passover seder and study of Hebrew and traditional sources that provide the framework for perpetuation of the Jewish people.

It has been estimated that in the early 1970s there were approximately three million Soviet Jews. Eli Wiesel characterized them as the "Jews of Silence." Those Jews are silent no more. Today, approximately one million have emigrated to Diaspora lands of freedom. Between 750,000 and 1,000,000 remain in the FSU and are able to practice their Judaism openly and with pride if they so choose. Approximately one million have immigrated to Israel and today comprise 20 percent of Israel's Jewish population and a quarter of its standing army. Despite complex social problems, the beneficial impact of FSU Jews on Israel's economy, politics, culture, and education is immeasurable.

5. *The FSU provides a fertile soil for the fruitful growth of Progressive Judaism.* The Jewish communities of the FSU are still in the early stages of development. Despite the efforts of a multiplicity of Jewish organizations, the majority of these Jews participate only marginally, if at all, in any Jewish organization. Under the Communist regime the attitude toward religion was usually summarized in Karl Marx's famous phrase, "Religion is the opiate of the masses." And in many areas of life in the FSU, vestiges of antireligious and anti-clerical sentiments still persist. Progressive Judaism appeals to those in search of Jewish identity in a modern environment. No other Jewish framework offers a more dynamic potential. The progress made in only a few years should energize us to mobilize the material and human resources that are essential for effective and rapid development of our

movement. This is the new frontier for creative contribution to the perpetuation of Jewish life.

I have referred to our participation in the Simchat Torah celebrations in Moscow in 1969. In the crowd, we met an old man who told us that every night he listened to the Voice of Israel radio broadcasts. "I lie in bed and hear the 11:00 P.M. news from Israel. At the close of the program, they play 'Ha-Tikvah' [The Hope]. When I hear the words and the music of 'HaTikvah,' I have faith that no matter how bad is the plight of Soviet Jewry, no matter how grievous the oppression and discrimination, there is, nevertheless, *hatikvah*—hope. The Voice of Israel broadcasts seven times during the course of twenty-four hours. For some reason, they have stopped playing 'HaTikvah' at the end of every broadcast and now play it only at the end of the 2:00 A.M. broadcast. As you see, I am old and sick and cannot wait up that late. When you get back to Israel, please contact the Israel Broadcasting Authority and ask them to do a favor for one old Jew in Moscow. Play 'Ha-Tikvah' again."

We in the WUPJ are privileged to lead and serve the Jewish people. Our task is to play "HaTikvah." Where the Jews are, there is history. Where there is history, there is a future. And where there is a future, there is hope.

Chapter Fourteen

Joining the World Zionist Organization and the Jewish Agency for Israel: Establishing ARZA and Arzenu

My personal involvement with the Jewish Agency for Israel–World Zionist Organization (JAFI-WZO) began during a sabbatical year in 1969–70. I had become friendly with Ted Lurie, the legendary longtime editor of the *Jerusalem Post*. He had asked me to write a number of articles and I had participated in several panel discussions subsequently published in the paper. One article of mine occupied the entire back page of the paper on December 31, 1969, projecting what I thought would be the character of the Israel-Diaspora relationship in the 1970s. In the article and in lectures delivered at the time, I rejected what was the predominant theme of American Jewish and even American Zionist leadership, which was referred to as the "Babylon-Jerusalem syndrome." Their contention was that American Jewry was analogous to the ancient Babylonian Jewish community at the time of the exile following the fall of the First Temple. American Jewry constituted a great independent center whose wealth, status, influence, and creativity would sustain, with financial and political support,

the smaller and weaker community of Israel. I rejected the
Babylon-Jerusalem concept and contended that a more ac-
curate metaphor would be "Israel is Broadway; America is
Off Broadway."

The article was reprinted widely in the United States. Many
of my Reform colleagues were incensed, and I received many
critical letters. In March 1970, we held a seminar with the
leaders of the movement who were in Jerusalem attending a
conference of the Central Conference of American Rabbis,
and my position was resoundingly attacked. The majority of
the American Jewish leadership contended that there were
two foci of equal weight—America and Israel. My formulation was considered a diminution of the status and importance of American Jewry.

However, the article that was so criticized by my Ameri-
can colleagues was read enthusiastically by Louis Pincus and
Leon Dulzin, respectively the chairman and treasurer of the
JAFI-WZO. At their invitation I met with them a number
of times. They solicited my views on the American Zionist
movement and on other issues relating to the character of the
American Jewish community. Toward the end of my sabbatical year, they invited me to become a member of the World
Zionist Executive and the Board of Governors of the Jewish
Agency. They stressed that the appointment was *ad hominem,*
that is on a personal basis. I accepted eagerly, and so in the
fall of 1970 I became a member of the American Section of
the Zionist Executive and the Board of Governors of the Jewish Agency. I was officially elected at the World Zionist Congress in 1972.

I considered the election to the Zionist Executive to be a
major personal and institutional achievement. As a youngster
in Cleveland, I had been active in the Young Judea youth
movement. Later on in Cincinnati, I served as director of Ha-
bonim, the Labor Zionist youth movement. I had studied the

history of the Zionist movement and was aware that prior to the establishment of the state, the Zionist Executive, which at that time was synonymous with the Jewish Agency Executive, served as the cabinet of the state-in-the-making. David Ben-Gurion, its chairman, automatically became prime minister of Israel; Moshe Shertok (Sharett), the chairman of the Department of Foreign Affairs of the Jewish Agency, became foreign minister; Eliezer Kaplan, the treasurer of the Jewish Agency, became finance minister. When I attended the first meeting of the Zionist Executive, I somehow felt myself to be in the presence of the great historic leaders of the Zionist movement. The small hall where the Zionist Executive met was called the Ben-Gurion Hall, and the larger hall, subsequently called the Weizmann Hall, was where Chaim Weizmann had been sworn in as first president of the Jewish state.

I considered it a rare privilege to be sitting at the same table where the founding fathers had made the fateful decisions regarding the establishment of the state and its future course.

In the course of my participation, I began to comprehend that it was not appropriate for me to be participating only as an individual. Why should not the entire Reform movement affiliate with the World Zionist Organization? I recognized that there would be much opposition, because even in those days the WZO had developed the unenviable reputation of being highly politicized and under the control of the Israeli political parties. Furthermore, I knew that many in the WUPJ leadership would not favor such a close identification with the WZO and its ideology. Some asked, Why do we have to join the WZO? Let us just join the Jewish Agency, which projected a more positive image. We explained that the only way for our movement to affiliate with the Jewish Agency was through the framework of the WZO, which comprised half of the Jewish Agency representation. In America, the United Israel Appeal was the conduit of the United Jewish Appeal and the Council of Jewish Federations. The rest of the world was represented through Keren Hayesod. These two entities, which together comprised 50 percent of the Jewish Agency representation (UIA, 30 percent; KH, 20 percent) were the primary funding organs for both the Jewish Agency and the WZO. After I made an initial investigation, it was clear that neither the United Israel Appeal nor the Keren Hayesod had an interest in incorporating a religious movement within their ranks. But by affiliating with the WZO we would not only identify with the Zionist movement but would also receive representation in the Jewish Agency.

The WZO constitution stipulated that there were two kinds of organizational affiliation:

1. *An international Zionist political movement*. Most of the Diaspora movements were identified with an Israeli political party. All its members were required to endorse the Jerusalem Program—an ideological statement defining the meaning of Zionism. This entitled members to participate in the elections to the World Zionist Congress. The elections determined the number of delegates each Zionist movement would send to the World Zionist Congress, which, in turn, would determine the positions of responsibility for which each party would be eligible. The Israelis comprised 38 percent of the delegates to the Zionist Congress. They were selected according to the votes received by the Israeli political parties in the general Knesset election prior to the convening of the Zionist Congress.

2. *An international organization*. Such organizations did not participate in the election process and its members were not required to endorse the Jerusalem Program. Because of the limited nature of its affiliation, members

of an international organization were not eligible to serve in elected positions in the WZO and Jewish Agency structures.

The WUPJ leadership determined that the only alternative open to it was the second type of affiliation—as an international organization. In that way we would not have to persuade all members of our worldwide movement to affirm the Zionist ideology by endorsing the Jerusalem Program. We would receive fifteen delegates to the World Zionist Congress, five to the Zionist General Council, and two members of the Zionist Executive, one in Jerusalem and one in New York. We would also be eligible to receive funding from the WZO budget for all our Zionist-oriented educational and youth programs.

The affiliation of the WUPJ to the WZO involved extensive negotiations, both because of internal questions within the WUPJ and also because the WZO recognized that affiliation of the Reform Movement would serve as a precedent for other religious streams.

We began the process on October 24, 1972, by inviting Louis Pincus to attend a meeting of the top leadership of the Reform movement in New York. In 1974 we invited Leon Dulzin, who after the death of Louis Pincus succeeded him as Chairman of the JAFI-WZO, to address the WUPJ Biennial in London. At the WUPJ governing body meetings I contended that the WZO was the most comprehensive, representative, democratic body within all of world Jewry. If we were critical, then we should express ourselves by joining the table and criticize it from within. I said, "To move the World Union to Israel and not to join the World Zionist Organization is like bringing the bride to the chuppah and not putting the ring on her finger." As I saw it, we had to take the step of officially getting married to the Jewish people.

In January 1976, at a meeting of the Zionist General Council under the chairmanship of Yitzchak Navon (subsequently elected president of Israel), the affiliation of the WUPJ to the WZO became official.

Once the WUPJ affiliated, the Conservative and Orthodox movements began the process of affiliation for their world bodies. The WZO leadership applauded the Reform Movement for precipitating a significant expansion of Zionism throughout the world. Had the WUPJ not established the precedent, there is little doubt that the other two world religious movements would not have affiliated.

After affiliation we did receive minimal budgetary assistance from the WZO for our emissaries to Australia, Great Britain, and the United States, as well as modest support for Diaspora youth movement study programs in Israel. However, because the chairmen and director generals of the WZO departments considered their primary loyalties to be to their own party movements and because in almost every case there were always budget deficits, we soon discovered that our requests for funding were never accorded equitable treatment.

The more we became involved with the actual day-to-day functioning of the WZO, the more we recognized that by limiting our status to an international organization we were limiting our influence and not expressing our legitimate weight in the Jewish world. Furthermore, we were not fulfilling as we should the obligation we had undertaken of inculcating Zionist ideology and commitment in our own membership.

Therefore, we began to think in terms of organizing a politically oriented Zionist movement within the Reform Movement. The Orthodox Zionist movement Mizrachi was our paradigm. Even though many Orthodox Jews were ideologically opposed to Zionism, Mizrachi, to its credit, had become a powerful and effective force for Zionism within the Orthodox world. The idea to establish a Reform political Zionist movement quickly gained momentum. By the fall of 1977, we had organized the Association of Reform Zionists of America (ARZA) and began to organize the international Reform Zionist organization.

According to the WZO constitution, recognition as an international Zionist movement requires membership in at least five countries. In 1980, Arzenu (International Federation of Reform and Progressive Religious Zionists) was established. It comprises Reform Zionist movements in Canada, the United States, Great Britain, Netherlands, South Africa, Australia, Switzerland, Argentina, Spain, Hungary, Germany, Russia, and Ukraine. Within the WZO, Reform Zionism functions as a *B'rit Olamit* (a World Zionist Union) called Arzenu and together with the WUPJ representatives is a faction in the WZO. In order to maintain its international character, the chairperson is a representative of a country outside the United States.

ARZA was launched at the UAHC Biennial in November 1977. We decided that we should immediately begin to plan for the elections in the World Zionist Congress to be held in February 1978. Within just two months, 9,000 members were recruited. When the elections were held, 11,900 people voted for ARZA, a firm indication that the movement had drawing power outside its own membership. This election result enabled ARZA to receive nine mandates for the Zionist Congress.

Our leadership decided that ARZA should offer resolutions on two major issues: equitable funding for our Zionist programs and equal status for the non-Orthodox movements in Israel. Four separate resolutions to four separate committees were presented. The World Zionist Congress rules provided that if a resolution was defeated within a committee, the sponsors had the right to present a *votum separatum* on all our resolutions to the plenary session. When our resolutions failed to pass in the committees, we announced that we intended to present a *votum separatum* in the plenary session. The Herut and Mizrachi delegates tried to prevent a vote from being held, on the grounds that the WZO constitution did not permit votes on religious issues. Nevertheless, a vote was called and the first resolution was adopted.

The Mizrachi and Herut delegates left the hall in anger and returned shortly thereafter, forming a snake dance and singing, *"Utzo eitzah v'tufar"* ("Your counsel shall be voided"). The delegates who supported the resolution in turn formed their own snake dance, singing. *"Hinei mah tov umah na-im"* ("How good and how pleasant it is for brothers to dwell together in unity"). When the two groups met head-on, fighting erupted. Planted pots on the stage were thrown and a general melee ensued. After intensive efforts, order was restored, and the second resolution went to the floor and was adopted. The texts of the two resolutions follow:

> *Resolution 61:* Congress confirms that all departments, authorities and programs of the WZO in Israel will be managed in accordance with the principle of equal status and identical treatment for every religious movement affiliated with the WZO, and for every Jew, regardless of origin or religious or ideological identification. Programs of a religious and educational character shall represent the pluralism which characterizes Jewish life throughout the world. Congress calls upon the State of Israel, as the homeland of the Jewish people, to put into practice the principle of assuring full rights, including equal recognition, for all rabbis and equal assistance to all trends in Judaism.

> *Resolution 63:* The WZO shall aid and assist the religious and ideological currents in their educational activities, so that the pluralism existing in Jewish life in Israel and the Diaspora is reflected. Jewish education shall emphasize the humanistic and moral values contained in Jewish culture and heritage.

After the two resolutions were adopted, the Mizrachi delegates walked out of the plenary session in protest, declaring
their intention to appeal to the Zionist court and threatening to leave the Zionist movement unless the two resolutions
were withdrawn.

We convened a meeting of our caucus together with some
of our allies from other parties. Leaders of the parties that
supported us urged us to withdraw the two resolutions that
had not yet come to the floor, on the grounds that a historic
victory had already been achieved. For the first time, resolutions advocating religious pluralism in Israel and equal rights
for rabbis of all streams had been adopted. To continue to pass
the additional resolutions would be overkill; consequently,
our caucus voted to withdraw the remaining resolutions. We
so informed the chairman, who reconvened the plenary session, and I was called upon to address the session. My brief
extemporaneous speech follows:

> I address my remarks to the members of Mizrachi who are
> here, and ask you to convey them to all members of Mizrachi
> who are not present. "Who is honored? He who honors his
> fellow man (*Pirkei Avot* 4:1)." We respect and honor our col-
> leagues in Mizrachi; we want them to honor and respect us.
>
> Some people have congratulated us for a "tremendous
> victory." We do not characterize what happened in terms of
> partisan victory and defeat. The resolution that was adopted
> was not a defeat for Orthodoxy. It was a victory for full par-
> ticipation in the Zionist cause by all movements in Judaism.
>
> Orthodox Judaism in general and Mizrachi in particular
> have made invaluable contributions to the preservation of
> Jewish life and the upbuilding of Zion. We applaud Mizrachi
> for its accomplishments. We appreciate you showing the way
> to Conservative and Reform Judaism. Had we been active in
> the Zionist movement, as you were fifty or seventy years ago,

the State of Israel and the condition of the Jewish people,
and the positions of our respective movements would have
been enhanced and the Jewish people thereby enriched.

Our insistence on equal status in the World Zionist Organization strengthens the sense of participation and commitment of significant segments of world Jewry in the majestic
drama of national rebirth. There cannot be full participation
in a democratic process if some elements believe they are
second-class citizens. So our joining the Zionist movement
and demanding equal status is good for Zionism. It will
encourage a vast increase in the ranks of Zionist membership
and supporters. It will inject a more intensive Zionist dimension in Jewish life throughout the world. And ultimately, even
if you members of Mizrachi do not accept it now, in time we
hope you will realize that it is equally good for Mizrachi.

We have much in common with Mizrachi, in one sense
more in common with you than with any other movement in
the Zionist family. We have a common enemy: our enemy is
Jewish ignorance and assimilation. We have a common objective: our objective is to inculcate in all Jews a perception of
being rooted in our religious sources. We share a common
conviction: for Zionism to endure and the Jewish people to
exist. Our Jewish religious heritage must be perpetuated.

You can help us. You can guide us. "Provide for yourself
a teacher and acquire a friend" [*Pirkei Avot* 1:6]. You have
been our teachers. We ask you to remain our friends, united
by the common bond of Zion. "God, Israel, and Torah are
one" [*Sefer Hazohar, Parashat Acharei Mot,* 73a]. Through
our combined efforts, God, Torah, and the people of Israel,
and the Land of Israel shall remain one.°

The media declared the passage of the resolutions and the
ensuing debate to be the highlight of the Zionist Congress. I

°Proceedings of the 29th World Zionist Congress (1978), 284–285.

have included the above remarks in full because they reflect the position that we in the Reform movement have adopted. Even as we demand our full rights, we extend our hands in respect and friendship to Orthodoxy.

In September 1978, ARZA held its First National Assembly. I was asked to deliver the keynote address. I decided that it was essential to define the meaning of Reform Zionism for individuals. Should we Reform Zionists distinguish between Zionism and being pro-Israel? What are the ideological and practical commitments a person must make that entitle him or her to be considered an American Zionist? Excerpts from my address follow:

> Over the years, the entrance of Reform Jews into the Zionist movement has represented a rejection of classical Reform's denial of Jewish peoplehood. As in the case of the First Zionist Congress, so this First National Assembly of ARZA symbolizes the acceptance of Zionism as a return to the Jewish people, even before it symbolizes a return of the people to its land. For Zionism is founded on the premise that the Jews are a people that can survive and thrive best in a framework conducive to collective life and action. *Shiva l'Tzion* (return to Zion) is essential because it provides the framework for the rejuvenation of the Jewish culture and the Hebrew language, as well as the means for the pursuit of Jewish destiny as a people acting in and through history. Zionism is thus both the stimulus and the means toward the collective redemption of the Jewish people.
>
> American Zionism holds a unique position within the World Zionist Movement. The confluence of the largest, most influential, and richest of world Jewish communities working as an organized force in the most powerful of nations, has accorded a special status to American Zionism. However, this very status has created a situation wherein

the stress has been placed on the pragmatic needs of fund-raising and political action, to the neglect of Zionist ideology, education, and programming. In the aftermath of the Yom Kippur War, the editor of *Commentary* characterized the spontaneous response of American Jewry as "instant Zionism," and the president of the American Zionist Federation proclaimed, "American Jewry has been Zionized." I question the accuracy of these generalizations. For if American Jews are all Zionists, then what distinguishes the Zionist organizations from the non-Zionist organizations?

I have simple criteria for determining whether or not a person is a Zionist. They are my own personal supplementary amendments to the Jerusalem Program to which every member of ARZA subscribes when joining. An American Zionist has to be able to say:

1. The existence and well-being of the State of Israel are indispensable to my existence as a Jew.
2. I am obligated to give my children an intensive Jewish education, which includes knowledge of spoken Hebrew.
3. I will seek extended educational and work experiences in Israel for myself and my family.
4. I would be pleased if one of my children or grandchildren decided to live in Israel.

I have purposely stated these criteria in a simplistic, personalized manner, because it is essential that Zionists stress the obligations of the individual. And I have purposely highlighted the family, because a person's highest values are manifest in what he seeks of and for his children. It is my hope that the members of ARZA will be distinguished by the Zionist mitzvot that they voluntarily assume as individuals. The other affiliates within the Union of American Hebrew Congregations are oriented toward special professional, age, or sex groupings. Only ARZA is established for the primary purpose of fostering a specific ideology and encouraging a specific pattern of personal commitment. ARZA aspires to the Zionist deed, on grounds that a person preaches what he practices.

I stress the primacy of the Zionist deed, even over and above ideology. Take the issue of *aliyah*. After the Six-Day War we drafted a resolution on Israel for the 1967 Biennial which, among other recommendations, advocated an *aliyah* program for the UAHC. This plank was immediately rejected by the resolutions committee on the grounds that it was so far-fetched that it was not even controversial. Five years ago a few committed persons took the initiative of organizing our Israeli youth into a settlement group that eventually led to the establishment of Kibbutz Yahel, the first Reform kibbutz. Our UAHC youth division immediately began the process of organizing an American *garin* (settlement group) , employing an emissary from Israel and fostering the kibbutz as a way of life for those of our young people who would be willing to accept the challenge. If instead of actually beginning the work, we would have debated the generality of *aliyah*, we would still be trying to pass a resolution. Today we have *aliyah* to Kibbutz Yahel and additional young people organized in *garinim* in America, South Africa, and Europe, who will soon join their fellows in the Arava Valley. Kibbutz Yahel has captured the imagination of our movement, funds are being raised from all over the world, and we are now planning a second kibbutz. Not only do we believe in *aliyah*, but we even have a resolution on *aliyah* adopted by the UAHC Board in 1976.

The Zionist believes in the mystique of *Eretz Yisrael*— the Land of Israel: Israel is not just another place of Jewish settlement. It is the unique setting where our people in Israel encountered God and where we encounter destiny. What happens in and to Israel is of significance far beyond

the number of persons involved. And what is true for the
Jewish people as a whole is especially true for Reform Judaism. What our movement does in relationship to Israel, what
happens in our movement and to our movement in Israel,
will shape the character of Reform Judaism in America
and throughout the world. It is in this perspective that the
organization of ARZA as a spearhead within Reform Judaism
assumes potentially historic proportions.

Because of time limitations, I will outline briefly what
I consider to be the major objectives of ARZA in the twin
spheres of Reform Judaism and Zionism. We should envisage
two primary functions for ARZA within Reform Judaism:

A. *To Zionize American Reform Judaism.* The term
   "Zionize" connotes the activation of Zionist ideology
   through education, political action and life experience.
   ARZA, through the support and expansion of existing
   programs and the creation of new ones in the congregation, community, and nation, should inform and
   sensitize our movement to the Zionist dimensions of
   Judaism. For us Zionism is not a separate or separable
   element, but an integral aspect of our faith and world
   outlook.

B. *To sustain the building of Progressive Judaism in Israel.*
   Reform Judaism has a message and a special approach
   to Jewish life. Our way of life is characterized by a
   spirit of religious liberalism, pluralism, and concern
   for social justice. We believe that our fellow Jews in
   Israel have demonstrated a need for our message and
   ways, adapted by Israelis to serve their own indigenous
   needs. A Jewish religious movement that does not play
   an active role in the central stage of the contemporary Jewish drama can not be considered authentic.
   We are one interdependent world movement. Israeli

> Progressive Judaism offers American Reform Judaism
> authenticity, credibility, inspiration and a cause.

ARZA's relationship to Progressive Judaism in Israel distinguishes it from other major Zionist groups in America. The
ZOA, the Labor Zionists, the Revisionists, all identify with
political parties in Israel, an anachronistic identification that
has little meaning for contemporary Diaspora Jews. On the
other hand, Hadasssah (and the World Confederation to
which it belongs) rejects identification with any Israeli political or ideological grouping and concentrates its energies on
providing health care and services. Only Mizrachi is predicated on an integrated approach, fostering a certain way of
life in Israel, establishing institutions and programs in which
their own members are recipients as well as contributors.
Discounting their politicization and their ideological stance,
they have much to teach us, and we would do well to learn.

The Zionist Congress resolutions on religious pluralism,
the direct result of Reform-Conservative cooperation, has
ramifications far beyond the vested interests of non-Orthodox religious movements. It augurs well for the potential
reinvigoration of the American and world Zionist bodies.
We inject new people, new ideas, new opportunities into
an organization that desperately requires re-energizing and
restructuring. We represent a dynamic synthesis in three dimensions requiring synthesis: a) Israel-Diaspora; b) religion-
peoplehood; c) universalism-particularism.

a) To a world Zionist movement some of whose members
still adhere to the classical Zionist theory of *sh'lilat hagalut*
(negation of the Diaspora), we offer the experience of an
affirmative Diaspora experience so essential to a creative
Israel-Diaspora cross-fertilization.

b) To a Zionist movement that attempted to preserve
Jewish distinctiveness without Jewish faith, we bring the

experience of a movement that has learned that the major components of God, Torah and Israel are inseparable. Just as Reform Judaism now understands that the dilution of peoplehood deprives Judaism of a *religious* factor, so must Zionism learn that the diminution of Judaism deprives Zionism of a vital *national* motivation.

c) To a Zionist movement that, under the pressures of ongoing crisis, has tilted in the direction of a right-wing coalition of militant politics and retrogressive religion, we inject a major element committed to the active integration of liberal politics and progressive religion.

We Jews are a people who specialize in the search for definitions. This Assembly is meeting at the time when historic decisions are being made concerning the definition of peace in the Middle East. From the perspective of Jewish eternity, just as historic are the definitions forged through deeds affecting the ideals, aspirations, and character of the Jewish people both in and outside the state. In the *Zohar* it is written, "When the people of Israel is worthy, the land is called after them—*Eretz Yisrael*. When the people is not worthy, the land is called by another name—*Eretz Canaan* (the Land of Canaan)."

ARZA in Hebrew means "toward the Land [of Israel]." May ARZA fulfill its name: may it become a force moving our people in the direction of being worthy of the land called *Eretz Yisrael*.

Chapter Fifteen

Controversies within the Movement

It is the duty of leaders of organizations to assume responsibility for advancing goals and objectives of the institutions they lead. Frequently these responsibilities lead to conflict or differences of opinion with other organizations within the same movement. The attempt to resolve such turf problems is an essential prerequisite to shaping the character of a movement. Conflicts reflect a complex blend of divergent ideological emphases, vested interests, and personality differences among individuals.

In general, within organizations, there is a tendency to mute the differences or to obfuscate them. My position has always been that it is important to confront the differences head-on, rather than to permit them to fester or generate ill will. It is essential to deal with the issues as they occur. Failing to come to terms both with the issues and with colleagues who espouse different positions can lead to indifference and lack of progress. While persons in positions of responsibility have every right to advance the objectives and interests of their institutions, they also have an obligation to consider the well-being and advancement of the movement. Therefore, the fundamental premise should be to assume that there is goodwill on the part of all participants and to hope that the process of attempting to resolve conflict will not only clarify issues, but also advance each institution and the movement as a whole.

One potentially explosive issue was the establishment of the Israel Religious Action Center. As we began to develop ARZA's program, we recognized that it was essential for it to identify with specific programs in Israel. Just to advocate support of Israel in general or even specifically the Israel Movement for Progressive Judaism was not enough. Just as the Hadassah women created their own medical institution in Israel, a cause with which they could identify and for which they could mobilize funds and generate interest, so we considered it essential for ARZA to sponsor a specific program within the IMPJ.

The area that we considered the most appropriate for Israel was that of social action. Our Religious Action Center in Washington had already demonstrated its capacity to take strong positions on key issues confronting American society. Its political and educational activities reflected the thrust of Reform Jewish ideology in America. Many of the leaders of ARZA were not only ardent Zionists, but also activists on American social issues. The issue that had given our movement the most visibility was that of pluralism—obtaining equal rights for non-Orthodox Judaism in Israel. The leadership of ARZA, together with representatives of the IMPJ and the WUPJ, therefore discussed conducting a feasibility study to determine how best to establish an effective social action program in Israel using the paradigm of the Religious Action Center in Washington.

In the fall of 1986, UAHC and ARZA jointly announced that they were establishing an ARZA Religious Action Center in Jerusalem. A fund-raising campaign was to be initiated to raise the $400,000 needed to establish the center. Despite the preliminary discussions, this announcement was made with no prior consultation, without the promised feasibility study, and not even with prior notification to the WUPJ or the IMPJ. The leadership of the IMPJ and the WUPJ reacted with astonishment. Although we were wholeheartedly in favor of an intensification of our struggles for rights in Israel, we adamantly rejected the idea that the social action program in Israel would be conducted under the aegis of the American movement.

It was inconceivable to us that Jews living outside Israel could determine the agenda on social issues for Jews living in Israel. Would the American movement permit Reform Jews in Jerusalem, Melbourne, or London to decide the stance on social issues in America? Conversely, should Jews in New York, Chicago, or Cincinnati determine the mandate for social action in Israel? For American Jews to assume responsibility for the decision-making process on Israeli social issues would be to deprive Israelis of the obligation and the right to take a stand on fundamental issues in their own society.

Having been involved in the controversy in the United States during the period when the Religious Action Center in Washington was being established, I stressed that it was essential for it to function within the policy positions of the Union of American Hebrew Congregations. We never conceived of the Religious Action Center as an independent institution, and as such, it would have quickly lost the support of the American movement. It would not have reflected the views of the movement, and in the final analysis, it would have become irrelevant. The essence of the Religious Action Center in Washington was that it spoke for the majority of Reform Jews on issues on which the movement had developed clear-cut policies.

Similarly, we believed that the Religious Action Center to be established in Israel had to function within the framework of policies adopted by the Israel Movement for Progressive

Judaism. While at times the dependence upon the IMPJ might affect and limit the positions to be taken, we considered that dependence essential in order that the movement speak with one voice on social issues. Interdependence with the IMPJ would impose structure, discipline, and obligations. However, that is a strength, not a weakness. I believed that in formulating positions the Religious Action Center spoke not only to Israeli society as a whole, but perhaps most important of all, to the movement it represented. It not only spoke *for* the movement, but it spoke *to* the movement. It thus became an educational force for inculcating social values.

The conflicting views led to heated discussions. On the one hand, it was essential to provide ARZA with an opportunity to support a specific project, but on the other it was essential that the project function within the framework of the IMPJ.

Given the goodwill of all parties involved, the differences were eventually reconciled. It was determined that the name would be the *Israel* Religious Action Center (IRAC). The policy board of the IRAC comprises representatives of all the Reform institutions—ARZA, the WUPJ, the IMPJ, and its respective constituent groups. It was agreed that ARZA would be listed as the sponsor, and ARZA determined that a percentage of its annual dues would go for support of the IRAC. The program today has been expanded and continues to demonstrate its effectiveness. It has become clear, just as it did in the case of the Religious Action Center in Washington, that the mandate in Israel is to create an exemplary democratic society. Whereas espousing rights for non-Orthodox movements remains a primary function, other social issues, such as concern for minority groups, rights of new immigrants, education, poverty, and the socioeconomic well-being of Israeli society, are also within its purview. IRAC's legal staff serves the needs of thousands of Israelis every year, and it has become a vital factor on the Israeli political scene.

Another major controversy between the WUPJ and the UAHC related to the establishment of the World Education Center in Jerusalem. The controversy revolved around an ongoing debate between Rabbi Alexander Schindler and myself, he in his capacity as president of the UAHC and I in my capacity as professional head of the WUPJ. I was committed to build institutions and programs in Israel. I was convinced that the best way to advance our cause was to construct buildings of meaning, with utilitarian purpose as settings wherein we could conduct a range of educational and cultural programs. It was clear to me from my experience that we would not be able to attract average Israelis to our congregations, because they were basically not interested in worship. In the Diaspora, when a Jew wanted to identify with his Jewishness, the probability is that he or she would join a synagogue, as the obvious symbol of Jewish identity. Even if a person did not actually attend services, at least an affiliation with a synagogue would be a way of manifesting one's Jewishness.

However, the average Israeli is by definition already identified as a Jew. He or she studies in Jewish schools, serves in the army, speaks the Hebrew language, and observes the national holidays, which are Jewish. These are all-embracing frameworks within which to identify as a Jew, and it is unnecessary to be affiliated with a synagogue. The average Israeli has rejected the religious factor as a key means of Jewish identity. If we, as a progressive movement, wanted to attract Israelis, the probability is that we would be able to attract them not to our religious services or to ritual observance, but to educational and cultural experiences that would enrich their life experience. That was the message I delivered to our colleagues when I proposed to build Beit Shmuel in Jerusalem as a cultural and educational center. I believed that if we provided Israelis with satisfying intellectual and educational experiences, perhaps they would also be attracted to other religious aspects of Jewish life.

In retrospect, perhaps the controversy between Schindler and myself was related to the roles we occupied. He, as president of the Union of American Hebrew Congregations, did not have to build buildings or institutions in order to perform his task effectively. Through the Maintenance of Union Membership campaign (MUM), the UAHC was assured of a steady annual income as a percentage of the dues paid by each member of a congregation. Schindler always maintained that he was not interested in buildings and that his task was to involve people and develop programs. In the course of our many conversations, I said that the Reform movement needed to prove that Israel is important to us, and therefore we should build institutions of aesthetic value and purpose that would provide the framework for creative educational and cultural programs. He maintained that the existing HUC-JIR building in Jerusalem was a sufficient statement and we were not in need of another. I countered that the building in Jerusalem, which had been erected by Professor Nelson Glueck, was basically just a center for archeological research, and it was not a structure that would advance the movement and inculcate educational and cultural content in the lives of Israelis who were not religious. (These conversations took place before HUC-JIR embarked on its system of requiring first-year students to spend the year in Jerusalem and before initiating the Israel rabbinic training program.)

I took, as an example, the Western Wall of the Temple Mount (the *Kotel* in Hebrew), which is today the most sacred site of the Jewish people. The *Kotel* is actually one of the outer walls of the Second Temple built by King Herod. What was the *Kotel*, if not a building? I contended that we needed a building both for the sake of the movement and to demonstrate that Israel is important enough for us to invest significant sums in order to establish our international headquarters there. We needed to prove to the Israeli public that the country is important to us, and one way to do that would be to erect buildings of beauty and purpose.

In my work as a regional director and as founder of the Religious Action Center, I had learned that it was easier to raise large sums for physical facilities than for programs and salaries. Major donors were prepared to give much larger sums for buildings that could be dedicated to their families than to fund programs within them.

The controversy between Alex Schindler and myself was never fully resolved. There were countless incidents that injected divisiveness and ill will between Fred Gottschalk (the president of HUC-JIR) and myself on the one hand and Schindler on the other, which eventually led to similar discord between the leadership of the WUPJ and the UAHC and between HUC-JIR and UAHC.

When a delegation of the UAHC board traveled to Israel and toured the site after we had begun construction and I had shown them the plans, I thought I had persuaded them of the justification for erecting our own education center. But I was mistaken. On reporting on their visit, they declared that "Hirsch is building a Taj Mahal. Even if he is able to raise the capital necessary to complete the building, he will never be able to raise the funds to maintain the facilities." The leadership of the WUPJ, many of whom were also leaders of the UAHC, accepted the view that the building was too ambitious and that the WUPJ would not be able to maintain it. They indicated that if that should prove to be the case, the UAHC would not take responsibility. It therefore urged that we hand over the building to the Israel Youth Hostel Association and let them manage it.

There were some leaders of the WUPJ who doubted that I could raise the necessary funds for construction and subsequently for maintenance. There were times when even I was concerned. Because of the rampant inflation at the time, the construction costs of Beit Shmuel, originally projected at $4.7 million, rose to $8 million.

In order to reassure our lay leaders, I informed them of my conversations with the Israel Youth Hostel Association, which had expressed an interest in managing the hostel and giving us 20 percent of their profit. I explained to them that our reason for not agreeing to their proposal was that we could not achieve our objective of being an educational-cultural center as well as a youth hostel without assuming responsibility for management of the entire institution. I assured our leadership that if after one year of operation our confidence in our ability proved to be unwarranted, I as a responsible leader would take the initiative to accept the offer of the Israel Youth Hostel Association.

Within the first year, Beit Shmuel quickly became the cultural center of Jerusalem. Thousands of people of all ages flocked to our premises every week for the cultural and educational programs. The WUPJ leadership took pride in having participated in the construction of the vibrant, dynamic center.

The controversies regarding the establishment of the Israel Religious Action Center and the construction of the additional campus in Jerusalem reflect issues that still pertain today. What are the obligations of the American movement, by far the largest, most influential, best-financed component, to its world movement? How should the interrelationships and mutual responsibilities be defined? The following are excerpts from letters I wrote, which I believe to be equally relevant to the situation today.

The first letter related primarily to the Israel Religious Action Center issue and was addressed to Charles Rothschild, the chairman of the board, and Rabbi Alexander Schindler, the president of the UAHC, signed by me as executive director of the WUPJ and by the WUPJ president Gerard Daniel:

> At the meeting of the North American Board on September 7, 1986, Rabbi Richard Hirsch stated that he was in favor of expanding and intensifying the existing programs of social concerns in Israel. As the founding director of the Religious Action Center in Washington, he welcomed the idea of increased initiative, counsel, and support from the American movement. However, one fundamental premise must be adhered to: effective social action in Israel must ultimately be formulated, conducted, directed, and implemented by people living in Israel. Otherwise we shall never build a strong, democratic, and indigenous movement in Israel and we shall never have the impact we want to have on Israeli society. The full message of Progressive Judaism cannot be delivered parcel post by resolutions adopted in New York or Washington, but only through the lives, deeds, and actions of Jews who are full participants in Israeli society.
>
> To what purpose is our worldwide united movement if each country can establish its own duplicate competitive program in Israel? Shall the European Board of the World Union or the Australian–New Zealand Union or Kadima of Canada, each of them now establish its own independent center in Israel? Is there not a significant difference between the American movement exercising leadership, partnership, and financial responsibility as an integral part of a worldwide movement and using its power and funds unilaterally? And should not the State of Israel serve as a central unifying factor for our movement rather than as a battleground for organizational turf fighting?

After the letter was received, it was agreed to hold discussions in New York. The following letter (excerpts) was sent October 9, 1986, by me to Rabbi Alexander Schindler and

the leadership of the UAHC, with copies to the WUPJ
leadership:

As background for our discussion, I have been remembering
the discussions we held in 1971. We were confronted then by
two basic questions: (1) what to do with the World Union for
Progressive Judaism, which was a rather ineffective organization (the total annual budget was less than $75,000); and
(2) how should we, as a movement, make an impact on and
contribute to the State of Israel.

In regard to the World Union, there were two fundamental alternatives—either to fold it up, and somehow or
other incorporate it into the UAHC, or else to try to make
a meaningful instrumentality of the World Union. It soon
became clear that the first alternative was impossible. There
was already considerable resentment by non-Americans of
the American domination of WUPJ affairs. Therefore, the
only realistic alternative was for the American constituents,
primarily the UAHC, to infuse personnel and funds.

We, simultaneously, determined to make a historic statement by moving the international headquarters of the World
Union to Jerusalem. In the meantime, our movement,
through the College, had acquired the rights to the land
adjacent to the College, and we, in the UAHC and World
Union, began to plan together with the College, our World
Education Center for Progressive Judaism. The two objectives meshed beautifully: to make a meaningful organization
out of the World Union, and to make an impact on Israel by
building a movement there, joining the World Zionist Organization, and establishing our World Center.

We recognized that if anything was to be achieved, the
UAHC would have to take the lead. We began to talk about
getting new professional and lay leadership for the World
Union. When it was suggested that I become the executive

head, my initial reaction was negative. I was pleased with my work as director of the Religious Action Center in Washington, and though I was fluent in Hebrew and was an ardent Zionist, I did not feel that I had the rich Jewish background required. In fact, I approached three other colleagues whom I considered to be more qualified than I to assume responsibility and to move to Israel, and only after each in turn refused, did I indicate that I would be willing to consider undertaking the assignment. I did so because I recognized that unless I practiced personally what I preached, my plans for the movement and my vision for Reform Zionism would not be implemented. In order to elevate the importance of the World Union, Rabbi Maurice Eisendrath would be elected as president of the World Union, even while he was still president of the UAHC.

I am very much in favor of significant expansion and intensification of our struggle for rights in Israel, but there are three fundamental questions that require much deliberation: (1) the auspices; (2) the program; and (3) the priorities. The program should not be undertaken by the American movement alone; the program should be tailored to the Israeli context; and the program should be implemented in relationship to the formulation of a set of priorities.

It has been difficult all these years to try to build a world movement and institutions in Israel in the face of the fundamental indifference of our major constituents. However, in the light of recent developments, the indifference has turned to competitiveness. What is the World Union without the American movement? If the American movement now wants to return to the first alternative we discussed in 1971 and, by ignoring the World Movement and the Israel Movement, take over the full responsibility and call all the shots for world Progressive Jewry, and for the Israel Movement, theoretically it has the power and the funds to do so, but I believe that the Progressive Jewish world would suffer. Within the Jewish Agency and the World Zionist Organization, and the World Jewish Congress, similar situations exist, and in each of those bodies, the American constituency, by far the strongest component, has exercised leadership, but if anything, has bent over backwards to include the rest of world Jewry and to give them a voice, a role and support. . . .

For me, the issue is clear-cut. To summarize: either we have a World Union, with its international headquarters in Israel, in which the American movement, including all its components, will take a leading role and primary financial responsibility, or let us close down the world movement. Either we have an Israel movement that is an integral part of a world movement, which serves as a major focus and cause for the world movement, or let us stop the pretense that we care deeply about what happens to and in Israel. . . .

Undoubtedly, we have all made mistakes, but now is not the time for personal or institutional recriminations. Now is the time for vision and cooperation. Let us create a situation where together with our colleagues in Israel and in the Diaspora, we reevaluate our goals and objectives, our successes and failures, and embark on new initiatives with a new sense of purpose.

Chapter Sixteen

Running for Office:
The Election Campaign of 1992

With each passing year, it became more obvious that the significance of Zionist political parties in the Diaspora was dissipating. The intricacies of Israeli politics were beyond the ken of most Diaspora Jews, and therefore they felt no kinship to them. Those who identified with Israel did so with the country in general and not always with any political party. Even those who held strong views on specific foreign policy issues or on domestic issues such as religion and state had no interest in affiliating with any particular Israeli political movement.

On the other hand, the religious movements that had joined the World Zionist Organization continued to grow in power. In America, the institutions that symbolized Jewish identity were the synagogue and the local Federation and its affiliates. The socialist and ethnic cultural identity that had served as the backbone of the Labor Zionist movement had all but disappeared. The religious movements were able to mobilize their forces to participate in the Zionist elections. They had at their disposal the pulpit and the synagogue bulletins. They could galvanize Diaspora Jewry around the ever-present, ever-controversial issues of religion and state in Israel. Many Diaspora Jews questioned their own right to participate in debates concerning foreign policy and domestic issues within Israel; however, with regard to the religion-state issue there was no debate. The status of the liberal movements in Israel was a legitimate concern for non-Orthodox Jews in the Diaspora. They had a vested interest in fighting for equal rights for non-Orthodoxy. Indeed, each new crisis brought greater and greater support for the liberal movements. The Federations recognized the inextricable relationship between their support of pluralism for religious movements in Israel and the annual Federation campaigns. During the elections to the World Zionist Congress of 1987, Arzenu mobilized thirty-three votes in America and twelve votes elsewhere in the world for a total of forty-five votes. The Conservative movement (Merkaz) in the United States received twenty-two votes.

The increasing strength of the synagogue-based Zionist movements and the decreasing strength of the Diaspora political parties were sufficient to discourage the two major political parties in Israel—Labor and Likud—from advocating elections in the Diaspora. It was universally agreed that the most distinctive characteristic of the World Zionist Organization, in contrast to most other organizations in Jewish life, was the holding of democratic elections. However, the theory of democratic elections was not as potent as the reality of the waning significance of the two major political groups. In addition, the political election campaigns cost significant sums of money. Each party was allocated funds by the WZO treasury for a membership recruitment campaign. The elections themselves called for huge sums for the polling process and the tabulation of the votes. There was concern that the convening of the election did not warrant the vast costs involved. Furthermore, the election campaign was conducive to a controversial advertising campaign that exaggerated the differences and injected divisiveness within Diaspora Jewish life. An additional factor was the charge that electoral lists compiled by the respective movements were often inaccurate, padded, and therefore invalid. There were also charges and countercharges of corruption in the voting process itself.

One result of all this was that the waning strength of the political parties and the ineffectiveness of the World Zionist Organization supported the Conservative and Reform movements' advocacy of democratic elections. The Reform and Conservative movements lobbied for the convening of elections against the wishes of all the political groupings in North America. Hadassah, the largest Zionist organization, claimed that its primary concern was the cost of the elections, but it was also afraid that it would lose votes. Consequently, Hadassah, and the Confederation of General Zionists to which it belonged, opposed elections, together with the Labor Zionist movement. The opponents of elections prevailed within the American Zionist Federation. Instead, they proposed an electoral college system that would in effect maintain the status quo from the previous elections of 1987. ARZA led the call demanding the retention of a fully democratic one-person one-vote electoral system. When it became clear that neither the American Zionist Federation nor its leading constituent parties would convene an election, the leaders of ARZA found themselves in a dilemma. Without an election, how could the Reform movement exert its growing strength within the Zionist movement, and how could the WZO constitution that mandated elections before each Congress be honored?

An idea began to germinate that the only way to keep alive the principle of democratic change was to run a candidate against the incumbent chairman, Simcha Dinitz of the Labor Party. Even though it was considered impossible for such a candidate to win, nevertheless the proposal evolved and began to attract support from within the ranks of the Reform movement. The leadership of the Shinui (Change) Party headed by MK Amnon Rubinstein and the Ratz Party headed by MK Shulamit Aloni supported the idea. (Subsequently, Shinui and Ratz merged and together with Mapam formed the left-wing Meretz Party.) But where were we going to find a candidate who could appeal to a broader audience?

It was Rabbi Eric Yoffie, now the president of the Union for Reform Judaism and at that time the executive director of ARZA, who after discussing the matter with his colleagues, met with me to propose that I accept the nomination to run against Simcha Dinitz. My initial reaction was to laugh. It would be preposterous for me to run. I immediately thought of dozens of reasons, among them, the prospect of certain defeat; my wife, Bella, would never agree that I do it; the Israeli political system would never tolerate a non-party person being elected chairman of the WZO and chairman of the Executive of the JAFI, let alone a Reform rabbi; the two political parties would immediately drop all differences and merge to prevent the loss of their monopoly over the political structure of the JAFI-WZO. Therefore, my initial response was firmly negative.

However, I said that I would go home to discuss it with my wife. When I suggested the idea to Bella, as I had foreseen, she immediately rejected it. Life as chairman would disrupt our home life. As it was, I spent long hours at the office and traveled abroad a great deal. The chairman's position was one that was beset with all kinds of political pressures, and the process itself tended to be both corrupt and corrupting. I would endanger my reputation. It was better to serve as chairman of the Zionist General Council (having been elected to that honorary position in 1987), playing an active role but standing above the fray rather than taking on the position of chairman of JAFI-WZO.

I assured Bella that I had no chance of winning. The only reason for becoming a candidate was to preserve the principle of democratic elections and to provide me with a platform from which I could advocate the radical reorganization of the WZO. Once I convinced her that there was no chance whatsoever and that the main reason to run was to fight for the principle of democratic elections, Bella consented.

The more I thought about it, the more I liked the idea. I had always advocated that it was important to do the right thing, even if one was not always clear what the right thing was. My career in social action had taught me that the only way to achieve rights is to fight for them. I was wont to quote a dictum from Ethics of the Fathers, "The reward of a good deed is the deed itself" (*Pirkei Avot* 4:2). I had always interpreted this to mean that when one performs a mitzvah, there is an inner reward. The dictum from Ethics of the Fathers continues, "One good deed fosters another." In other words, to do right nurtures that right.

So, after considerable deliberation, Bella and I agreed that I would become a candidate. However, I promised her that under no circumstances would I ever actually serve. We joked about how this was like *The Mouse that Roared* (a famous story that became a movie by Leonard Wibberley about a small nation that declares war on the United States) or the old joke about how Israel could solve its economic problems by declaring (but losing) war on the United States.

A few weeks before the World Zionist Congress convened, Bella met a distinguished activist in the Likud Party who told her that he intended to vote for me and that he knew that many other delegates to the Congress would break party discipline to vote for me if there was a secret ballot. Under certain circumstances, he told her, it would be possible for your husband to win. Bella could not wait until she got home. She called me at the office and told me to come home immediately. In great anger she said, "I thought you promised me that you wouldn't win." I said, "I did—I have no chance." Bella's final words were, "If you're in, I'm out!" Fortunately for our relationship, we were never confronted with the moral dilemma of what to do had I won. In a public statement issued in June 1992, prior to the Congress, I gave my rationale for becoming a candidate:

> I was asked to become a candidate for the position of chairman of the World Zionist Organization by friends who are deeply concerned about its future. Zionism as a historical political movement has triumphed, but the Zionist Organization is in decline. A primary reason for the continued existence of the WZO today is to meet the needs of Diaspora Jewry. As long as it is run on the basis of the interest of the major political parties in the Knesset, it is unable to fulfill this purpose. The convoluted structure of the WZO based on outdated political realities is characterized by lack of efficiency, frustration, and waste of resources. New leadership representing world Jewry is necessary to initiate change and innovation, to reinforce the democratic process, to advance the commitment to Zionist Jewish education, and to strengthen the ties between Diaspora Jews and Israel.

Many ideological and political factors contributed to my decision to run against Dinitz. Among them was my belief that the true partnership in world Jewry is between Israel and the Diaspora, not between Zionists and non-Zionists. The structure of the JAFI at the time belied that principle. From the Diaspora perspective, the Zionist groups and the synagogue movements participated, not as representatives of the Diaspora, but as representatives of the World Zionist Organization. Within Israel the representation within the Jewish Agency stemmed from the relative strengths of the Zionist parties in the Knesset. Thus, Diaspora Jewry was not fully reflected in the composition of the delegates to the Jewish Agency, and Israeli society was not fully reflected in the composition of the Israeli delegation. In theory, the Diaspora representation could have included leadership of the religious movements as well as the Zionist organizations; however, internal politics precluded that from happening. Conversely, the Israeli delegation could have included representatives from the worlds of business, academia, municipal government, arts, and culture, but the reality of Israeli politics prevented it.

Another issue was the premise that the chairman of the JAFI-WZO should be from the same political party as the government. Until Likud won the general election of 1977 and the assumption of power by Menachem Begin, all chairmen of the JAFI-WZO had been appointed by the Labor Party. The accepted premise was that the cooperation of the government was so essential to the effective functioning of the Jewish Agency that only members of the same party would be able to coordinate policies. I persistently and categorically stated that this was a false premise. The reality of the democratic political process of coalition building in Israel was such that ideological differences *within* each of the parties were no less divisive than the ideological differences *between* the parties. In great measure it depended upon the character, attitudes, and beliefs of the individuals who held key positions. In the final analysis, cooperation was not dependent so much on affiliation as upon mutual commitment to the common cause of Israel and world Jewry. The accepted arrangement was that the two major parties divided the key positions between them. The candidates for the major roles were appointed according to the political composition of the Knesset. So long as the Labor Party was in power, the chairman of the JAFI-WZO was selected by the Labor Party, and the treasurer was selected by the Likud. Once the Likud came to power in 1977, the functions were reversed, and the Likud had the right to select the chairman, while the Labor Party selected the treasurer.

The parties were mandated to send the names of nominees for positions of responsibility to an "Advise and Consent" committee appointed by the UIA–Keren Hayesod. The committee interviewed the candidates and in most instances gave approval. The candidates for positions of responsibility were not selected by public tender or through a search, but invariably came from the lists of political party candidates. In most instances, they were lackluster persons who had not succeeded within the Knesset or the government and were selected by the political party so as to provide them with a job.

I never accepted this premise. I believe that a close working relationship between individuals is founded on a commitment to common goals and a good interpersonal working relationship rather than on party identification. In fact, there never was a neat pattern in the party relationships. Leon Dulzin, appointed chairman of the JAFI-WZO during Menachem Begin's administration, broke with the Likud to declare the establishment of a new liberal party. Simcha Dinitz (Labor) functioned during part of his administration with Yitzhak Shamir (Likud) as prime minister. Avraham Burg (Labor) functioned with Benjamin Netanyahu (Likud) as prime minister, just as Sallai Meridor (Likud) functioned as chairman with Labor's Ehud Barak as prime minister.

I was convinced that the entire process needed radical revision. I was keenly aware of the politicization within Israeli society. Clearly the chairman had to be a person well versed in the political process and capable of operating in the maelstrom of Israeli politics. To select a person for the leadership of the Jewish Agency from within the political party system did not necessarily produce the most effective leaders. Nor did it mean that persons selected had any particular qualifications. To be successful in an Israeli political party election did not mean that a person would be able to relate to Diaspora Jewry, nor that he or she would be able to work effectively with Diaspora Jewish leadership. In fact, over the years we had unfortunately gained enough experience to realize that the differing mentalities of Diaspora and Israeli Jewry often led to personal conflict and misunderstanding. Furthermore, I maintained that the Israeli political parties had no right to presume that they could control the institutions of world Jewry. I posited that if someone outside the political parties were to run as a candidate, this could shake up the current system and demonstrate that change was not only possible, but was even essential.

However, I correctly prognosticated that with the possibility of a nonpolitical candidate entering the fray, a number of developments would ensue. In the first place, the Labor and Likud parties would unite for a common aim. Within the context of the Israeli political system, the two parties were radically divided on numerous issues, such as territorial compromise, economic policy, and religion-state controversies. However, the ideological differences would be subsumed within the context of the issues confronting the leadership of the JAFI-WZO. I contended from the very beginning that ultimately, no matter what ideological differences existed, the two parties would unite against the candidacy of an outsider. There were too many jobs of influence and political patronage at stake to sacrifice their privileged positions.

We had established Hasiah Hachadashah, the "New Faction," which consisted of Arzenu, the international Reform Zionist movement, Shinui, Ratz, and Hanoar Hatzioni. For several months prior to the World Zionist Congress, we carried out negotiations with the Likud Party. They had been unable to find a suitable candidate to stand against Simcha Dinitz. Some of the leadership of our New Faction believed naïvely that in the absence of finding a suitable candidate, the Likud would come to support my candidacy against Dinitz, and for some time, some of their leadership actually indicated they might be willing to do so. However, I never believed that this would be possible. Some two months before the Congress, the Likud proposed to revive a constitutional possibility that the World Zionist Congress be led by a president as well as by a chairman. The last person to hold the office of president was Nahum Goldman, who had served in this role from 1956 to 1968. However, since his resignation, the position had remained unfilled. The Likud proposed that if we supported their candidate for chairman, they would support my candidacy for president. After long negotiations, we agreed on a formula that was acceptable to both parties. However, we insisted on one proviso: the person to be nominated for chairman of the Executive should be a person of integrity and committed to the same goals we espoused. A prerequisite was that the candidate be known for his liberal attitude to religion and state. Without insisting on our right to name the person, in effect we had predicated our acceptance on the principle of advise and consent. We proposed one name only, MK Dan Meridor, a respected and experienced public figure and ex-minister. But he never agreed.

The Likud proposed a number of alternative candidates. Some of them were interested and some were not. I met with two of them, but in reality the Likud never was able to find a candidate worthy of our support. In the absence of recruiting a suitable candidate, some members of the Likud came to the New Faction and said they would support my candidacy. However, it was clear that even though we would receive significant support beyond the membership of our own New Faction, we would fall woefully short of winning the election.

My initial prognostication was proved correct. Immediately prior to the opening of Congress, Likud and Labor signed a deal. The Likud agreed that Simcha Dinitz would be reelected as chairman and Hanan Ben Yehuda would be elected treasurer.

We were extremely disappointed that at no time did the Likud come to our faction to forewarn us of their intentions to strike a deal with Labor. The deal was signed with no contact with us, nor did anyone attempt to offer any explanation afterwards.

Another consequence, for which I was prepared, was that I and other leaders would be attacked personally. Immediately after I had made the decision to become a candidate, I communicated with Simcha Dinitz and Yehiel Leket, then secretary-general of the World Labor Zionist Organization. I met each of them separately and informed them that my decision to become a candidate was based on principles and they should not see it as a personal attack on them in any way. I undertook to make no public statements of a personal character against either of them and said that I wanted to retain their friendship. They could not understand why I, or anyone else for that matter, would want to fight a losing cause. They said that they would make every effort to meet our demands for democratic elections and for reorganization, but that by my competing against the Labor Party for chairman it would be more difficult to accept our demands for change. They warned that a heated election campaign was not conducive to conciliation on matters of public policy. They also warned me that it was likely that the campaign would turn personal, and even though they would try to prevent it, some personal attacks would inevitably be directed against me.

I told them that I was aware of the pitfalls. I reminded them that I had refused to run initially but had decided to do so because of the principles involved. I expressed the hope that at the end of the campaign they would consider my candidacy to have been to the benefit of the World Zionist Organization.

My candidacy was not universally welcomed within our own Reform movement. Some of our rabbis had been active in the Labor Zionist movement, as indeed was I until I moved to Israel. The Reform movement had always seen a

parallel between its own social idealism and that of the Labor movement, particularly regarding the kibbutz movement.
The establishment of the Reform kibbutzim Yahel and Lotan
as well as Har Halutz would not have been possible without
the active cooperation of the leadership of the Labor kibbutz
movement. To oppose Labor Zionism in a direct election was
considered by a number of our leading rabbis as a betrayal of
basic principles, and they expressed themselves in numerous
communications. In April 1992, a letter signed by several distinguished Reform rabbinical leaders was sent to the entire
Reform rabbinate. The letter read in part:

> Differences over elections for the upcoming World Zion-
> ist Congress have jeopardized this historical alliance. ARZA
> insisted upon direct elections while all the other American
> Zionist groups have agreed to compromise and develop
> another democratic option. The conflict between the Reform
> and Labor Zionist movements is not a simple one. Mistakes
> and wrong assumptions have been made by both sides. But
> to concede our place in the future leadership of the World
> Zionist Organization or, even worse, to be a party to the
> ascendancy of forces of right wing ideology is to compromise
> our ultimate interests and principles.
>
> As committed Reform Jews who also appreciate the
> ideological vision and state-building role of the Labor Zion-
> ist Movement, we are particularly distressed by the current
> dispute. We believe that it is our role, yours and ours, to urge
> the leaders of both movements to find a way to reconcile
> their differences. Both too should strive to maintain their
> natural alliance with the Conservative Movement, Hadas-
> sah, and others, each an enlightened partner to a coalition
> founded on the principles of pluralism.
>
> We would urge you to join us in calling upon the leader-
> ship of ARZA today to consider moving towards a mutually

agreed upon formula for compromise and reconciliation. Time is running out. Let us each call or write our leaders and representatives today. This done, we can then with integrity ask the same of our former partners in Labor.

The leaders of the New Faction and I myself received many oral and written communications urging us to withdraw my candidacy. The most painful to me personally came from a close friend and outstanding leader, S. Zalman Abramov, author of the book *The Perpetual Dilemma*, published by the World Union for Progressive Judaism. Abramov also served as chairman of the Board of Overseers of the Hebrew Union College–Jewish Institute of Religion in Jerusalem and had great influence within our movement. On June 15, 1992, he wrote a letter to Professor Alfred Gottschalk, then president of HUC-JIR. His letter was given broad distribution. The following are extracts from his letter:

> It seems that the obsession of ARZA is beyond cure. Their position contradicts all tenets of Reform philosophy, that is to say, keeping away from involvement in party politics.
>
> Unlike the dignified and honorable stand of the Conservative Movement, the Reform have turned their back on the only party which has consistently espoused the cause of pluralism in general and of the Reform Movement in particular.
>
> Labor is the only element that can be relied upon in the future. Supporting a Likud candidate would also run counter to the sentiments of the majority of the Reform membership in Israel and will close the gates of the kibbutz movement to any Reform attempts to cooperate with it.
>
> I have never been a member of the Labor Party. Nor have I voted for it. However, in the present situation to pressure a belated anti-Labor policy is unfair, harmful and the Reform Movement will, no doubt, pay a high price for it.

The closer we came to the Congress, the more pressure was exerted on me to withdraw. I was visited by individuals and groups of rabbis who maintained that I was destroying the very foundations I had built for the development of the Reform movement in Israel. The day the World Zionist Congress convened, a group of rabbis met with our leadership in my office and offered a compromise, which in essence was the same as the electoral college proposal made by the Labor movement and Hadassah, a proposal rejected again and again by ARZA.

One hour before the election was due to take place, I delivered another speech before the Congress. Here are extracts translated from the Hebrew:

> I rise to criticize but not to condemn, to be constructive and not destructive, and to unite and not divide. I rise to tell you why we have decided to put up a candidate and why I accepted the candidacy.
> This is the Thirty-Second World Zionist Congress. In Hebrew numbering, the number thirty-two is *lev*—heart. In most cultures the heart is considered the seat of the soul and the mind the seat of knowledge. But in Hebrew there is no such dichotomy. The heart and the mind are one and they are inextricable. Let us be frank. Over the years we have permitted a great gap to divide heart from mind, word from deed, intention from reality.
> From its very inception the WZO encouraged every Jew to pay one shekel, to register and vote in shaping the future of the Jewish people. We proudly proclaim that we are the only Jewish organization in the world that holds elections. . . . But in reality, for this Congress no elections were held in the Diaspora, except for two countries with a total of nine delegates—Belgium and Peru. In Israel, elections

were held for the Knesset, but only a minute number of
Israeli citizens realize that in casting their ballot they were
also electing 38 percent of the delegates to this Congress.
What a paradox! Those who do vote are not aware of the significance, and those in the Diaspora who do know were not
given the opportunity to vote.

It was clear to us in ARZA that if we did not press for an
election this time, no democratic election would ever be
held again. . . . Now that the Zionist Court has reaffirmed
the constitutional requirement for elections, I hope we
all agree that the democratic nature of the WZO has been
strengthened. . . . In keeping with the Court's decision let us
now proceed to devise an equitable and effective system of
elections, both in Israel and in the Diaspora.

During the next Congress, we shall be celebrating the
one-hundredth anniversary of the WZO and shortly after, entering the twenty-first century. For us Jews this can
represent a new era that will, hopefully, be marked by a key
factor—that of demography. It is projected that by early in
the new century, the majority of Jews in the world will reside
in Israel. The twenthieth century was characterized by the
establishment of the State of Israel. The twenty-first century
should be secured by ensuring the continuity of the Jewish
people and the Jewish heritage. For this, the State of Israel is
central to both ideology and practice.

The Jewish world will not be able to respond effectively to
the challenges of the twenty-first century with the tools of the
previous century—not the World Zionist Organization, not the
Jewish Agency, and not the World Jewish Congress. None of
them separately nor all of them together are adequate to meet
the needs of the new era. New conditions call for new structures. . . . There will be no justification for overlapping and
competitive worldwide frameworks. There will be no justification for artificial delineation between Jews and Zionists.

Most of the recommendations for reorganization of the
WZO have been minimal. They do not begin to respond
to the needs of the new era. . . . I call for the creation of a
covenant of partnership between Israel and the Diaspora,
incorporating all the major international political, cultural,
and religious organizations.

Who should take the lead in restructuring world Jewry
if not the World Zionist Organization? In the process of
restructuring world Jewry we shall restructure ourselves.
If we can commit ourselves to work toward this end, then
this "Congress of the Heart" can fulfill the promise of the
prophet Ezekiel: "I will give you a new heart and put a new
spirit into you" (Ezekiel 36:26).

The election was the major, perhaps the only, excitement of
the Congress. The New Faction convened caucus after caucus to discuss the political situation. Emissaries came from
all the other parties to meet with us, and we sent emissaries
to them. Round-the-clock discussions were held with leaders
of the Labor Party in an attempt to reconcile the differences.
The election, originally scheduled for the morning session of
10:00 A.M., was postponed to the afternoon while a negotiating
team, headed by Rabbi Alexander Schindler, president of the
UAHC, met with Simcha Dinitz to try to agree to a formula
on the basis of which I would withdraw my candidacy. I did
not myself attend the negotiating meetings. Instead, on the
morning of the election I prepared my speech to be delivered
before the Congress. In fact, I prepared two speeches—one
predicated on a situation whereby we accepted a compromise
and I would withdraw honorably; the second, a speech going ahead with the election. Finally, after hours of fruitless
negotiations, the discussions broke off. We were willing to
compromise if the Labor Party would commit itself to a full
democratic election process in the following Congress. But

as they refused to make such a commitment, we therefore decided to proceed with the election.

If the truth be told, I was relieved. I would have felt a terrible sense of anticlimax had a compromise resolution been arrived at. We had gone through an intensive period of campaigning over issues of principle. I was convinced that no matter what compromise would be achieved, the reality of the World Zionist Organization's condition was that it was against the interest of the major parties to convene elections in the Diaspora. Therefore, no agreement for full democratic elections would ever be implemented. I have always believed that it is important to fight for principles and that the process of fighting for rights is no less important than attaining them. The essence of democracy is in the electoral process, not only the election itself, but the debate over issues, persons, and policy.

Raya Yaglom, the president of the Women's Internation Zionist Organization, chaired the plenary session preceding the elections. After some introductory remarks, she called upon the Zionist movement to unite. She publicly asked our movement to withdraw my candidacy, since it was a hopeless cause and it was clear that all the other factions supported the re-election of Simcha Dinitz. She spoke to me from the podium directly and in person and called upon me to withdraw my candidacy. She hoped that I would do so for the sake of unifying the Congress. But it was clear that none of us wanted to withdraw. Without hesitation, I walked up to the podium and informed her that we chose to continue with the election.

Yaglom then called upon one representative from each faction to speak on behalf of a candidate. All the faction representatives spoke on behalf of Simcha Dinitz. Rabbi Alexander Schindler spoke on behalf of my candidacy. Then each of the candidates was allocated a brief period of time to present his case. The session was adjourned following the representations of the candidates and the voting commenced. When the booths closed, the votes were counted. The results were 382 votes for Simcha Dinitz, 101 votes for me, and 11 abstentions. Our delegates were overjoyed with the results. Including the abstentions, at least 43 persons had broken party discipline by not voting for Dinitz.

After the booths had closed, someone came running up to me and said, "Where were you? You were the only one of our delegation who did not vote." The truth is that so many people had engaged me in conversation during the balloting that I had forgotten to vote! How fortunate it was that the results turned out as they did. Otherwise, we might have lost by one vote and I, the candidate, would have single-handedly been responsible for the defeat. What a relief!

In the final analysis, the election process was constructive and salutary. I believe that we won a great victory. Certainly the Zionist movement did not lose by it, and neither did the Reform movement.

Chapter Seventeen

Reorganization of the World's Jewish Organizations

The Jewish Agency for Israel and the World Zionist Organization were created to advance interdependence between Israel and the Diaspora. Their primary purpose was to offer a framework within which the Diaspora would participate in the upbuilding of Zion, and Israeli Jewry would participate in the enriching of Jewish life in the Diaspora. The guiding principle is *Kol Yisrael arevim zeh bazeh*, "Every Jew is responsible for one another." There has to be an enduring partnership between Israel and the Diaspora, one grounded in mutual responsibility and shared destiny.

Over the years, the organizational structures of world Jewry have assumed different forms in order to meet changing conditions. Following the First World War and the Balfour Declaration of 1917, the World Zionist Organization leadership recognized that they needed the support of the world Jewish community in order to achieve their objectives. At the time, heated ideological conflicts divided world Jewry. The majority of Jews in Western democratic countries were opposed to Zionism. They maintained that the Emancipation of the Jews, especially in Eastern European and Arab countries, was the right way to ensure a secure Jewish future. In their view, Zionism, with its call to reconstitute the Jews as a people in their ancient homeland, was the antithesis of Emancipation, because its objective was to encourage Jews to leave the countries in which they were living.

The Zionists, then very much in the minority, were desperate for the financial and political support of Jewish leadership in the West, particularly that of the United States. Led by the president of the World Zionist Organization, Dr. Chaim Weizmann, the Zionists managed to persuade the leading non-Zionist Jewish philanthropists of the day to support their struggle on humanitarian grounds. However, the non-Zionists, led by Louis Marshall, a prominent American Jewish leader, were unwilling to work within the framework of the WZO, because that would imply a commitment to Zionist ideology. As a compromise, the Jewish Agency was created as a roof organization for cooperation between Zionists and non-Zionists. Article Four of the League of Nations Mandate for Palestine stipulated "that an appropriate *Jewish agency* shall be recognized as a public body for the purpose of advising and cooperating with the administration of Palestine" (italics added)—hence the name. Established in 1929, the Jewish Agency did not function as had been anticipated. Louis Marshall, the guiding spirit of the non-Zionists, died on his way home from the founding meeting. The worldwide depression intervened. The Nazi Party under Adolf Hitler came to power in Germany, eventually leading to the Second World War and the Holocaust.

The plans of the founders were never implemented. Until the establishment of the State of Israel in 1948, the WZO assumed full responsibility for the Jewish Agency, and its executive also served as the executive of the Jewish Agency. Following the war, David Ben-Gurion, then chief executive of both the Jewish Agency and the WZO, decided that it was essential to mobilize the support of the non-Zionist Jewish philanthropists. He began to propound the hypothesis that the only "true Zionists" were those who chose to live in Israel; all others were friends and supporters. With the establishment of the state, he advocated the disbanding of the WZO. Even though the WZO rejected Ben-Gurion's proposals, the WZO's status and influence were significantly diminished. In Israel, the pre-state functions of the WZO were taken over by the government. In the Diaspora, most leadership roles were assumed by the non-Zionists. New fund-raising mechanisms were created that transferred responsibility from the Zionists to the philanthropic establishment. For their part, the non-Zionist leadership recognized that the Zionist hypothesis had been vindicated by historical events and that it was now the obligation of the entire Jewish community to rescue Jews in distress, to bring as many as possible to Israel, and to strengthen the fledgling Jewish state. Diaspora Jewish communal and defense agencies took over many of the functions of the WZO, such as political action and public information, which until then had been the exclusive domain of the Zionists.

The Six-Day War ushered in a new era of cooperation. The threat of annihilation and the subsequent victory had galvanized the entire Jewish world and created new conditions that required that the covenant between Israel and the Diaspora be strengthened in a renewed working partnership.

Diaspora Jewish leadership was no longer satisfied with a role limited to fund-raising. Most of them were not members of the WZO, and they resented a condition that some, recalling early American history, saw as "taxation without representation." Unlike their predecessors who, following the Second World War, the Holocaust, and the establishment of the state, gave of their material resources unconditionally, the new generation of Diaspora leaders insisted on greater involvement in the decision-making process and in monitoring program expenditures. This was a legitimate and salutary development.

The WZO leadership, led by South African–born Louis Pincus, and the Diaspora leadership, led by Max Fisher, embarked on extended discussions in order to redefine the relationship. These discussions were enshrined in a Reconstitution Agreement signed in June 1971 and later ratified by the Knesset through an amendment to the Law of Status in June 1976.

The newly reconstituted Jewish Agency was restructured along the same lines as the original, with parity between the WZO and its philanthropic partners in the Diaspora, the United Israel Appeal in the United States and Keren Hayesod (KH) in the rest of the world. The WZO was allocated 50 percent of the representation on all governing bodies, the UIA (today the Jewish Federations of North America [JFNA]) 30 percent, and Keren Hayesod 20 percent. A program for delineation of functions was approved, with the Jewish Agency assuming responsibility for immigration and absorption, settlement, and other tasks in Israel, and the WZO assuming responsibility for educational and organizational tasks in the Diaspora.

Once I had become active in the Jewish Agency for Israel–World Zionist Organization, I recognized that the existing organizational structures did not meet the primary goals of the major Jewish institutions. In December 1975, the United Nations adopted the infamous resolution declaring that "Zionism is racism." World Jewry was appalled. In early 1976, a special emergency conference was convened jointly by JAFI-WZO and the Israeli government. The conference decided that the most effective response to the resolution would be to develop a large-scale program of strengthening the Jewish state.

At the conference I proposed a resolution that we embark on a new immigration initiative. At the time *aliyah* was at a low point. The Ministry of Absorption, which had been established after the Six-Day War, and the Jewish Agency's Department of *Aliyah* and *K'litah* (Immigration and Absorption) were engaged in constant bickering over their respective areas of responsibility. The competitiveness between the government and the Jewish Agency had become both embarrassing and counterproductive. My resolution recommended that a special commission be appointed to bring order to the process of immigration and absorption and clarify the respective institutional responsibilities.

The resolution was unanimously approved and in due course a commission was appointed. Major General Amos Horev, the president of the Technion, was appointed chairman. Prime Minister Rabin appointed me to the commission. I was informed that I represented four constituencies: new immigrants, the Jewish Agency, the American Jewish community, and for the first time, Reform Judaism. I joked that it reminded me of my Washington experiences. When it came to appointing persons to important political positions in the 1960s, we were said to be searching for an African American nun named Goldberg (representing four constituencies: women, blacks, Jews, and Catholics).

The Horev Commission held intensive discussions for more than six months and formulated a series of recommendations. Unfortunately, for the most part, the recommendations were never implemented. However, for me it was an important learning process in the ways both the government and the Jewish Agency functioned in their complex interrelationship.

By the 1990s I had become convinced that it was essential to introduce radical change into the governance of the Jewish Agency, because its structure no longer reflected the reality of Jewish life. In 1992, I wrote an article called "The Israel-Diaspora Connection: Reorganizing World Jewry to Meet the Needs of the 21st Century." The article provoked intense discussion. Various seminars were convened in which public figures and WZO leaders participated. In stating my case for radical change I made the following points:

Zionism as a historical, political movement has triumphed. Paradoxically, however, the World Zionist Organization manifests all the symptoms of a sick organization. Its reputation has reached a nadir in both Israel and the Diaspora. Its leaders have a negative self-image and they themselves do not consider the organization to be an effective instrument of change. Its officers reveal low morale and high frustration. Individuals are too often selected for leadership roles because of their party affiliations rather than a demonstrated commitment. Efforts to restructure the WZO are blocked by turf wars. Ideological and institutional issues are not confronted, but compromised.

In most of the Diaspora countries, elections to the WZO are either not held or are marked by corruption. In Israel, only a minute portion of the electorate realizes that in voting for the Knesset, they are also voting for 38 percent of the delegates to the World Zionist Congress. The WZO constitution, originally formulated to encourage dynamic change within a democratic process, has been exploited to prevent change and to maintain the status quo.

Ideological controversy was at the root of the establishment of the Jewish Agency in the 1920s. In those days, a Jewish state was a dream, the viability and desirability of which was passionately discussed. Today the Jewish state is both an indisputable fact and the prime factor influencing Jewish life throughout the world. Today's controversies relate to ideological perceptions of what is in the best interests of the Jewish people and the State of Israel. These controversies are reflected in issues concerning the budget priorities of the world Jewish community. How should the Jewish people spend the funds it mobilizes? How much should stay in local communities and for what purposes? How much should go to Jews elsewhere in the world and for what purposes?

The issues of funding today reflect the pre-state debates between Zionists and non-Zionists, and the ongoing conflicts between those who give priority to state-building and those who give priority to preserving Jewish life wherever Jews live. However, unlike the confrontations of the past, the positions adopted on such ideological controversies are not dependent on whether a person is a card-carrying Zionist or not, or whether a person lives in Israel or the Diaspora. Some people, both Zionists and Israelis, have gone to the length of telling Diaspora Jews to stop contributing their money to Israel and to retain their funds for Jewish education in their own communities and for combating the tide of assimilation. Conversely, there are some fund-raisers who advocate much higher allocations for Israel. However, with regard to the argument over Zionism, no respectable Jewish leader today would declare him- or herself to be an anti-Zionist.

There is an ideological battle which must be waged within world Jewry. A high percentage of Jews, maybe even the majority, have not yet accepted the message or implications of Zionism. Many Jews are indifferent to Israel, even as many others are indifferent to their Jewish heritage. Even among the rabbinate and the intellectual leadership a form of neo-non-Zionism has developed. The Zionist dimension in Diaspora Jewish education is minimal and in some educational institutions non-existent. In the hope that some vestiges of ideological difference among the WZO-KH-United Jewish Communities partners can be resolved, how can these differences best be reconciled? I believe they must be brought out into the open and discussed in detail so as to take joint action.

The respective mission statements of the Jewish Agency and the WZO are essentially identical in content and intent. Whatever institutional differences do remain do not justify the perpetuation of separate and divisive infrastructures.

Therefore, I propose the creation of a new democratic world body to advance the interdependence of Israel and Diaspora. The new body should be based on an Israel-Diaspora partnership formula rather than on the present WZO-UJC-KH partnership.

As I envisage it, the new body would incorporate the Jewish Agency and the World Zionist Organization so as to create a real unified institutional framework (which most people believe already exists). Neither Diaspora Jewry nor the Israeli public understand the organizational or ideological differences between the WZO and the Jewish Agency and in Israel, the word *Hasochnut* (the Agency) is freely used to describe both organizations.

It is essential to retain both the ideology and the terminology of Zionism in the name of a new body. The new combined organization could be called the World Zionist Agency or in Hebrew *Hasochnut HaTzionit Haolamit* or a similar name.

Even if agreement could be reached on this proposal in principle, the actual process of reconstitution would be long, and controversial. The proposal will inevitably meet with strong opposition from many quarters. It will be alleged that the ideological emphasis of Zionism will be diluted. I contend that just the opposite will occur: Zionism as a historical political *movement* has triumphed; Zionism as an *organization* is desperately in need of revitalization.

I see no other way. The status quo is a recipe for continued friction. Separation of the Jewish Agency and the WZO would inevitably weaken both organizations. It could eventually lead to the demise of the World Zionist Organization and the contraction of the Jewish Agency into a purely philanthropic organization. Only merger into one organization can ensure a true democratic partnership between the Diaspora and Israel, and for Diaspora Jewry it will encourage a greater participatory role in the decision-making process.

The article began to make waves. Some people were incensed. Those among our New Faction supporters who thought it would be interpreted as a call to dismantle the WZO were proved right. However, others thought it was a positive contribution and stimulated thinking concerning the need for reorganizing the WZO and the Jewish Agency. Many individuals indicated that they were in fundamental agreement that major changes had to be initiated. On the basis of these conversations, we convened three all-day seminars at Beit Shmuel in which representatives of all the Zionist factions participated as well as people from outside the WZO framework. These meetings were summarized in a written report, which was widely disseminated.

I was under no illusions. My proposal was considered too radical by most leaders in the JAFI-WZO and it never made much headway. Over the years, dissatisfaction among the partners became more intense. The UJC-KH partners were adamantly committed to depoliticizing the Jewish Agency. Many of them considered the WZO an anachronism and were determined to stop funding it from UJC-KH sources. For their part, the WZO partners distrust the ideological commitment of the leadership to Israel. They point to the decreasing percentage of funds allocated to Israel by local communities. They refuse to accept the premise that the Jewish Agency should be governed by criteria established for voluntary nonprofit agencies in the Diaspora.

The differences came to a head in June 2009. The report of a Jewish Agency committee on governance issues was accepted by the General Assembly of the Jewish Agency. The report recommended that the current representation of the constituents—that is 50 percent WZO, 30 percent JFNA, 20 percent KH—be continued. The Jewish Agency would continue to subsidize the WZO until 2013, after which it would expect the WZO to be financially independent. It was also decided that the chairperson and deputy chairperson of the Jewish Agency Executive could not serve in any capacity with the WZO.

I was an outspoken critic of the last proviso. I maintained that it was a serious mistake and would lead to divisiveness and controversy between the Jewish Agency and the WZO. As chairman of the Zionist General Council, I devoted my address at the opening plenary session to the subject. A resolution was overwhelmingly adopted calling for continued discussion of this one central issue. However, the JFNA leaders were adamant and the chairman, Natan Sharansky, was unanimously elected as chairman under the specific understanding that his responsibilities exclusively concerned the Jewish Agency.

The following are excerpts of my address before the Zionist General Council in June 2009 (translated from the Hebrew original):

> We have been told that American Jewish leaders are motivated by their desire to eliminate politics in the selection of the top leadership of the Jewish Agency. This statement reflects a misunderstanding of the divergent cultural experiences and systems of governance between American Jewry and Israel. It is important to delineate these differences.
>
> In the Diaspora communities, Jewish identity is based on volunteerism. Jewish identity is a question of personal choice. In that sense not only converts to Judaism may be designated as "Jews by choice," but every person in the Diaspora is in effect a "Jew by choice." Leadership is chosen in a self-selecting process by which persons volunteer to give of their time, efforts, and material resources. Rarely is there a contested election. In almost every instance, a small nominating committee selects the leaders based on the criteria of who can best advance the interests of the various Jewish institutions.

In Israel, Jewish identity is not a private, but a public matter. An Israeli citizen is obligated to serve in the army, to pay taxes, to participate in the culture, and to use the Hebrew language. The Jew in Israel is a Jew by no-choice. Jewish identity is an integral dimension of Israeli citizenship. Therefore, in contrast to the Diaspora, in Israel, leaders are selected through a process of elections among political parties. The WZO, as the institution that was the precursor to the establishment of the state, is grounded in a political structure closely related to the state framework.

Therefore, JAFI represents a distinctive blend of two divergent systems—the volunteerism of the Diaspora and the political process of Israel. That is why JAFI has special legal status with the Israel government that is enshrined in Knesset legislation and perpetuated through the officially recognized Coordinating Committee of the Government of Israel and the Jewish Agency, which meets at least three times a year. No other Jewish organization is privileged to enjoy such a status and relationship.

The head of JAFI-WZO is one of the key positions in the Jewish world. The person selected should undisputedly be of the highest caliber. Unfortunately, a major disability in both the voluntary system of the Diaspora and the political system of Israel is that the most qualified persons often do not want to serve or in many cases are not electable.

I understand the perspective of our American partners. It would be easier to have an organization grounded in the American system of volunteerism such as that of the American Jewish Joint Distribution Committee ("the Joint"). However, to transform JAFI into another Joint would be to create yet another philanthropic organization that would duplicate each other's work. That would eliminate or diminish the Israeli-WZO political dimension, but unfortunately, it would also eliminate the Israeli political process: the unique involvement, commitment, concern, and support of state institutions and the fruitful collaboration between the government and the Jewish Agency.

The people who serve as the full-time leadership of an organization set the tone and the content of its mission. In many ways they also personify the organization's message. They are responsible for formulating policy issues and bringing them before the board. That is why in the American Jewish Federation framework a major function of the lay board is to seek top professionals. In an international organization like JAFI, whose board of governors convenes only three times a year, the role of chairman is critical.

We believe that the appointment of separate heads of JAFI and the WZO will inevitably lead to conflict over issues, policies, programs, and financing. This in turn would lead to institutional and ideological competitiveness and in all likelihood would exacerbate the existing differences between the two institutions.

In the final analysis, reorganization of structure is not the major challenge confronting world Jewry. The reorganization of American Jewish institutions more than a decade ago has not proved to be the overwhelming success for which its leadership strived. Nor have the strategic plans adopted by JAFI and the WZO plan for restructuring significantly changed the status and the impact of our institutions among world Jewry. By now we should have learned that to change organizational structures without revitalizing goals, programs, and leadership is not necessarily a recipe for success.

The recent shocking failures in the world economy have dashed outmoded theories and made many institutions anachronistic. In the geopolitical sphere, even the United States, the hitherto unchallenged superpower, will have to learn to shift to a multi-polar world order in which China, India, the Far East, and Middle East nations will demand an ever-increasing share of political power and economic influence.

The crisis in the global economy has already had a traumatic impact on Jewish organizational life in the Diaspora. The most visible consequences have been severe reductions in staff and budget. These changes represent the tip of the iceberg. Many institutions will be forced to rethink their goals and structures. The crises have precipitated changes that, in many instances, should have been introduced in any case. Jewish day schools, as well as rabbinical seminaries and university programs offering a Jewish education, are in jeopardy. Students who had planned careers in Jewish professional life—rabbis, educators, and communal workers—may have to replan their career objectives. Some international and national organizations may be forced to reevaluate their relationship to similar institutions that are competitive. Already some synagogues have been compelled to consider merging with others, not only within movements, but even between synagogues in the Reform and Conservative movements.

Of special interest is the impact of the current situation on Israel-Diaspora relations with the Jewish Agency and the WZO. The funding of the Jewish Agency has been dependent on contributions from the JNFA and the Keren Hayesod. Over the years the Federation system has been weakened. The numbers of donors has declined and the real value of the funds contributed has declined with it. Major givers are giving proportionally less to Jewish causes and more to general causes. A growing number of American Jews, especially among the younger generation, are indifferent to Israel, even as among the younger generation of Israelis there is an increasing disinterest in world Jewry. In general, we sense a growing social and cultural distancing between the Diaspora and Israeli communities.

Whereas in previous generations, it was a weak Israeli community that was dependent on the strong North American Diaspora, the balance has been reversed. Not only is the population of Israel the largest in world Jewry, but its economy is strong and no longer in such desperate need of financial support from the Diaspora. The need to rescue Soviet Jewry in Operation Exodus and Ethiopian Jewry in Operations Moses and Solomon no longer propels Diaspora Jewry to raise massive emergency funds. As a consequence of the new reality in both Israel and the Diaspora, significantly less funds are allocated to Israel. Instead Jewish communities are devoting more attention to funding their domestic programs in order to fulfill the needs of their own local communities.

The radical changes in the Jewish condition should motivate responsible leadership to work toward equally radical changes in Jewish institutional life. Alvin Toffler taught us in his book *Future Shock* that organizations or even nations that do not change in response to the kaleidoscopic changes in society are destined to disappear or become irrelevant.

To illustrate the kind of radical changes I believed should be considered by the World Zionist Organization, I offered the following proposals regarding the relationship between the WZO and the Jewish National Fund and the World Jewish Congress. The following are excerpts from my address to the Zionist General Council in June 2007:

> The Jewish National Fund (Keren Kayemet LeYisrael) was established by Theodor Herzl and the Fifth Zionist Congress in 1901 to serve as the instrumentality for purchase and development of land in Eretz Israel. To this day, the JNF is theoretically under the exclusive control of the WZO. All the leaders are selected at the same time and in the same electoral process as the leadership of the WZO.

In Israel, the JNF has achieved remarkable success and is a powerful force in shaping land development in the country. It has offices in every major Jewish community in the world. Like so many Jewish families worldwide, when I was a child growing up in Cleveland, Ohio, my parents kept a little blue tin on the table—a *pushke*—and we were taught to put spare coins in it at least once a week and on special family occasions. Today the JNF engages in massive fund-raising efforts all over the world and raises many tens of millions of dollars annually throughout the Diaspora. In the United States it is even engaged in countering anti-Zionism on university campuses. They have learned the lesson that the WZO never learned. Major donors are attracted to large, dynamic, and visionary development projects.

In order to be effective, an organization requires three fundamental characteristics: a clearly defined program and mission, well-qualified leadership, and financial support to achieve the objectives.

The JNF has successfully acquired all three characteristics. The WZO needs to adopt an entirely new approach to the Jewish National Fund; we should embark on a collaborative process to coordinate and integrate the work of the JNF and the WZO both abroad and in Israel. Similarly with the World Jewish Congress. This, like the WZO, is a worldwide representative umbrella group, comprising representatives of Israel and Diaspora communities. The mission statements of the World Jewish Congress and the World Zionist Organization are almost identical. In fact, for many years, Dr. Nahum Goldman was simultaneously president of both organizations. During the Cold War, Jewish organizations functioning under the rubric of "Zionism" were anathema to the USSR and the other East European countries. However, under the rubric of "Judaism," representative Jewish organizations were able to negotiate with Eastern European governments on the plight of the Jews. Thus, the rationale for continued existence of two separate organizations was justifiable.

However, since the breakup of the Soviet Union and the affiliation of some countries of the former Eastern bloc with the European Union, that rationale is no longer valid. Furthermore, from the Zionist perspective, to permit the nations of the world to distinguish between Jew and Zionist is unacceptable. Our assumption is that all the leaders of the World Jewish Congress are Zionists and that, in turn, all Zionists are committed to fighting anti-Semitism and securing Jewish rights wherever Jews live.

Therefore, since our proclaimed agendas are the same, it is time for closer collaboration between the World Jewish Congress and the WZO, with the objective of considering an eventual merger. This is a challenge that could presage a renewed vision and more effective governance for world Jewish organizations.

Just as in Israel, changing political and social conditions have resulted in a realignment of Israeli political forces, so the radical changes in the condition of world Jewry require realignment of world Jewish organizations.

Until now, we in the WZO and JAFI partnership have stressed what Diaspora Jewry can do for Israel. But tomorrow, the basic questions will be: What can Israel do to sustain and strengthen world Jewry, and how will Israel and the Diaspora working in the closest partnership perpetuate the Jewish people and the Jewish heritage?

The reality is that no one organization, no matter how comprehensive, can encompass all of world Jewish interests. The distinctive characteristic I choose to call "Jewish peoplehood" encourages a multiplicity of ways to preserve Jewish identity. In previous articles, I have coined the phrase "the perpetuation mood." I believe that Jewish survival is motivated by an instinctive compulsion for perpetuation.

The State of Israel has enhanced the perpetuation mood in our time. By its very existence, and the continuing threat to its existence, Jewish life has become more exuberant, vital, dynamic, and yet more tenuous. The Jewish reality invariably leads to continuing calls to change the reality. We confront at one and the same time the centrifugal forces pulling away from Jewish perpetuation and the centripetal forces compelling collective responsibility for Jewish perpetuation.

The establishment of the Jewish state was never a goal in itself. The ultimate goal of Zionism is to keep the Jewish people alive. Our task is to create the programs, develop the leadership, and mobilize the funds to achieve that objective, using Israel as the framework, the inspiring campus of a vibrant Jewish people learning and living to fulfill the vision of the prophet Jeremiah: "For I am mindful of the plans I have made concerning you—declares the Lord—plans for your welfare, not for disaster, to give you a hopeful future" (Jeremiah 29:11).

Epilogue

In discussing the historic significance of the movement for Progressive Judaism in Israel, I have often referred to an early Zionist movement called BILU. This was the first movement of young pioneers from Eastern Europe to organize as a settlement movement in 1882. Before that, Jews who had settled in the Land of Israel had come for religious reasons—to pray, to study, and to wait for the Messiah or to die and be buried in the Holy Land.

The BILU rejected the religious approach. Instead, they adopted a political objective: to establish settlements of Jews who would farm the land and form indigenous communities. Since these early pioneers had no training in agriculture and since the conditions in Palestine were so harsh and inhospitable, they experienced hardship, disease, and frustration. Some were unable to endure and returned to Europe, but others courageously persisted. The pioneering efforts of the BILU inspired others to follow. This entire early period of settlement became known as the First Aliyah, and it set the stage for other waves of immigration to follow. The efforts of those early pioneers were considered heroic, because the fledgling settlements they created demonstrated the potential. Indeed, had their pioneering efforts not succeeded, it is likely that Theodor Herzl's proposals for a Jewish state would not have been considered feasible.

Why do I compare the early efforts of Progressive Judaism in Israel to the BILU? Because we too have endured opposition and frustration, but through it all, we have persevered. Like the BILU, we too are comparatively few in number. But also like the BILU we have demonstrated the potential. We have demonstrated that without the participation of Progressive Judaism, Israel would be incomplete and nonrepresentative, just as without our being in Israel we would be peripheral to Jewish destiny. I am convinced that the ramifications of our efforts will yet reverberate with greater resonance in both Israel and the Diaspora.

I have yet another purpose in referring to the BILU movement. The word "BILU" is based on a verse from Isaiah 2:5, *Beit Yaakov l'chu v'neilchah b'or Adonai* ("House of Jacob, come and let us walk by the light of the Lord"). "BILU" is an acronym of the first letter of the first four Hebrew words: "House of Jacob, come and let us walk." Because the members of BILU did not consider themselves religious, they purposely left out the last two words of the verse: *b'or Adonai*, "by the light of the Lord." During the same decade the BILU was organized in Eastern Europe, the Central Conference of American Rabbis was organized in the United States. By an amazing coincidence, the CCAR selected as the motto to be inscribed on its emblem four words from the same verse in Isaiah. But since in those days the Reform rabbis were consciously trying to expunge Zionism and Jewish peoplehood from their vocabulary, they deleted the first two words—*Beit Yaakov*, "House of Jacob" (representing Jewish peoplehood)—but they did retain the last four words of the verse: *L'chu v'neilchah b'or Adonai*, "Come and let us walk by the light of the Lord."

I consider this to be remarkable. The identical verse from Isaiah was used by the first Zionists and by the first Reform anti-Zionists.

Today I see this coincidence as prophetic. We are challenged to complete the cycle and to eliminate the dichotomies. The entire Jewish people is desperately in search of wholeness and unity of purpose. In order to flourish, we require all components: people, land, faith, culture, language, common goals, and shared destiny.

Today, our movement can inculcate in *K'lal Yisrael* a passionate commitment to strive to fulfill the entire clarion call.

That is our message. That is our mission.

"House of Jacob, come and let us walk (together) by the light of the Lord."

Appendix 1:
Glossary of Terms and Abbreviations

ARZA	Association of Reform Zionists of America
Arzenu	International Federation of Reform and Progressive Religious Zionists
CCAR	Central Conference of American Rabbis
HUC-JIR	Hebrew Union College–Jewish Institute of Religion
IMPJ	Israel Movement for Progressive Judaism
IRAC	Israel Religious Action Center
JAFI	Jewish Agency for Israel
JFNA	Jewish Federations of North America
JNF	Jewish National Fund (Keren Kayemet LeYisrael or KKL)
KH	Foundation Fund (Keren Hayesod)
MARAM	Council of Israel Progressive Rabbis (*Mo-etzet Rabbanim Mitkadmim*)
MUM	Maintenance of Union membership
Nahal	Fighting Pioneer Youth (Noar Halutzi Lohem, an IDF brigade)
NFTY	National Federation of Temple Youth
NRP	National Religious Party (Israel)

UAHC	Union of American Hebrew Congregations (now URJ)
UIA	United Israel Appeal
URJ	Union for Reform Judaism (North America; formerly UAHC)
WIZO	Women's International Zionist Organization
WUPJ	World Union for Progressive Judaism
WZO	World Zionist Organization

Appendix 2:
Institutions and Programs of Progressive Judaism in Israel

Over the years the Progressive movement in Israel has developed many interrelated institutions and programs. The following is a listing of the Progressive movement's scope.

Hebrew Union College–Jewish Institute of Religion

The Jerusalem campus is an academic center for the training of rabbis, cantors, and Jewish educators. There are special programs for training professional Jewish leaders for North America and Israel. Among the facilities on the prize-winning campus are the Abramov Library, the Academic Center, a museum of archeology, and the Hebrew Union College Biblical and Archaeological School.

World Union for Progressive Judaism

On the HUC-JIR campus are the international headquarters of the World Union for Progressive Judaism, the umbrella organization of Reform, Liberal, Progressive, and

Reconstructionist movements in more than forty countries around the world. Also situated on the campus is Beit Shmuel, a youth hostel and educational and cultural center; and Mercaz Shimshon, a conference center housing residential accommodation, theater, and hall, with a panoramic view over Jerusalem's Old City.

Israel Movement for Progressive Judaism

The national offices are housed in Beit Shmuel.

Leo Baeck Educational Center in Haifa

Established in the 1930s by Rabbi Meir Elk, a liberal rabbi from Germany, and expanded into a magnificent campus, the Leo Baeck Educational Center is today considered a leading high school in Israel and a major center pioneering innovative educational programs and integrated activities for the entire Haifa community.

TALI School, Jerusalem

TALI is a Hebrew acronym for "intensified Jewish studies." A successful, high-standard public school integrating studies and programs in the spirit of liberal Judaism with the curriculum authorized by the Ministry of Education.

Israel Religious Action Center (IRAC)

This organization is the public and legal advocacy arm of Progressive Judaism in Israel. Its message is to advance the cause of religious freedom, pluralism, social justice, and civil liberties for all. Its legal staff has won several landmark High Court rulings in religious-state issues, and its professional staff fight for the rights of new immigrants and other minority groups who are in need of outside advocacy.

Netzer Olami

A worldwide young adult Reform Zionist movement under the auspices of the World Union for Progressive Judaism. Netzer Olami has activities for youth in all the countries that are constituents of the World Union.

IMPJ Youth Movement (Telem Noar)

Thousands of children aged eight to eighteen participate in weekly educational and social activities that emphasize experiences in Jewish tradition, culture, and democracy.

Project Mechina

A nationally recognized study program for young Israelis, who spend a year in the program after graduating from high school prior to entering military service. The program includes Jewish study, leadership development, social action, and community service.

Summer Camp Programs

Many hundreds of children participate in an overnight summer camp, called Havaya (Experience), where children have experiences in living in a Progressive Jewish environment combining study and sun 'n' fun.

Batei Midrash

Many hundreds of adult Israelis engage in regular adult education programs studying classic Jewish texts—Bible, Talmud, and Jewish philosophy—in all our centers in Israel.

Education Outreach

The Progressive movement promotes programs in Jewish studies in the public schools, produces educational materials for teachers and students, and helps train the teachers to use them. It encourages classes for pupils of bar or bat mitzvah age whose secular parents would otherwise not encourage their children to participate in the bar or bat mitzvah experience.

Young Adult Leadership Forum

A framework for young adults (aged twenty to thirty-five) dedicated to developing new forms of communal participation and activism.

Early Childhood Education

Many dozens of kindergartens throughout the country, which stress experiences in observance of the Sabbath, the Festivals, and Jewish tradition.

Administration

The IMPJ sponsors a Biennial Conference for the entire movement and all its institutions. A *Vaad Artzi*, a national commission, and a *Hanhala*, an executive committee, meet regularly to formulate movement policy.

MARAM (Israel Council of Progressive Rabbis)

Gives guidance to development of siddurim and *machzorim* and creative liturgy for other occasions. It oversees the rabbinic *beit din* (rabbinic court) for issues of *ishut* (personal status) with special emphasis on conversion.

Communal Settlements

Kibbutz Yahel—in the Arava
Kibbutz Lotan—in the Arava
Har Halutz—in the Upper Galilee

Synagogues and Community Centers in Israel

Location	Name
Carmiel	Yedid Nefesh
Even Yehuda	HaShahar
Gezer	Birkat Shalom
Haifa	Ohel Avraham
	Or Hadash
	Shirat HaYam
Herzlia	She'arei Kedem
Jerusalem	Har-El
	Kol Haneshama
	Mevakshei Derech
Kiryat Ono	Brit Olam
Kiryat Tivon	Ma'alot Tivon
Mevasseret Zion	Mevasseret Zion

Modi'in	Yozma
Nahariya	Emet Veshalom
Netanya	Natan-Ya
Ra'anana	Ra'anan
Ramat Hasharon	Darkei Noam
Rishon Lezion	Achvat Yisrael
Rosh Ha'ayin	Bavat Ayin
Tel Aviv–Jaffa	Daniel Centers for Progressive Judaism
	Beit Daniel–Tel Aviv
	Mishkenot Ruth Daniel–Jaffa
Tzur Hadassah	Tzur Hadassah
Zichron Ya'akov	Sulam Ya'akov

Appendix 3:
Leaders of the World Union
for Progressive Judaism

Beginning in 1999 the lay leader bore the title chairperson of the board, and the professional head was named president. Upon his retirement, Rabbi Richard G. Hirsch was named honorary life president.

President / Chairperson of the Board

1926–1938	Dr. Claude G. Montefiore
1938–1953	Rabbi Dr. Leo Baeck
1954–1959	Hon. Lily H. Montagu
1959–1964	Rabbi Dr. Solomon B. Freehof
1964–1970	Rabbi Dr. Jacob K. Shankman
1970–1972	Rabbi Dr. Bernard J. Bamberger
1972–1973	Rabbi Dr. Maurice N. Eisendrath
1973–1980	Rabbi Dr. David H. Wice
1980–1988	Gerard Daniel
1998–1995	Donald Day
1995–2000	Austin Beutel
2000–2005	Ruth Cohen

| 2005–11 | Steven Bauman |
| 2011– | Michael Grabiner |

Executive Director / President

1960–62	Rabbi Hugo Gryn
1962–72	Rabbi William A. Rosenthal
1972–99	Rabbi Dr. Richard G. Hirsch
1999–2000	Rabbi Richard A. Block
1999–2001	Rabbi Dow Marmur (acting president)
2002–2008	Rabbi Uri Regev

| 1999– | Rabbi Richard G. Hirsch—Honorary Life President |

Appendix 4:
Leaders of the
Israel Movement for
Progressive Judaism

Chairpersons

1969–1972	Herbert Bettelheim
1972–1979	David Riegler
1979–1980	David Cohen
1980–1986	Nissim Eliad
1986–1992	Bruria Barish
1994–1998	Yonatan Livni
1998–2000	Rabbi Mordecai Rotem
2000–2002	Yonatan Livni
2002–2006	Paula Edelstein
2006–2010	Prof. Avraham Melammed
2010–	Yaron Shavit

Directors-General

1976–1980	Rabbi Adi Assabi
1980–1985	Rabbi Mordecai Rotem

288*For the Sake of Zion*

1986–1992	Rabbi Meir Azari
1992–1993	Amir Shacham
1993–1994	Maggi Barturah
1994–1997	Tzvi Timberg
1997–2000	Menahem Leibovic
2000–2002	Rabbi David Ariel-Yoel
2002–2009	Iri Kassel
2009–	Rabbi Gilad Kariv

Appendix 5:
Leaders of Arzenu
(International Federation
of Reform and Progressive
Religious Zionists)

Chairpersons

1980–1986   Rabbi Dow Marmur
1986–1991   Rabbi Michael Stroh
1991–1996   Rabbi David Lilienthal
1996–2002   Dr. Harvey Zimmerman
2002–2008   Mark Anshan
2008–   Joan Garson

Executive Directors

1983–1991   Rabbi Michael Boyden
1991–2002   Paula Edelstein
2002–   Dalya Levy

Appendix 6:
Leaders of ARZA (Association
of Reform Zionists of America)

Presidents

1978–1984	Rabbi Roland Gittelsohn
1984–1989	Rabbi Charles Kroloff
1989–1993	Norman Schwartz
1993–1995	Marcia Kayne
1995–2004	Philip Meltzer
2004–2008	Rabbi Stanley Davids
2008–	Rabbi Robert Orkand

Executive Directors

1977–1983	Rabbi Ira Youdovin
1983–1992	Rabbi Eric Yoffie
1992–2004	Rabbi Ammiel Hirsch
2004–2008	Rabbi Andrew Davids
2010–	Rabbi Daniel Allen

Index

Jesus, as Messiah in Christianity, 79
Jew-by-choice
  halachic definition of, 98–99
  use of, as phrase, 35–36
Jewish Agency for Israel (JAFI), ix, 11
  creation of, 255, 256, 260
  Department of *Aliyah* and *K'litah* (Immigration and Absorption), 258–259
  efforts toward depoliticizing, 263
  election of Hirsch, as chairman of Department for the Former Soviet Union (FSU), 185
  in encouraging immigration of Jews, 185
  former Soviet Union (FSU) Department of, 104–105
  funding of, 267
  future for, 46
  Institute for Jewish Studies establishment of, under auspices of, 105
  joining, xxiv
  leadership of, 266
  legal status of, 265
  membership in, 14
  mission statement of, 261–262
  need for change in, 259–262
  primary purpose of, 255
  Reform movement as member of, 116
  report of committee on governance issues, 263–264
  restructuring of, 258
  separation of World Zionist Organization (WZO) and, 262
  Settlement Department, 163
  Silver's representation of, 3
  structure of, 242
  subsidization of World Zionist Organization (WZO), 263–264
Jewish Agency for Israel-World Zionist Organization (JAFI-WZO)
  appointment of chair, 243
  Dulzin as chair of, 244
  emergency conference of 1976 and, 258–259
  involvement of Hirsch with, 209
  issues confronting leadership of, 245
  political structure of, 240
  responsibility for, 256–257
  selection of chairman/treasurer for, 243
  Sharansky as chairman of, 264
Jewish aspirations, Israel as fulfillment of, 29
Jewish communal organization, relationship with Christian counterparts, 79
Jewish demography, projection of, 16
Jewish ethnic identity, 21
Jewish expectations, growing gap between Israeli reality and, 29–30
Jewish faith, acceptance of, 94
Jewish Federations of North America (JFNA), 137, 179
  contributions to Jewish Agency, 267
  decline in donor base, 46
  leaders of, in North America, 25–26
  Orthodox contributions to, 26–27
  restructuring, 258
  source of leadership, 26

Kelman, Naamah
  as dean of HUC-JIR, 173
  immigration of, to Israel, 173
Kelman, Paula, 171
Kelman, Wolfe, 171
Kennedy, John F., 34, 73
  assassination of, 73–75
Keren Hayesod, 212
  Advise and Consent committee
    appointed by, 244
  contributions to Jewish Agency,
    267
  future for, 47
  restructuring, 258
Kfar Shmariyahu, start of congregation in, by Zemer, Moshe,
  167
Khartoum conference (1967), position of Arab League at, 56
Khirbet Kerach (Beit Yerach), 158
  archeological excavations at,
    xxxi
Kibbutz, 158
  life in, 165–166
  renewal of Jewish ritual obser-
    vance in, 161
Kibbutz Beit Hashita, 158
Kibbutz Ginegar, xxx–xxxi
Kibbutz Hazorea, xxx–xxxi
Kibbutz Lotan, 283
  establishment of, 165, 248
Kibbutz movement, 157. *See also*
  Reform kibbutz movement
  leaders of, 158
  relationship between Reform
    Judaism and, 160–161
  in search for authentic Judaism,
    161
Kibbutz Shefayim, Israel Movement for Progressive Judaism
  at, 175

Kibbutzim Yahel, 283
  dedication of, 164–165
  establishment of, 164,–165, 221,
    248
Kibbuz Gezer, 171
Kindergartens, initiative of Israel
  Movement for Progressive
  Judaism in starting, 173
King, Martin Luther, Jr., xxxviii
Kippah
  elimination of, by classical Re-
    formers, 6
  as symbol of Jewish peoplehood,
    6
K'lal Yisrael (worldwide commu-
  nity of Jews), 275
  commitment of Jews to, 35
Klatzkin, Jacob, on the Diaspora,
  40
Klausner, Yosef, xxxi
Knesset
  democratic and civil character of
    legislation, 19
  Jewish identity issue and, 99
  Law of Return and, 100–101,
    120–121
  National Religious Party in, 8,
    18
  rights of, to pass judgment on
    religious acts performed by
    Jews abroad, 53
  strengths of Zionist parties in,
    242
  as tool of the Orthodox religious
    parties, 121–122
Kogan, Zinovy, as president of
  Hineini, 202
Kol HaNeshama
  establishment of, 171
  notoriety of, 172
Kollek, Teddy, 142, 145